Publisher: Robert Ipsen

Editor: Carol Long

Managing Editor: Micheline Frederick

Text Design & Composition: North Market Street Graphics

Library of Congress Cataloging-in-Publication Data:

Marcus, Evan, 1962–
    Blueprints for high availability : designing resilient distributed systems / Evan Marcus, Hal Stern.
        p.   cm.
    ISBN 0-471-35601-8 (cloth)
    1. Electronic data processing—Distributed processing. 2. System design. I. Stern, Hal, 1962– II. Title.

QA76.9.D5 M357 2000
004'.36—dc21   99-053030

Printed in the United States of America.

10 9 8 7 6 5 4 3

ISBN 0471-35601-8

Contents

Foreword

Steps Toward an Always-On Network

Everywhere we look, networks matter. Around the world, the global Internet and related information networks are transforming every aspect of business, government, education, and culture. With so much happening, at such astounding speed, it's easy to forget that the Internet and network computing are still in their infancy. We sense that even more dramatic changes are still to come, and that we have caught only a brief glimpse of the technology's ability to improve our lives.

Compare today's computer networks, for example, to the global long-distance telephone network. A ten-key pad of buttons gives us access to virtually anyplace on earth, and a worldwide directory system helps us to quickly locate businesses and individuals. When we use this system, its incredible complexity is almost entirely invisible to us. Moreover, we expect this global network and its familiar dial tone to always be available. We take it for granted that the network is always on.

High availability systems, the subject of this book, represent one of the chief means to achieving the goal of always-on computer networks. This branch of systems engineering began with the need to ensure the availability of critical applications running within organizations. As information networks became more central to doing business, the number of applications deemed critical to doing business expanded and the demand for high availability systems increased. Today, with the walls of the organization coming down and businesses everywhere extending their networks and applications to the Internet, the availability of networked systems has become a top priority. In the context of e-business, downtime puts you out of business. Not only do you lose money the instant the system fails, you risk losing the attention and loyalty of your on-line customers.

The positive side of all this is that high-availability technology has dramatically improved to meet the e-business challenge. Clustering and failover software, once limited to exotic and extremely expensive hardware, is now available, at a much lower cost, for standard hardware and open, flexible operating environments. New management software makes it easier and more cost-effective for businesses to monitor and control availability. New guidelines and methodologies, such as those outlined in this book, are helping businesses and solutions designers intelligently build high availability into their networks.

For all that's state of the art in high availability, there can be no better guides than the authors of this book. Evan Marcus of VERITAS Software and Hal Stern of Sun Microsystems are true experts in the field of high availability, as well as hands-on scientists who understand the challenges faced by systems designers, solutions providers, and IT and e-business managers. If you represent any of those groups, you can rely on this book for information on the technologies and methods you'll need to design and implement high availability systems. In other words, this book will help you transform the vision of always-on networks into a reality.

Dr. Eric Schmidt
Chairman and CEO, Novell, Inc.

Preface

Technical books run the gamut from code listings sprinkled with smart commentary to dry, theoretical tomes on the wonders of some obscure protocol. When we decided to write this book, we were challenged to somehow convey nearly 15 years of combined experience. What we've produced has little code in it; it's not a programmer's manual or a low-level how-to book. Availability, and the higher concepts of resiliency and predictability, demand that you approach them with discipline and process. This book represents our combined best efforts at prescriptions for developing the disciplines, defining and refining the processes, and deploying systems with confidence. At the end of the day, if a system you've designed to be highly available suffers an outage, it's your reputation and your engineering skills that are implicated. Our goal is to supplement your skills with real-world, practical advice. When you see "Tales from the Field" in the text, you're reading our (only slightly lionized) recounts of experiences that stand out as examples of truly bad or truly good design.

We have sought to provide balance in our treatment of this material. Engineering always involves trade-offs between cost and functionality; between time to market and features; and between optimization for speed and designing for safety. We treat availability as an end-to-end network computing problem; one in which availability is just as important as performance. As you read through this book, whether sequentially by chapter or randomly based on particular interests and issues, bear in mind that *you* choose the trade-offs. Cost, complexity, and level of availability are all knobs that you can turn; our job is to offer you guidance in deciding just how far each should be turned for any particular application and environment.

We would like to thank the entire editorial team at John Wiley & Sons. Carol Long believed in our idea enough to turn it into a proposal, and then she coached, cajoled, and even tempted us with nice lunches to elevate our efforts into what you're reading now. Special thanks also to Christina Berry and Micheline Frederick for their editorial and production work and suggestions that improved the overall readability and flow of the book. You have been a first-rate team, and we owe you a debt of gratitude for standing by us for the past 18 months.

From Evan Marcus

This book is the product of more than 2 years of preparation and writing, more than 7 years of working with highly available systems (and systems that people thought were highly available), and more than 15 years of general experience with computer systems. Having worked in technical roles for consulting companies specializing in high availability and for software vendors with HA products, I found myself answering the same kinds of questions over and over. The questions inevitably are about getting the highest possible degree of availability from critical systems. The systems and the applications that run on them may change, but the questions about availability really don't. I kept looking for a book on this subject, but never could find one.

In 1992, I became intimately involved with Fusion Systems' cleverly named *High Availability for Sun* product, believed to be the very first high availability or failover software product that ever ran on Sun Microsystems workstations. It allowed a predesignated standby computer to quickly and automatically step in and take over the work being performed by another computer that had failed. Having done several years of general system administrative consulting, I found the concept of high availability to be a fascinating one. Here was a product, a tool actually, that took what good system administrators did and elevated it to the next level. Good SAs worked hard to make sure that their systems stayed up and delivered the services they were deployed to deliver, and they took pride in their accomplishments. But despite their best efforts, systems still crashed, and data was still lost. This product allowed for a level of availability that had previously been unattainable.

High Availability for Sun was a tool. Like any tool, it could be used well or poorly, depending on the knowledge and experience of the person wielding the tool. We implemented several failover pairs that worked very well. We also implemented some that worked very poorly. The successful implementations were on systems run by experienced and thoughtful SAs who understood the goals of this software, and who realized that it was only a tool and not a panacea. The poorly implemented ones were as a result of customers not mirroring their disks, or plugging both systems into the same power strip, or running poor-quality applications, who expected *High Availability for Sun* to solve all of their system problems automatically.

The people who successfully implemented *High Availability for Sun* understood that this tool could not run their systems for them. They understood that a tremendous amount of administrative discipline was still required to ensure that their systems ran the way they wanted them to. They understood that *High Availability for Sun* was just one piece of the puzzle.

Today, even though the product once called *High Availability for Sun* has changed names, companies, and code bases at least three times, there are still people who realistically understand what failover management software (FMS) can and cannot do for them, and others who think it is the be-all and end-all for all of their system issues. There are also many less-experienced system administrators in the world today, who may not be familiar with all the issues related to rolling out critical systems. And there are managers and budget approvers who think that achieving highly available systems is free and requires little or no additional work. Nothing so valuable is ever that simple.

The ability to make systems highly available, even without failover software, is a skill that touches on every aspect of system administration. Understanding how to implement HA systems well will make you a better overall system administrator, and make you worth more to your employer, even if you never actually have the chance to roll out a single failover configuration.

In this book we hope to point out the things that we have learned in implementing hundreds of critical systems in highly available configurations. Realistically, it is unlikely that we have hit on every single point that readers will run into while implementing critical systems. We do believe, however, that our general advice will be applicable to many specific situations.

Some readers may begrudge the lack of simple, universal answers in this book. There are two reasons for this. One is that the issues that arise at each site, and for each computer system, are different. It is unreasonable to expect that what works for a 10,000-employee global financial institution will also work for a 10-person law office. We offer the choices and allow the reader to determine which one will work best in his or her environment. The other reason is that after 15 years of working on, with, and occasionally for computers, I have learned that the most correct answer to most computing problems is a rather unfortunate, "It depends."

We have made the assumption that our readers possess varying technical abilities. With rare exceptions, the material in the book is not extremely technical. I am not a bits-and-bytes kind of guy (although Hal is), and so I have tried to write the book for other people who are more like me. The sections on writing code are a little more bits-and-bytes-oriented, but they are the exception rather than the rule.

We have also chosen to define a lot of terminology, both in the text and in the Glossary. Our definitions are not exhaustive or particularly technical. The intent is for someone who is new to some of these terms to understand them within our context. If you need more information about some of the terms or topics, there are more in-depth works on all of them. We are not assuming a tremendous breadth of technical experience from our readers; if you have technical experience, then feel free not to read the more basic sections.

When I describe this project to friends and colleagues, their first question is usually whether it's a Unix book or an NT book. The honest answer is both. Clearly, both Hal and I have a lot of Unix (especially Solaris) experience. But the tips in the book are not generally OS-specific. They are very general, and many of them also apply to disciplines outside of computing. The idea of having a backup unit that takes over for a failed unit is commonplace in aviation, skydiving (that pesky backup parachute), and other areas where a failure can be fatal, nearly fatal, or merely dangerous. After all, you wouldn't begin a long trip in your car without a spare tire in the trunk, would you? Busy intersections almost never have just one traffic light; what happens when the bulbs start to fail? Although many of our examples are Sun- and Solaris-specific, we have included examples in NT and other Unix operating systems wherever possible.

Throughout the book, we offer specific examples of vendors whose products are appropriate to the discussion. We are not endorsing the vendors—we're just providing their names as examples. And rather than cluttering the book with URLs, we have created Appendix B, listing URLs for the vendors and other web sites we make reference to.

First and foremost, my gratitude goes to my family. Without the love, support, and understanding (or at least tolerance!) of my wife Carol and my daughters Hannah and Madeline, there's no way I could have written this book. A special note of thanks, too, to our family and friends, who pretended that they understood when I missed important events to stay home and write. See, it really was a book!

Additional thanks to Michael Kanaval (we miss you, Mike) for his inspiration and some excellent examples; to Joseph J. Hand, who helped with some of the NT material; to Michael Zona and John Costa for some of the backup stuff; to Mark Fitzpatrick and Bob Zarrow for some of my early and ongoing education in failover and general HA stuff; and to Mindy Anderson and Eric Burgener for clustering and SANs. Thanks, too—for general support, enthusiasm, and tolerance—to my parents Roberta and David Marcus, my in-laws Gladys and Herb Laden (now can I have that recipe?), and Ed Applebaum, Ann Sheridan, and Dinese Christopher, and everyone else at VERITAS and elsewhere who made suggestions and showed general enthusiasm and interest in this project. Special thanks to Mark Fannon and Evan Marks for excellent technical review and general help.

Thanks go out to the countless customers, users, and technical colleagues I've worked with over the years, with special thanks to the people at Morgan Stanley Dean Witter, Bear Stearns, Deutsche Bank, J. P. Morgan, Sun Microsystems, VERITAS Software, Open Vision, and Fusion Systems.

And a really big thanks to Hal Stern for being my personal door opener. In mid-1997 I finally made the decision to write this book. Having never written a book before, I knew that I needed help. I e-mailed Hal, looking for initial guidance from someone who had written a successful book. He wrote back and asked if perhaps we could collaborate. I thought long and hard for about 2 nanoseconds and then replied with an enthusiastic "Yes!" It was Hal's idea that we begin the writing process by creating a slide presentation. Our original set of 250 slides quickly grew to over 400, which we still present at technical conferences each year. By presenting the slides, we were able to determine what content was missing, where questions came up, and how the content flowed. It was a relatively (very relatively) easy job to then turn those slides into the book you see before you. Hal also originally contacted Carol Long at Wiley, got us on the agenda at our first technical conferences, and approached Eric Schmidt to write the Foreword. This book would still just be an idea in my head without Hal.

From Hal Stern

My introduction to reliable systems began nearly 10 years ago, when I worked with the Foxboro Company to port their real-time, industrial control system from proprietary hardware to the Sun platform. You never really consider the impact of a hung device driver or failed disk drive until the device driver is holding a valve open on a huge paint mixing drum, or the disk drive is located along the Alaskan oil pipeline under several feet of snow. As the Internet has exploded in popularity, reliability and "uptime engineering" are becoming staples of our diet, because web surfers have caused us to treat most problems as real-time systems. As system administrators we have to decide just how much money to pour into reliability engineering, striving for four-nines (99.99 percent) or five-nines (99.999 percent) uptime while management remarks on how cheap hardware has become. There are no right answers; everything is a delicate balance of management, operations, money, politics, trust, and time. It's up to you to choose the number of nines you can live with. I hope that we help you make an informed choice.

This book would not have been possible without the love and support of my family. To my wife Toby and my children Elana and Benjamin, a huge thank-you, a big hug, and yes, Daddy will come out of his study now. I also want to thank the following current and former Sun Microsystems employees for educating me on various facets of availability and for their ideas and encouragement: Carol Wilhelmy, Jon Simms, Chris Drake, Larry McVoy, Brent Callaghan, Ed Graham, Jim Mauro, Enis Konuk, Peter Marcotte, Gayle Belli, Scott Oaks, and Wendy Talmont. Pete Lega survived several marathon sessions on complexity, recovery, and automation, and his inputs are valued. Chris Kordish and Bob Sokol, both of Sun Microsystems, reviewed the manuscript and offered their comments and guidance. Larry Bernstein, retired vice president of network operations at AT&T, challenged me to learn more about "carrier grade" engineering; it was an honor to have had discussions with a true Telephone Pioneer. Avi Nash and Randy Rohrbach at the Foxboro Company gave me a firsthand education in fault tolerance. Various individuals at Strike Technologies, Bear Stearns, Fidelity Investments, Deutsche Bank, Morgan Stanley Dean Witter, and State Street Bank proved that the ideas contained in this book really work. I thank you sincerely for sharing engineering opportunities with me, even if confidentiality agreements prevent me from listing you by name. A special thank-you to George Spehar, a true gentleman in every sense, for offering his sage management and economic decision-making advice. Ed Braginsky, vice president of advanced technology at BEA Systems, has been a good friend for eight years and a superb engineer for longer than that. His explanations of queuing systems, transaction processing, and asynchronous design, along with the thoughts of BEA cofounder Alfred Chuang, have been invaluable to me. Of course, thanks to Mom and Pop for teaching me the importance of being reliable.

Finally, a huge thank-you to Evan Marcus. We became acquainted while working on a customer project that required sniffing out performance problems during the wee hours of the morning. I'd never met Evan before, yet he was driving me around New Jersey and providing a steady patter at all hours. I should have recognized then that he had the stamina for a book and the power of persuasion to have me join him in the endeavor. Evan, thanks for your patience, understanding, and unique ability to prompt me out of writer's block, winter doldrums, and extreme exhaustion. It's been a pleasure traveling, working, and teaching with you.

Introduction

Quality is job 1.
–Ford Motor Company advertising slogan

Despite predictions in the 1970s (and extending into the 1980s) that computers would make everyone's lives easier and give us all more leisure time, just the opposite seems to be taking place. Computers move faster, thanks to faster and faster CPUs, and yet the business world seems to move even faster. Computers are expected to be operational and available 7 days week, 24 hours a day. Downtime, even for maintenance, is no longer an option.

With the unprecedented growth and acceptance of the Internet, average people expect to be able to buy clothing or office supplies on the web at 4 A.M., while in their underwear. And if they can't buy from your web site, they will buy from your competitor's. Uniform resource locators (URLs) are part of the culture; they are written on the sides of city buses, and even four-year-olds know www.pbs.org and www.disney.com.

Adding to the complexity is the globalization of the Internet and the web. Even if there are quiet times for web servers in the United States, those times are filled by users in Europe and the rest of the world. National borders and time zones essentially disappear on the web.

The amounts of data that businesses are being called on to save and manage are growing at astounding rates. The consulting organizations that monitor such things estimate that online data will grow 70 to 75 percent per year for the next few years. That data must be accessible quickly at all hours of the day or night, if not for your company's European operation, then for its U.S. personnel. As the amount of data grows, the price of storage devices continues to drop dramatically, making it feasible for companies to store all their data.

But what happens when the systems crash? What happens when disks stop turning? What about when your network stops delivering data? Does the business stop? Must your customers visit your competitor's web site to order their Barbie dolls? Should you just send your employees home? For how long? Can you recover? When? And how come this stuff never seems to happen to your competitors? (Don't worry—it does.)

The media frenzy surrounding the Y2K problem did do some good. The fear of all computers everywhere failing made the average Joe appreciate (even if just a little bit) the direct effect that computers have on his daily life. While that lesson may be quickly forgotten, at least the impact was there for a short time. As a result, the people who allocate money for the management of computer systems have a little bit more of an appreciation of what can happen when good computers do go bad.

Why an Availability Book?

The Y2K problem is certainly not the only issue that has caused problems or at least concerns with computer availability; it just happens to be the best-known example. Some of the others over the last few years include:

- Terrorist attacks in New York, London, and other large cities, such as the 1993 bombing of New York's World Trade Center

- Satellite outages that brought down pagers and other communication devices

- Attacks by various computer viruses

- Natural disasters such as floods, tornadoes, and earthquakes

- Introduction of the euro

- The Dow Jones Industrial Average passing 10,000 (sometimes called D10K)

- Emergence of the Internet as a viable social force, comparable to TV or radio as a mass market influence

Obviously the impact of each of these issues has varied from negligible (D10K) to serious (virus attacks). But again, each calls attention to the importance and value of computers, and the impact of failures. Downtime on the

Internet is like dead air on a television station; it's embarrassing and a mistake that you only make once.

Our Approach to the Problem Set

In this book, we will take a look at the elements of your computer systems that can fail, whether due to a major event such as the ones just listed, or due to rather mundane problems like the failure of a network router or corruption of a critical file. We will look at basic system configuration issues, including, but not limited to, physical placement of equipment, logical arrangements of disks, backing up of critical data, and migration of important services from one system to another.

We will take an end-to-end perspective, because systems are an end-to-end proposition. Either everything works, or nothing works. Rarely is there any middle ground. Your users sit in front of their computer screen, trying to run applications. Either they run or they don't. Sometimes they run, but too slowly. We'll look at performance only to the extent that an exaggerated performance problem smells like an availability issue. When an application runs too slowly, that may still be an availability issue, since the user cannot get his or her job done in a timely manner.

We will also take a businesslike approach, never losing sight of the fact that every bit of protection—whether mirrored disks, backup systems, or extra manpower for system design—costs real money. We have tried to balance costs and benefits, or at least help you to balance costs and benefits. After all, no two sites or systems are the same. What may be important to you may not matter a bit to the guy down the hall. One of the hardest jobs facing designers of highly available systems is scoping out the costs of a particular level of protection, which are frequently higher than the people running the business would like. In an era where computer hardware prices shrink logarithmically, it's hard to explain to management that you can't get fault-tolerant system operation at desktop PC prices. Our goal is to help define the metrics, the rules, and the guidelines for making and justifying these cost/benefit tradeoffs. Availability is measured in "nines"—99.99 percent uptime is "four nines." Our goal is to help you choose the number of nines you can achieve with your engineering constraints, and the number you can afford within your budget and cost constraints.

We'll frequently refer to cost/benefit or cost/complexity trade-offs. Such decisions abound in technology-driven companies: Buy or build? Faster time to market or more features? Quick and dirty or morally correct but slower? Our job is to provide some guidelines for making these decisions. We'll try to avoid taking editorial stances, because there are no absolutes in engineering design.

What's Not Here

Many things are missing from this book, some of which may be missed, but all of which were omitted for specific reasons:

- We mention products, but we do not judge them. Product references are not endorsements; we mention them so that you have the opportunity to evaluate the best-known players in a particular market. Products change rapidly, vendors change rapidly, and we prefer not to make judgment calls about products. After all, we both work for vendors of these products. We prefer to outline the questions to ask, to make you a better evaluator of your own issues.

- There aren't prescriptions or recipes that you can copy and try out in your machine room. Partly this is because there are no one-size-fits-all solutions, and partly it's because describing only the solution evades a discussion of the skills needed to build it.

- There's not much code, as in programming snippets. When you're customizing a failover solution, you're going to be writing some code and fine-tuning scripts to match your environment. Our goal is to convey discipline, process, and methodology to establish the requirements for this code-slinging. You'll find this book a level more abstract than a programmer's guide.

- You won't find complete answers to all of your questions. Some topics can only be addressed in *your* machine room, with *your* business and *your* requirements. If we help you make choices you can live with, we feel that we've done our job.

Our Mission

This book actually comes with a Mission Statement. It's not a rambling paragraph about curing all the world's ills; it's a short, snappy reflection on what we're prompting you to do. When we wrote the book, this statement was never far from our thinking. We believe that every bit of information in the book is related to this statement:

> **High availability cannot be achieved by merely installing failover software and walking away.**

In fact, the best way to ensure that you stick to our mission statement is to follow this piece of advice: **Build your systems so that they never have to**

failover. Yes, of course they will failover, but if you make failover the very last resort, you will truly maximize your availability.

Of course, some sanity must be added to the last statement. You can't just throw money at your systems to make them work better. At some point, the additional money will not provide commensurate benefits. The key is to:

- **Price out your downtime**

and then use that figure to

- **Determine how much you can afford to spend to protect against service outages**

Remember that reliability engineering costs money; it's far more than what you'll spend on hardware or system software. It's an operating system/independent cost, and one that hasn't come down as a function of cheaper memory or larger disks.

Those messages are probably the most important statements in this entire book. Together they build a message that balances system needs with the harsh realities of budget limitations.

The Availability Index

Another way of making the point about balancing downtime with cost is to look at availability as a curve. The more you spend, the higher you move up the curve. Be sure to note, however, that the incremental costs to move from one level to the next increase as you move up the curve.

We've chosen four places along the curve, as shown in Figure 1.1, that are the most common stopping points:

1. *Basic systems.* These are systems that do not employ special measures to protect their data. Backups are taken, but nothing more. When an outage occurs, the support personnel work to restore the system, but are doing so without any prior planning.

2. *Redundant data.* Some level of disk redundancy is employed to protect the data against the loss of a disk. RAID-5 provides less protection than full mirrors, but both provide data redundancy. The redundancy may be delivered through hardware or software, and with many other bells and whistles.

3. *System failover.* A model where two systems are employed to do the work of one. The extra system acts as a standby or backup machine that takes over for the primary system, should the primary system fail.

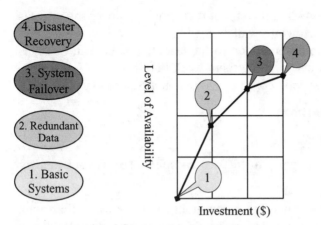

Figure 1.1   The availability index.

4. *Disaster recovery.* In addition to systems at the main site, a second set of systems is maintained at a backup site. In the event the main site becomes unusable, the systems in the backup site are brought up in place of the primary systems.

Moving from one level to the next requires significantly more money and equipment than was needed for the level before it. You have to look at your systems and decide what level each needs to be at. After you have chosen a level, you can work out the details and choices within that level.

Note that the graph is a curve, rather than a straight line. That curve reflects the law of diminishing returns. After you protect against the cheaper and easier-to-fix problems, the cost (and complexity) of the next level of protection increases, flattening out the curve.

Summary

Computer systems are very complex. The solutions that make them work best are complex too. They require planning, work, testing, and a general ongoing effort by knowledgeable people at every level of implementation. Applications must be tolerant of failures and inappropriate inputs. Hardware must be able to automatically recover from failures. And since systems change, if you want this functionality to always be present, you must regularly test your recovery procedures. Do they still work? Do they still work as quickly as they should? If they do not work as expected, the time to find out is not when something has gone wrong and the pressure is on.

Our goals are to help you design your systems for maximum availability and predictable downtime and recovery times. We will look at these systems from end to end; and from network, system, and application perspectives.

Organization of the Book

We take a very layered approach to systems, and that layered approach follows in the organization of this book. We look at each type of component separately, starting with disks and moving up through systems into software and finally disaster recovery.

In many of the chapters, you will find sidebars that we call "Tales from the Field." They are generally true-to-life experiences that we have lived or seen at real users of computer systems. Some of them are funny; all of them help make a point clearer. We hope that you learn from the mistakes and examples that we have seen and sometimes suffered through.

Chapter 2 takes a look at the concept of resilience, and explains exactly what we mean by it, as well as what can go wrong with the various components of your system. This chapter also looks at cost/risk trade-offs.

Chapter 3 contains our 20 key design principles for attaining resilience and high availability. We refer back to these principles throughout the book.

Chapter 4 looks at data storage. We discuss disks and disk arrays, and the ways to logically arrange them to maximize your protection against hardware failures, including the use of RAID hardware and software.

Chapter 5 is the first of three chapters related to computer systems. We look at the hardware components and design necessary to build systems that can failover.

In Chapter 6, we look at failovers and the software that manages them. We look at the implications of building your own failover software, and at some of the inherent complexities that accompany the use of this software.

Chapter 7 examines the myriad of different failover configurations—the good, the bad, and the ugly.

Chapter 8 reviews networking concepts and discusses the various elements of making your networks stand up to various failures, in both hardware and software.

Chapter 9 looks at some of the more common data management services that your systems provide, such as databases and web servers, and how to layer them on top of hardware and failover software systems.

Chapter 10 reviews techniques for replicating data, and applications to other systems across a network.

Chapter 11 focuses on application reliability. What are the issues involved in making your applications recover properly after a server has failed and recovered? What should you do to make your applications more resilient to external system faults and internal (logical) problems?

Chapter 12 is dedicated to backups. How do you take them, why do you take them, and how do you handle the tapes and the hardware?

Chapter 13 looks at some of the less technical issues related to system resiliency, such as personnel management; maintenance plans; vendor management; configuration and spare parts management; security; and environmental issues like data centers, power, cooling, and physical space.

Chapter 14 examines disaster recovery issues, ranging from legal and personnel issues to practical issues like whose application gets restored first at the DR site.

Chapter 15 is our parting shot—a quick summary and some thoughts about what comes next.

Finally, there's a glossary that quickly goes through some of the terms in the book, and a list of URLs for vendors and other useful sources.

▶Key Points

We will end each chapter with a few bullet points that we believe sum up the key messages from that particular unit. For Chapter 1, it's really quite easy:

- High availability cannot be achieved by merely installing failover software and walking away.
- Build your systems so reliably that they never have to failover.
- Figure out how much downtime costs on your systems, and then use that figure to determine how much you can afford to spend to protect against that downtime.

CHAPTER 2

What Is Resiliency?

In this chapter we will discuss:

- What resiliency is
- How we measure availability
- Ways to quantify the costs associated with downtime
- The things that can go wrong in a typical server environment

Throughout this book we use the term "resiliency" in terms of overall system availability. We see resiliency as a general term similar to "high availability," but without all the baggage that "HA" carries along with it. High availability once referred to a fairly specific range of system configurations, usually involving two computers that monitor and protect each other. During the last few years, however, it has lost much of its original meaning; vendors and users have co-opted the term to mean whatever they want it to mean.

To us, resiliency and high availability mean that all of a system's failure modes are known and well-defined, including networks and applications. They mean that the recovery times for all known failures have an upper bound; we know how long a particular failure will have the system down. While there may be certain failures that we cannot cope with very well, we know what they are and how to recover from them, and we have backup plans for use if our recoveries don't work. A resilient system is one that can take a hit to a critical component, and recover and come back for more in a known, bounded, and generally acceptable period of time.

Measuring Availability

When you discuss availability requirements with a user or project leader, he or she will invariably tell you that 100 percent availability is required: "Our project is so important that we can't have any downtime at all." But the tune usually changes when the project leader finds out how much 100 percent availability costs. Then it becomes a matter of money, and more of a negotiation process.

As you can see in Table 2.1, for many applications, 99 percent uptime is adequate. If the systems average an hour-and-a-half of downtime per week, that may be satisfactory. Of course, a lot of that depends on when the hour-and-a-half occurs. If it falls between 3:00 and 4:30 Sunday morning, that is going to be a lot more tolerable on many systems than if it occurs between 10:00 and 11:30 Thursday morning, or every weekday afternoon at 2:00 for 15 or 20 minutes.

One point of negotiation is the hours during which 100 percent uptime may be required. If it is only needed for a few hours a day, then that goal is quite achievable. For example, when brokerage houses trade between the hours of 9:30 A.M. and 4:00 P.M., then during those hours, plus perhaps three or four hours on either side, 100 percent uptime is required. A newspaper might require 100 percent uptime during production hours, but not the rest of the time. If, however, 100 percent uptime is required $7 \times 24 \times 365$, the costs become so prohibitive that only the most profitable applications and large enterprises can consider it.

Table 2.1   Measuring Availability

PERCENTAGE UPTIME	PERCENTAGE DOWNTIME	DOWNTIME PER YEAR	DOWNTIME PER WEEK
98%	2%	7.3 days	3 hours, 22 minutes
99%	1%	3.65 days	1 hour, 41 minutes
99.8%	0.2%	17 hours, 30 minutes	20 minutes, 10 seconds
99.9%	0.1%	8 hours, 45 minutes	10 minutes, 5 seconds
99.99%	0.01%	52½ minutes	1 minute
99.999%	0.001%	5.25 minutes	6 seconds
99.9999% ("six 9s")	0.0001%	31.5 seconds	0.6 seconds

As you move progressively to higher levels of availability, costs increase very rapidly. Consider a server ("*abbott*") that with no special measures taken, except for disk mirrors and backups, has 99 percent availability. If you couple that server with another identically configured server ("*costello*") that is configured to take over from *abbott* when it fails, and that server also offers 99 percent availability, then theoretically, you can achieve a combined availability of 99.99 percent. [Mathematically, you multiply the downtime on *abbott* (1 percent) by the uptime on *costello* (99 percent); *costello* will only be in use during *abbott's* 1 percent of downtime. The result is 0.99 percent. Add the original 99 to 0.99, and you get 99.99 percent, the theoretical uptime for the combined pair.]

Of course, in reality 99.99 percent will not occur simply by combining two servers. The increase in availability is not purely linear. It takes time for the switchover (usually called a *failover*) to occur, and during that period, the combined server is down. In addition, there are external failures that will affect access to both servers, such as network connectivity or power outages. These failures will undoubtedly decrease the overall availability figures.

The rule of thumb for costs is that as you move one line down the chart, costs increase from 5 to 10 times, and the multiplier also increases as you move down the chart.

Defining Downtime

Definitions for downtime vary from gentle to tough, and from simple to complex. Easy definitions are often given in terms of failed components, such as the server itself, disks, the network, the operating system, or key applications. Stricter definitions may include slow server or network performance, the inability to restore backups, or simple data inaccessibility. We prefer a very strict definition for downtime: *If a user cannot get his job done on time, the system is down.*

The system is provided to the users for one service: to allow them to work in an efficient and timely way. When circumstances prevent a user from doing this work, regardless of the reason, the system is down.

Causes of Downtime

In Figure 2.1, we examine the various causes of downtime. One of the largest regions on the graph is planned downtime. It is also one of the easiest segments to reduce. Planned downtimes are the events, usually late at night, when the system administrators add hardware to the system, upgrade operating systems or other critical software, or rearrange the layout of data on disks. Sometimes planned downtime is just a preventative reboot to clean up logs, temporary directories, and memory.

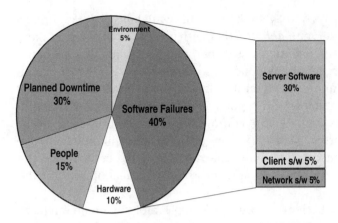

Figure 2.1   Causes of downtime.

Source: IEEE Computer April 1995

Most of these events can be performed with the system up nowadays; disks can be added to hot pluggable disk arrays without interrupting services. Many (though sadly not all) critical applications can be upgraded without service interruptions. In a failover environment, which we will discuss in much more detail later, one machine in a failover pair or cluster can be upgraded while its partner continues to operate. Then, the upgraded cluster member can take over the server role, while the first machine is upgraded. The only service interruption comes during the switchover of services, called a *failover*. Several vendors produce disk and logical storage and volume management software that can enable on-line management of data layout and volumes, with no interruption to service at all.

The people factor is another major cause of downtime. People cause downtime for two closely related reasons. The first reason is that they sometimes make dumb or careless mistakes. The second reason that people cause downtimes is that they do not always completely understand the way a system operates. The best way to combat people-caused downtime is through a combination of education and intelligent, simple system design. By sending your people to school to keep them up to date on current technologies, and by keeping good solid documentation on hand and up to date, you can reduce the amount of downtime they cause.

Possibly the most surprising region on the chart is hardware. Hardware causes just 10 percent of system outages. That means that the best RAID disks in the world and the most redundant networks can only prevent about 10 percent of your downtime. In fact, besides disk and network failures, hardware outages also include central processing unit (CPU) and memory failures, loss of power supplies, and internal system cooling.

The most obvious common causes for system outages are probably software failures. Altogether, software is responsible for 40 percent of system downtime.

Software bugs are perhaps the most difficult source of failures to get out of the system. As hardware becomes more reliable, and methods are employed to reduce planned outages, their percentages will decrease, while the percentage of outages attributed to software issues will increase. As software becomes more complex, software-related outages may become more frequent on their own. Of course, as software development and debugging techniques become more sophisticated, software-related outages should become less prevalent. It will be very interesting to see whether software-related downtime increases or decreases over time.

What Is Availability?

At its simplest level, availability, whether high, low, or in between, is a measure of the time that a server is functioning normally. We offer a simple equation to calculate availability:

$$A = \frac{\text{MTBF}}{\text{MTBF} + \text{MTTR}}$$

Where A is the degree of availability expressed as a percentage, MTBF is the *mean time between failures*, and MTTR is the *maximum time to repair* or resolve a particular problem.

Some simple observations:

- As MTTR approaches zero, A increases toward 100 percent.
- As the MTBF gets larger, MTTR has less impact on A.

For example, if a particular system has an MTBF of 100,000 hours, and an MTTR of 1 hour, it has a rather impressive availability level of 100,000/100,001, or 99.999 percent. If you cut the MTTR to 6 minutes, or $\frac{1}{10}$ of an hour, availability increases an extra 9, to 99.9999 percent. But to achieve this level of availability with even 6 minutes of downtime, you need a component with an actual duration between failures of 100,000 hours, which is better than 11 years.

Let us restate that last statistic. *To achieve 99.9999 percent availability, you are permitted just 6 minutes downtime in 11.4 years.* That's 6 minutes in 11.4 years over your entire system, not just the one component we happen to be examining. Given today's technology, this is unachievable for all practical purposes, and an unrealistic goal. Downtimes of less than 10 minutes per year (about 99.998 percent) are probably achievable, but it would be very difficult to get much less than that. In addition to well-designed systems, a significant degree of luck will surely be required. And you just can't plan for luck.

Luck comes in many flavors. Good luck is when your best developer happens to be working late on the night that his application brings down your critical servers, and he fixes the problem quickly. Good luck is when the water pipe in the ceiling breaks and leaks water over one side of your disk mirrors but doesn't affect the other side. Bad luck (or malice) gets you when someone on the data center tour leans on the power switch to a production server. Bad luck forces a car from the road and into the pole in front of your building where the power from both of your power companies comes together. Bad luck is that backhoe outside your window digging up the fiber cable running between your buildings, as you helplessly watch through your office window.

"M" Is for Mean

The key term in MTBF is *mean time*. A mean time between failures number is just that, a mean. An average. If a disk drive has an MTBF of 200,000 hours (almost 23 years), that does not mean that every disk rolling off the assembly line is guaranteed to work for exactly 23 years, and then drop dead. When the government announces life expectancy figures, it certainly doesn't mean that every man in America will die when he reaches the age of 79.6 years. For every person who doesn't make it to his 50th birthday, there is going to be someone whose picture makes it onto *The Today Show* for surpassing his (or her) 100th birthday.

Means are trends. If you look at all the disks that roll off the assembly line during a given period of time, the average life expectancy of a disk, before it fails, is about 23 years. That means, however, that some disks may fail the first day, and others may last 40 years (obsolescence aside). It also means that if you have a large server, with, say, 500 disks in it, on average you will lose a disk every 200,000/500 or 400 hours. Four hundred hours is only about 16½ days. So, you will be replacing a disk, on average, every 2½ weeks.

A statistical mean is not enough to tell you very much about the particular members of a population. The mean of 8, 9, 10, 11, and 12 is 10. But the mean of 1, 1, 1, 1, and 46 is also 10. So is the mean of 12,345, −12,345, 47,000,000, −47,000,000, and 50.

The other key number is *standard deviation*, or sigma (σ). Without going into a long, dull explanation of standard deviation calculations (go back and look at your college statistics textbook!), sigma tells you how far the members of a population stray from the mean. For each of the three previous examples (and treating each like a complete population, for you statistics nerds), σ is: 1.414214, 19.6, and 29,725,411. For the sake of completeness we offer one more example: the mean of 9.99, 10.01, 9.999, 10.002, and 9.999 is still 10, and the standard deviation is 0.006419. As these comparisons illustrate, the closer the members of the population are to the mean, the lower sigma becomes. Or in other words, the lower sigma is, the more indicative of final results the mean is. (You can unclench your teeth now; we have finished talking about statistics.)

When looking at hardware components, therefore, you'll want MTBF figures that are associated with low standard deviations. But good luck in obtaining MTBF numbers; most hardware vendors don't like sharing such data. If you can get these numbers, however, they will tell you a lot about the quality of the vendor's hardware.

The same guidelines that apply to MTBFs also apply to MTTRs. If it takes your administrator 15 minutes to recover from a particular problem, that does not necessarily mean it will take him 15 minutes every time. Complications can set in during the repair process. Personnel change, and recovery times can increase while the new people learn old procedures. (Conversely, as an administrator becomes more adept at fixing a particular problem, repair times can decline.) System reboot times can increase over time, too, as the system gains additional components that need to be checked and/or reinstalled at boot time.

Many aspects of MTTRs can be out of your control. If you need a critical component to repair a server, and that component is on back order at the vendor, it could take days or possibly weeks to acquire it. Unless you have alternative sources or stock spare parts, there isn't anything you can do but wait, with your system down. In many shops, system administration is a separate job from network administration, and it is performed by a totally separate organization. If the system problem turns out to be network-related, you may have to wait on the network folks to find and fix the problem so you can get your system running again. Or vice versa.

Usually the amount of acceptable downtime determines the level of availability required. In general, you don't hear about local phone service outages. The phone companies have mastered the art of installing upgrades to their infrastructure without causing any perceptible interruptions to phone service. Acceptable outages in a telephone network are in the subsecond range.

On a trading floor, outages in the subminute range can be tolerated (usually not well, though) before impact is felt. Regulatory issues concerning on-time trade reporting kick in within two minutes. The market moves every few seconds, possibly making a profitable trade less interesting only a few seconds later. In a less critical application (decision support for marketing, for example), tolerable outages may be up in the one- or two-day range. You'll need to understand what downstream systems are affected by an outage. If the decision support system is driving a mass mailing that has a deadline 48 hours away, and it takes 4 hours to finish a single query, your uptime requirements are stronger than if the mailing deadline is in the next month. Design your support systems, and spend your money, accordingly.

Sometimes, user expectations enter into the equation. If your users believe that the system will be down for an hour while you fix a problem, and you can fix it in 20 minutes, you are a hero. But if the users believe it should take 10 minutes, the same 20-minute fix makes you a goat. Setting expectations drives another downstream system, namely, what the users will do next. If they're convinced they'll be live again in an hour, you have to deliver in that hour. In one of the original *Star Trek* movies, Captain Kirk asked Engineer Scott if he always multiplied his repair estimates by a factor of four. Scotty's response was, "Of course. How do you think I keep my reputation as a miracle worker?"

Failure Modes

In this section, we will take a quick look at the things that can go wrong with computer systems and that can cause downtime. Some of them, especially the hardware ones, may seem incredibly obvious, but others will not.

Hardware

Hardware points of failure are the most obvious ones—the failures that people will think of first when asked to provide such a list. And yet, as we saw in Figure 2.1, they only make up about 10 percent of all system outages. However, when you have a hardware outage, you may be down for a long time if you don't have redundancy built in. Waiting for parts and service people makes you a captive to the hardware failure.

The components that will cause the most failures are moving parts, especially those associated with high speeds, low tolerances, and complexity. Having all of those characteristics, disks are prime candidates for failures. Disks also have controller boards and cabling that can break or fail. Many hardware disk arrays have additional failure-prone components such as memory for caching, or hardware for mirroring or striping.

Tape drives and libraries, especially DLT tape libraries, have many moving parts, motors that stop and start, and extremely low tolerances. They also have controller boards and many of the same internal components that disk drives have, including memory for caching.

Fans are the other components with moving parts. The failure of a fan may not cause immediate system failure the way a disk drive failure will, but when a machine's cooling fails, the effects can be most unpredictable. When CPUs and memory chips overheat, systems can malfunction in subtle ways. Many systems do not have any sort of monitoring for their cooling, so cooling failures can definitely catch even the best-monitored systems by surprise.

It turns out that fans and power supplies have the worst MTBFs of all system components. Power supplies can fail hard and fast, resulting in simple downtime, or they can fail gradually. The gradual failure of a power supply can be a very nasty problem, causing subtle, sporadic failures in the CPU, memory, or backplane. Power supply failures are caused by many factors, including varying line voltage and the stress of being turned on and off.

To cover for these shortcomings, modern systems have extra fans, extra power supplies, and superior hardware diagnostics that provide for problem detection and identification as quickly as possible. Many systems can also "call home." When a component fails, the system can automatically call the service center and request maintenance. In many cases, repair people arrive on site to the complete surprise of the local staff.

Of course, failures can also occur in system memory and in the CPU. Again, some modern systems are able to configure a failed component right out of the system without a reboot. This may or may not help intermittent failures in memory or the CPU, but it will definitely help availability when a true failure occurs.

There are other hardware components that can fail, although they do so very infrequently. These include the backplane, the various system boards, the cabinet, the mounting rack, and the system packaging.

Environmental and Physical Failures

Failures can be external to the system as well as internal. There are many components in the environment that can cause system downtime, yet these are rarely considered as potential points of failure. Most of these are data-center related, but many of them can impact your servers regardless of their placement. And in many cases, having a standby server will not suffice in these situations, as the entire environment may be affected.

The most obvious environmental problem is a power failure. Power failures (and brownouts) can come from your electric utility, or they occur much more locally. A car can run into the light pole in front of your building. The failure of a circuit breaker or fuse, or even a power strip, can shut your systems down. The night cleaning crew might unplug some vital system in order to plug in a vacuum cleaner, or their plugging in the vacuum cleaner may overload a critical circuit.

The environmental cooling system can fail, causing massive overheating in all of the systems in the room. Similarly, the dehumidifying system can fail (although that failure is not going to be as damaging to the systems in the room as a cooling failure).

Most data centers are rats' nests of cables, under the floor and out the back of the racks and cabinets. Cables can break, and they can be pulled out. And, of course, a change in the laws of physics could result in copper no longer conducting electricity. (If that happens, you probably have bigger problems. . . .)

Most data centers have fire protection systems. Halon is still being removed from data centers (apparently if they get one more Halon "incident," that's it!) but the setting off of one of these fire protection systems can still be a very disruptive event. One set of problems ensues when the fire is real, and the protection systems work properly and put it out. The water or other extinguishing agent can leave a great deal of residue, and can leave the servers in the room unfit for operation. Halon works by displacing the oxygen in the room, which effectively chokes off the fire. Of course, displaced oxygen could be an issue for any human beings unfortunate enough to be in the room at the time. Inergen Systems are newer and more friendly to oxygen-breathing life and are becoming more popular. And the fire itself can cause significant damage to the environment. One certainly hopes that when a fire protection system is put into action the fire is real, but sometimes it isn't, and the fire protection system goes off when no emergency exists. This can leave the data center with real damage caused solely by a mistake.

The other end of the spectrum is when a fire event is missed by the protection system. The good news is that there will be no water or other fire protection system residue. The bad news is that your once-beautiful data center may now be an empty, smoldering shell. Or worse.

Another potential environmental problem is the structural failure of a supporting component, such as a computer rack or cabinet. Racks can collapse or topple when not properly constructed. If shelves are not properly fastened, they can come loose and crash down on the shelves beneath them. Looming above the cabinets in most data centers are dusty ceilings, usually with some cabling running through them. Ceilings can come tumbling down, raining dust and other debris onto your systems.

Many data centers have some construction underway, while active systems are operating nearby. Construction workers bring heavy-duty equipment in with them, and may not have any respect for the production systems that are in their way. Cables get kicked or cut; and cabinets get pushed slightly (or not so slightly) and can topple. While construction workers are constructing, they are also stirring up dust and possibly cutting power to various parts of the room. If they lay plastic tarps over your equipment to protect it from dust, the equipment may not receive proper ventilation, and overheat.

And then there are the true disasters: earthquakes, tornadoes, floods, bombs and other acts of war and terrorism, or even locusts.

It is important to note that some high-end fault-tolerant systems may be impacted by environmental and power issues just as badly as regular availability systems.

Network Failures

Networks are naturally susceptible to failures because they contain many components and are affected by the configuration of every component. Where, exactly, "is" your network? In the switch? The drop cables? Bounded by all of the network interface cards in your systems? Any of those physical components can break, resulting in network outages or, even more maddeningly intermittent network failures.

Networks are also affected by configuration problems. Incorrect routing information, duplicated host names or IP addresses, or machines that misinterpret broadcast addresses can lead to misdirected packets. You'll also have to deal with redundancy in network connections, as you may have several routers connecting networks at multiple points. When that redundancy is broken, or its configuration is misrepresented, the network appears to be down.

When a network that you trust and love is connected to an untrusted or unmanaged network, you run the risk of being subject to a denial of service attack or a network penetration attempt. These type of attacks happen within well-run networks as well. Security mogul Bill Cheswick asks attendees to his talks if they leave their wallets out in the open in their offices. Nary a hand goes up. Then he asks how many leave unprotected network access points like twisted pair wall jacks in open offices, and you see the tentative hands raised. Access to the network is valuable and has to be protected while still allowing user activity to proceed without onerous overhead.

Finally, networks use a variety of "core services" or basic information services that we lump into the network fabric. Naming systems like NIS or DNS, security and authentication servers, or host configuration servers for hosts requiring DHCP to boot and join a network will bring down a network if they are not functioning or are giving out wrong answers. As we'll see in Chapter 8, building resilient networks is a complex task and requires many cost/benefit choices.

Database System Failures

Like any complex application, database systems contain many "moving parts." These moving parts are not found in fans or disk drives, however: They are the interrelated subapplications that make up any large enterprise application. The heart of a database system is the server process, or database engine, the main and primary database component that does the reading and writing to the disk, manages the placement of data, and responds to queries with (we hope) the correct answers. If this process stops working, all users accessing the database stop working. The database engine may be assisted by reader-writer or block manager processes that handle disk I/O operations for the engine, allowing it to execute database requests while other processes coordinate I/O and manage the disk block cache.

Between the users and the database server sits the listener process. The listener takes the incoming queries from the users and turns them into a form that the database server can process. Then, when the server returns its answer, the listener sends the answer back to the user who requested it.

The users, at their client workstations, run their end-user application, which is almost always one level removed from the actual SQL (simple query language) engine. The end user application translates the user's request into SQL, which is then sent across the network to the listener. Well-written end-user applications also shield the user from the dreary complexities of the nearly perfect grammar that SQL requires, and from ordinary problems with the database, such as server crashes and other widespread downtime.

Obviously, the failure of any of these processes in the chain will cause the database to be unavailable to its users. Possible failures can include:

Application crashes. The application stops running completely, leaving an error message (we hope) that will enable the administrators to determine the nature of the problem.

Application hangs. A more insidious problem with databases or other systems that have significant interaction with the operating system is when a component process, such as a listener, reader-writer process manager, or the database kernel, hangs waiting for a system resource to free or gets trapped in a deadlock with another process. Some very long-running database operations (such as a scan and update of every record) may appear to make the system hang when they are really just consuming all available cycles.

Resource shortfalls. The most common resource shortfall to strike most database environments is inadequate disk space. If the space allocated to the database fills up, the database engine may crash, hang, or simply fail to accept new entries. None of these is particularly useful in a production environment. If the database itself doesn't fill, the logs can overflow. There are logs that are written into the database disk space itself, and others that may be written into regular file system space. When data cannot be written to either type of log, the database will not perform as desired; it could hang, crash, stop processing incoming requests, or act in other antisocial ways.

Database index corruption. A database server may manage terabytes of data. To find this data quickly on their disks, database servers (and filesystems, for that matter) use a confusing array of pointers and links. Should these pointers become corrupted, the wrong data can be retrieved, or worse, the attempt to retrieve data from an illegal space can result in the application or the system crashing completely. Data corruption problems are fairly unusual because most good RDBMSs have consistency checkers, which scan the database for corruption on start-up.

Buggy software. Almost by definition, software has bugs. (There is an old saw in computing that says all programs have at least one bug in them and can be shortened by at least one line. By extension, that means that all programs can be cut down to one line in length, and that line will have a bug in it!) Software is written by humans, and most of us, from time to time, make mistakes. Bugs can impact the system in various ways, from a simple misspelling in a log entry to a fatal bug that crashes the server and/or system. When trying to solve a problem, always consider the possibility that it was caused by a bug. Don't just assume that all problems were caused by bugs, but at the same time, don't strike "bug" from the list of possible causes for almost any problem. And these bugs can occur at any point in the subapplication chain, server processes, listener processes, client SQL engines, user applications, or even with the user's keyed input.

Web Server Failures

The bugs that can strike a database can also affect a web server. Of course, many web servers are part of client/server applications that query backend database servers to service client requests. So, anything affecting the database server will have an adverse effect on the web server as well. However, there are many other places within the web server environment where things might go awry.

There are many new places for bugs to crop up, including in the CGI, Perl, Java, or Active/X code that manages the web page. If some set of circumstances causes a common gateway interface (CGI) program to get stuck in a loop, the web page it manages will never display, most likely causing the user to try another site.

New technology turns up all over the world of web servers. Much of this technology has been tested in a relatively short time by lots of users, and so it is often quite reliable. However, "web server" refers to a collection of applications: the httpd or web server that handles requests for items on a web page (hits) and returns the HTML or image files; the CGI scripts that get executed to generate web pages or take action on forms or other postings from web clients; and whatever backend database or file servers are used to manage the content and state information on the web site. A failure in any of these components appears to be a web site failure.

Sitting in front of the web server, load-balancing hardware and software may be used to distribute requests over multiple, identical web servers, and on the client side a proxy cache server sits between a client and server and caches commonly accessed pages so that requests don't have to go outside of the client's network. Again, these systems can fail, making it appear that the web server has gone away.

Much like database servers, disks, filesystems, and logs can fill; memory or CPU can be exhausted; and other system resources can run out, causing hangs, crashes, nonresponsiveness, and other nasty behavior.

How do your CGI programs react if they cannot write to a file? Or if they don't get a response from some upstream application? Make sure they continue to operate.

File and Print Server Failures

When file and print servers fail, clients will hang or experience time-outs. A time-out can mean that a print job or a file request fails. The time-out can also lead to wrong answers or data corruption. For example, using Network File Systems (NFS) soft mounts, a write operation that times out will not be repeated. This can lead to holes in data files that will only be detected when the file is read. NFS soft mounts, and other misbehavior by NFS clients, is discussed more in Chapter 11.

The failure of a print server can result in lost jobs, hung jobs, or damaged jobs that require resubmitting. All the while, the user who has requested the job is not being served; based on our definition of downtime, the print server is down to the user.

Cost/Risk Tradeoffs

The only way to convince the people who control the purse strings that there is value in protecting uptime is to approach the problem from a dollars-and-cents perspective. In this section, we provide some ammunition that should help make the case to even the most stubborn manager.

The Costs of Downtime

The most obvious cost of downtime is probably not the most expensive one. The most obvious cost of downtime is lost user productivity, and the actual cost is dependent upon what work your users perform on the affected systems.

If your users are developers, then perhaps the cost seems to be nothing more than the time and carrying cost for the idled developers. Of course, for a large development organization, those costs can be quite significant. A developer may be paid $500 to $1000 a day, though that figure may vary significantly depending upon innumerable factors. It is quite reasonable that idling a group of 50 developers for a week could cost $250,000.

But even the $250,000 is nothing more than the direct cost of the developers' idle time. Not taken into account is the overtime required to make up for the lost time, to ensure that delivery deadlines do not slip. If your developers are consultants, or other hourly employees, then at time-and-a-half, the overtime costs could exceed an additional $375,000. These figures do not take into account factors such as fatigue from working all that overtime, or the impact on morale.

On the other hand, rather than pay the overtime, you might elect to slip your project deadlines a week to make up for the outage. (Does that ever actually

Table 2.2 The Costs of Downtime

INDUSTRY	BUSINESS OPERATION	AVERAGE DOWNTIME COST PER HOUR
Financial	Brokerage operations	$6.45M
Financial	Credit card/sales authorization	$2.6M
Media	Pay per view TV	$150K
Retail	Home shopping (TV)	$113K
Retail	Home catalog sales	$90K
Transportation	Airline reservations	$89.5K
Media	Telephone ticket sales	$69K
Transportation	Package shipping	$28K
Finance	ATM fees	$14.5K

Source: Dataquest, Perspective, September 30, 1996.

happen?) The costs of slipping deadlines are not as obvious or as easily stated as employee carrying costs, but they are just as real.

For production users, costs will obviously vary depending on the line of work performed on the affected servers. For equities traders in large trading firms on Wall Street, the number often quoted for downtime during the trading day is $2 million per 20-minute outage. One assumption in that $2 million number is that all trades made on the trading floor are profitable. Consider that the outage could have prevented a trader from making a money-losing deal, thus saving the firm money. Wall Street firms are oddly loathe to discuss this possibility.

Of course, the traders' salaries and carrying costs are lost, and while many traders do make a lot of money, very few of them can bring in $2 million dollars every 20 minutes. A trading firm's loss is not as easily quantifiable as the loss to the development organization, because the trading firm's losses are also composed of *opportunity losses*.

Opportunity losses refer to the loss of a chance to do *something*, regardless of its outcome. The something could be trading shares of stock, verifying a credit card transaction, or something more mundane like selling a product on the Internet. Without close monitoring, it is almost impossible to know what the opportunity losses are when a system goes down.

But you don't need to precisely quantify a loss to know that a significant loss has occurred.

Imagine that you wish to order an $80 sweater from one of those catalog clothing stores, via telephone (or the Internet). When you call, the operator politely tells you that their systems are down, so could you please call back in a couple of hours? But you want your sweater now. So you call a different catalog company, and order your sweater from it. The direct loss to Company 1 is clear; it is the price of the sweater that you didn't buy from it. But there are other, more indirect, costs. You took your business to its competitor; this helps the competitor, so not only did Company 1 lose $80, but Company 2 made an extra $80. Assuming that Company 2 serviced your order satisfactorily, which will you call next time you want a sweater? Most likely, Company 2. More losses to Company 1. And when your friends ask you where you got that nice new sweater, and you tell them Company 2, the losses to Company 1 increase. They increase further if you tell the whole story, convincing your friends to go to Company 2. Multiply that by the number of customers who may call during the system outage, and you can see that the impact is significant, though perhaps impossible to quantify precisely.

Explaining the Problems to Management

Once you understand the direct and indirect costs of downtime, and assuming that you are not the actual purchasing decision maker, you need to explain to management what must be done to close the holes in your environment.

First, explain the levels of availability to management, then assign costs to each of them. Look at the whole picture; plan complete scenarios. Consider problems that might occur (we discuss them throughout this book), and look at them from a wide perspective. For example, if your entire building is under water, your users will not be able to get to their desks and phones, and so you may not need your computer systems running at all. Therefore, total building loss may not be an eventuality you need to plan for.

Next, decide on the risks that are worth taking. That means spending smart, on the things that will have the most beneficial effects and that are most likely to occur.

Finally, make and justify recommendations. Unless management has specific opinions, and assuming that your recommendations make good financial sense, they will likely be given serious consideration.

One of the greatest challenges in explaining the risks and costs to your management is convincing them not to wait to learn from their own experience. Explain in detail what can happen. Make sure that you balance your dire predictions against the likelihood that these events might occur, and against the costs to the business if these events do occur. Many companies don't properly plan for outages until they occur, when management finally begins to understand the real cost of the outage. Then it may become an iterative process: A disaster occurs; the company plans for it to occur again. A new unplanned outage occurs and the company once again develops a response. Nothing is planned for that hasn't already occurred. Most companies operate in this reactionary manner, and it is always a lose-lose scenario. If the outages could be planned for, they may not occur at all.

This lack of prior planning is human nature. A great example of how this planning doesn't occur until the disaster strikes is taking backups of laptops and other portable computing resources. Most companies don't regard this as a serious issue until the CTO's laptop disk crashes. Then, suddenly, laptop backups become an issue worthy of attention.

Levels of Availability (The Availability Continuum)

It is important to remember that the levels of availability we will discuss are not discrete in nature. There are a great number of incremental steps and combinations of technologies that can add (or in some cases decrease) general system availability. The levels we describe are fairly arbitrary, but they do represent real scenarios.

Level 1. Regular Availability: Do Nothing Special

The most basic level of system protection is essentially no protection at all. No special measures are taken to protect systems or disks from outages. Level 1 may include backups, but nothing more. You deal with downtime as it comes, with no special planning at all. This level is sufficient for many applications, but it can result in outages lasting days in some cases. You may also lose data. If you suffer a disk failure near the end of a day, before backups are taken, an entire day's worth of work on the failed disk is gone. If your systems are in any way tied to revenue generation, direct or indirect, this level should probably be deemed totally unsatisfactory.

Level 2. Increased Availability: Protect the Data

Level 2 is not significantly different from Level 1, except that it includes some sort of online data protection. This means employing RAID technology; most often this means complete disk mirrors, but it also can mean a lesser level of protection such as RAID-5 (parity RAID). No single disk failure will result in lost data, because the data is stored on more than one physical disk. And when system backups are regularly taken, even the loss of two disks will not cause the loss of data. Backups will also protect the data against corruption caused by user error.

Other system component failures will still result in downtime that can last days, but the most critical system resource—the data—will be protected.

Level 3. High Availability: Protect the System

Level 3 is what is commonly called *High Availability* or HA. In an HA configuration, we take two separate servers and loosely couple them together, forming a cluster. When combined with protected disks, the server is provided with duplicates of every system component. If any single component fails, it can be automatically or manually replaced by its duplicate.

Some downtime still occurs in HA configurations, but in most cases it is of a limited duration. Uptimes exceeding 99.98 percent can be achieved at Level 3, and even higher levels are possible when additional protections are implemented. Designing an end-to-end HA system requires network design, supporting system considerations, system and network management considerations, and audits to be sure that you have covered all bases.

One trade-off in implementing availability at this level is that a certain degree of complexity is added to the environment, and complexity makes systems harder to manage. The other trade-off is cost. You're adding redundancy, and that requires money for the systems, networks, time to engineer them, and people to run them. Many of our discussions in this book focus on what level of protection you get for a given cost, and what the potential benefits of that investment are.

Level 4. Disaster Recovery: Protect the Organization

Discussed in more detail in Chapter 14, disaster recovery is the highest and most expensive level of system protection. When you implement disaster recovery, you protect against the total loss of your building or site of operations by having an alternate site some distance away from the main site. You will need all of the hardware necessary to operate your systems in reserve at the backup site, along with policies and procedures to maintain this site, and to get your data and applications so that they can become operational quickly after a disaster has occurred at the main site.

Fault-Tolerant Systems

Another level of system protection (which, however, falls outside the scope of this book) is fault tolerance. A fault-tolerant server is a specialized piece of hardware that is built from double- and triple-redundant components in a single system. If a component fails entirely, another steps in to take its place without interruption. This usually means that the components work in parallel. If a component begins to give spurious or inaccurate results, those results can be compared against other identical components in a democratic system of sorts, and the bad component can be configured out of the system.

In a well-designed fault-tolerant system, no hardware failure should result in any downtime whatsoever. The only component that should be able to cause downtime is software. A bug in a critical application or in the operating system could still cause system downtime, as could a major external incident, such as a long-term loss of power, a fire, or some other environmental problem.

Since system hardware failure theoretically cannot cause downtime in a fault-tolerant system, the question is whether the added availability is worth the high cost of such a system. The costs for fault-tolerant systems can range into the millions of dollars. Fault-tolerant systems often use older and more mature (and better-tested) components that may not deliver the same level of performance as standard systems.

TIME RUNS OUT

In 1993, a bug turned up in the operating system of one of the major manufacturers of fault-tolerant servers. It seemed that a clock counter overflowed; it occurred on every one of this manufacturer's servers throughout the world, as the zero hour passed through each time zone. The only way to fix the problem was to reboot the system.

Of course, as soon as you reboot a fault-tolerant system, you lose any claim to 100 percent uptime.

—Evan

Balancing Risk and Rewards

It is a rare enterprise where the money allocated to solve availability problems is unlimited. Trade-offs inevitably must be made between the acceptable amounts of risk and the resources that can be allocated to minimizing those risks. Consider these simple guidelines as you choose which components to invest your protection resources in first. Protect the components that:

Fail the most often. Obviously, the components that fail the most frequently have the greatest potential for causing service interruptions. Look at the ones with the lowest MTBF numbers, and those with the most moving parts.

Are hardest to replace. Consider the gasket buried deep in your car engine. It fails once in 200,000 miles, and costs 69 cents in materials.

Unfortunately, replacing the gasket requires pulling the engine out of the car and dismantling half of it to get to the gasket. Then, once it is replaced, the engine must be rebuilt and reinstalled. If the car manufacturer could develop a gasket that lasts twice as long without needing any maintenance, even if the cost increases to $1.99 or more, car owners would save tremendous amounts of money, time, and aggravation. If at a cost of $25, the gasket could be changed more easily, that would be even better. The same is true with computers; while there may not be components that take a week to replace, components have varying ease of access and replacement. Choose components that last a long time and that are easy to replace.

Have the greatest impact when they fail. One way to do this is to introduce smarter components that respond to failures around them. In the past, if a cooling fan failed, the system would in turn eventually overheat and then fail, without any warning. Modern systems have extra cooling capacity and fans that know when one of their brethren has failed. The fans can kick into higher gear, increasing their cooling ability, while notifying the system administrators of the failure. In this way, a failure that once would have had tremendous impact can be taken in stride, with minimal effect on users.

You will get a better return on your protection investments by protecting the components whose failure will have the greatest impact on downtime and system management and repair times. Look at what fails the most, or whose failure hurts the most, and spend there. Generally this means protecting your data first, and your data access second. For many companies, losing their critical data means shutting the doors and going home, so the data must be protected regardless of the cost. However, once you get past the obviously critical resources that need protection, the rules become a little fuzzier. You have to balance spending against the likelihood of a particular failure, and the effect of the loss of particular system. In many environments, it doesn't make sense to spend $1 million or more to protect a development system. (But in your environment, it might.)

Don't Overspend

Like so many pieces of good advice, this one is much easier said than done. Don't overspend. Don't waste limited financial resources protecting against events that are too massive to overcome. And don't defend against an impossible situation. For example, no matter how smoothly the salesman talks, don't spend $500,000 to install that Godzilla shield around your data center. Godzilla's not coming. Almost certainly.

Of course, a Godzilla attack is an extreme case. Every event that could cause downtime has a likelihood, just as every protective measure you could take has a real dollar cost to it. If a Godzilla shield is at one end of the scale, then data backups are at the other end. And every point on the scale has a cost associated with it. You need to determine where on that scale your operation needs to be.

Also beware of defending against every conceivable combination of disasters. Engineers enjoy discussing cascading what-if scenarios, and while these make for entertaining academic exercises, they have little basis in reality. Do you need to be concerned about a case where a disk fails at the same time your DBA deletes a critical database table, while terrorists attack the building during a thunderstorm on a Sunday morning? Almost certainly not. Each of those scenarios may be interesting separately, but the odds of them happening simultaneously is akin to winning the lottery two or three times in a row. When plotting events against this scale, consider independent groups of events to be much less likely to occur than any event occurring alone.

Examine your environment. Look at what can realistically fail. Look at how these failures will affect the environment. Consider the likelihood of these events. Strive to minimize the impact of any failure, starting with the worst and most likely scenarios, and working toward the least critical ones.

▶Key Points

- *Components fail.* Face that fact, and plan for it, and be sure that you know the different failure modes of all of your components, from disks to systems to applications.

- *Beware of mean values, and look at maximum values instead.* Know the longest period that you can afford to be down and the worst-case time to fix a problem.

- *Protection against failures costs money, as does downtime.* Finding the right balance between the insurance provided by redundant systems and the potential cost or loss of business caused by failures is the art of designing highly available systems.

CHAPTER 3

Twenty Key System Design Principles

There's never time to do it right; always time to do it over again.
—Unknown

In this chapter (and with an apology to David Letterman's famous "Top Ten" lists) we are going to look at what we see as the fundamental rules for designing highly available and resilient servers. These rules apply to most computing environments and are not particularly technical. They are, however, sound strategies, and if followed will result in saved money, increased uptime, and happier, more productive users.

So, from the Home Office in Fair Lawn, New Jersey, we present our Top Twenty Key System Design Principles to maximize system availability:

#20: Spend Money . . . but Not Blindly

Quality costs money. A Rolls Royce costs more than a Yugo. A pint of Ben & Jerry's or Häagen-Dazs costs more than half a gallon of grocery-store-brand ice cream with those little pieces of ice in it. But we've had the opposite financial trend in the computer industry: More powerful computers cost less each year, while they grow in memory and disk capacity. This trend frequently creates the misconception that availability should somehow be cheaper and easier than in the past. It's not; it still costs money because availability is a quality issue, not a commodity issue.

Your job, as a designer of reliable systems, is to explain to management the costs of various levels of protection. In order to achieve this added value and added quality, management must expect to spend money. If you can't spend the money, you aren't going to be able to achieve very much additional availability.

Analyze the options we offer throughout this book. Consider which ones will make the most sense for your environment. Prioritize them, balancing the cost with the expected overall improvement. Then wholeheartedly attack the ones you have selected, with an open wallet.

Balance your spending with a return on investment criteria set. How much payback do you expect on a new investment in hardware or process engineering, in terms of increased uptime or reduced maximum time to repair?

#19: Assume Nothing

High availability does not come bundled with your systems. Achieving a production level of end-to-end system availability requires directed effort at redundancy engineering, processes for management, testing, integration, and application level assessments. None of these things are done for you by the vendors "out of the box." Nothing can simply be dropped into an environment and be expected to add quality or availability; without the up-front engineering work, the exact opposite is true.

Don't expect product features that work in one situation to continue to operate in other, more complex environments. You add constraints when you add reliability, and you'll have to test, set, and verify the bounds of operation. Above all else, don't assume that applications developers are aware of or sensitive to your planned production environment or the operational rules you'll impose there. Part of the availability design job is doing the shuttle diplomacy between applications developers, operations staff, and network management crews.

#18: Remove Single Points of Failure

A Single Point of Failure (SPOF) is a single component (hardware, firmware, software, or otherwise) whose failure will cause some degree of downtime. You can imagine the SPOF as the weakest link in a chain. When that one link breaks, regardless of the quality of the rest of the chain, the chain is broken. There are obvious potential SPOFs, such as servers, disks, network devices, cables; most commonly these are protected against failure via redundancy.

There are other, equally dangerous, second-order SPOFs that also need attention. Walk through your entire execution chain, from disk to system to application to network and client, and identify everything that could fail: applications, backups, backup tapes, the physical machine room, the building, interbuilding ways used for network cable runs, wide area networks, and Internet service providers. Reliance on external services, such as DHCP or DNS can also be a SPOF.

A NET BY ANY OTHER NAME

While we were teaching our availability course, a system administrator related his experience with redundant Internet connections. Insisting on no single points of failure in its entire networking chain, his company had routers from different manufacturers connected to different Internet Service Providers (ISPs) so that they'd be safe from router bugs or ISP headaches. Nevertheless, his primary connection to the outside world had failed. It turned out, unfortunately, that the secondary ISP chosen happened to resell access from the same upstream provider as the failed primary ISP. Both Internet connections were down because the SPOF was located at the Internet access wholesaler.

—Hal

There are many other SPOFs to consider, and many of the ones discussed briefly above have many other facets we have not yet addressed. We will address many of these through the course of the book.

#17: Maintain Tight Security

Entire books and multiday seminars have been written on maintaining a high level of system security. We do not intend to supplant any of them. Making your systems secure is a necessary but not sufficient reliability requirement. You need to do it, to prevent data corruption and unauthorized access, but it doesn't do much to reduce the impact of a failure. Without duplicating the state of the art in security books, we'll discuss the key issues you need to manage in Chapter 13.

#16: Consolidate Your Servers

The trend over the last few years in many computing circles has been to consolidate servers that run similar services. Instead of having many small single-purpose machines or lots of machines running a single instance of a database, companies are rolling them together and putting all the relevant applications onto one or more larger servers with a capacity greater than all of the replaced servers. This can significantly reduce the complexity of your computing environment. It leads to fewer machines that require backups; fewer machines that require reboots; and overall, fewer things that can fail.

Sometimes many small servers are the right answer, especially when the services can be easily replicated and the server recovery approach is to just "stick a new server in there." This is certainly the trend with NT server farms, and we'll provide guidelines for choosing between consolidation or small-scale replication in Chapter 10.

Consolidation is, however, a powerful force for improving the simplicity and manageability of an environment. It comes with the cost of having to invest even more engineering effort in making the larger, consolidated server more reliable and robust. The moral of the story is "Go ahead and put all your eggs in one basket, just make sure the basket is built out of titanium-reinforced concrete."

#15: Automate Common Tasks

Many experienced system administrators know that they can save themselves a lot of time and effort by automating the most commonly performed mundane tasks. Automation can also prevent simple errors like typos, helping to guarantee successful completion of the tasks. Automated tasks run faster than tasks performed by a human operator and reduce manpower requirements.

The rule for automation is that investing in the development of tools ensures that your skill set and environment don't get stuck at one point in time; you can continue to improve the environment with the existing staff by freeing your people from repetitive and less-than-challenging tasks they've mastered. The downside is that you're accepting responsibility for maintaining and updating all of these tools as soon as you depend on them.

#14: Document Everything

The importance of good, solid documentation simply cannot be overstated. Documentation provides audit trails to work that has been completed. It provides guides for future SAs so that they can take over systems that existed before they arrived. It can provide the SA and his management with accomplishment records. (These can be very handy at personnel review time.) Good documentation can also help with problem solving.

Documentation includes run books, procedures, development documentation, operation manuals, application error guides, and anything else that a new developer or SA might need in order to get the systems to work. It should be well-written, with no assumptions about applications or processes, and should be aimed at multiple audiences over time.

1. The first audience is the author himself. Documentation aimed at the software author makes it much easier for the author to go back and debug problems in his own code that may occur years later. When you look back at two- or three-year-old work (system design and layout, or programs), it can be almost impossible to remember why you did something *this* way, and not *that* way. Write comments. Write manuals, even if they are just a couple of pages long.

2. The second audience is somewhere in the future. The people who maintain the systems and the applications today aren't going to be around forever. And you can't assume that any experienced personnel will be around to mentor newcomers. You must prepare for a massive exodus of your experienced people. A popular sign on many system administrators' desks reads: "Remember, 100 years from now, all new people!"

3. The third audience is management. Keeping good notes, and documenting your work helps demonstrate to management that you were diligent, and shows what measures were taken to keep the systems running and productive. If a system does not meet the requirements set forth in the documentation, it should be easy to figure out why, and what must be done to make the system compliant.

Make sure that documentation is stored on paper too. If the system is down when you need the manuals, you're not going to be able to get to them. Keep them in binders so that they can be easily changed and updated. Once the documentation is written, don't forget to review it on a regular basis. Bad documentation is worse than none at all. In a crisis, documentation is likely to be followed verbatim. If it's wrong, things can go from bad to worse.

Documentation is a lot like castor oil. Everybody agrees to its importance, but nobody likes it. That makes it all the more important that the documentation be written and maintained.

THE BOOK OF EVAN

When I worked for one Wall Street trading firm, the tradition was for departing System Administrators (SAs) to create, say, "The Book of Evan," in which the soon-to-be-dearly-departed describes in detail all of his projects. In this way, the SA who takes over the projects has a way to get started, and to know what's going on. Once an SA gave notice, he'd spend the last two weeks of his employment writing his Book. This is an excellent way to ensure a clean passing of the torch from one generation to the next.

—Evan

#13: Establish Service Level Agreements

Before disaster hits, many organizations like to put written agreements in place with their user community to define the levels of service that will be provided. Some agreements include penalties for failing to meet, and rewards for greatly exceeding, agreed-to service levels.

Service level agreements might deal with the following areas:

- *Availability levels.* What percentage of the time are the systems actually up?

- *Hours of service.* During what hours are the systems actually critical? On what days of the week?

- *Locations.* Are there multiple locations? Can all locations expect the same levels of service?

- *Priorities.* What if more than one system is down at the same time? Who gets priority?

- *Escalation policy.* What if agreements cannot be met? Who gets called? After how much time has elapsed?

These agreements are usually the result of considerable negotiations between (and often significant pain to) both customer and service provider.

Be very careful to avoid agreeing to levels of service that you cannot realistically provide. You cannot guarantee levels of system availability that are measured from the users' perspective unless you have authority and responsibility for every component that brings data from the servers to the users. If even one component is outside of your control, you cannot be assured of meeting expected levels of service; if that component fails, who will fix it? Have they delivered a service level agreement to you or to your users?

#12: Plan Ahead

Specifically, we are talking about planning for emergencies and crises, as well as for the operational cases not covered by your automated tools. At some point, there will be multiple failures or complex, never-before-seen-in-the-wild problems that require human intervention. If you have a plan ready that dictates what you'll do, and how you'll try to resolve the problems or situation, you'll be able to step through the issues. If, on the other hand, you're prioritizing and coordinating in real-time, you leave yourself open to myriad variations on your theme of "fix it now!"

Any kind of documented recovery plans should be approved by management and key personnel, and may be part of a service level agreement. Keep these plans off-line, in binders, and in multiple locations so that the acting, senior person on-site can execute to them when required.

GET I.T. RIGHT!

In a sales organization where I once worked, the IT department announced via e-mail that it would be taking the internal e-mail system down for the entire upcoming weekend. As the upcoming weekend was the last weekend of the calendar quarter, and since the sales organization worked on a quarterly calendar, a very angry e-mail was issued from the Senior VP of Sales. The IT department quickly found a reason to reschedule the downtime.

—Evan

#11: Test Everything

Not only crisis plans need to be tested—so do all new applications, system software, and hardware modifications. Ideally, testing should take place in a production-like environment, with as similar an environment to the operational one as possible, and with as much of the same hardware, networks, and applications as possible. Even better, the same users should perform the tests. The tests need to be performed with the same production network configuration and loads, and with the same user inputs and application sets. User simulation and performance modeling tools may help to generate the first few tests in a quality assurance environment, but you're going to want to test out an application in an environment that looks and feels "live" before really turning the system "on."

Be sure that you test at the unit level (what if this disk fails?); at the subassembly or subsystem level (what if we unplug this disk array or pull out this network connection?); at the complete system or application layer; and then on a full end-to-end basis.

Tests need to be repeated on a regular basis. Environments change, and the only way to be sure that everything works and works together is to test it. Otherwise problems will occur in production that will inevitably lead to downtime. Adopting a regular testing policy is akin in popularity to eating asparagus boiled in castor oil. But no matter how unpopular or distasteful documentation and testing are, they are still preferable to downtime. You'll catch many problems in the earlier tests that may be buried or harder to find in the more complex, later tests.

#10: Maintain Separate Environments

Keep your production and development environments separate and independent. Not just the servers, but the networks, and the users. Development users should not be permitted access to production equipment, except during the first few days of a new rollout (and even then, only under carefully controlled and monitored conditions). Without separate environments, it is not possible to enforce change control in your production environment. Be prepared to equip and operate up to six different environments:

1. *Production.* In production, changes are made only with significant controls. Everything in production needs to work all the time. If something doesn't work, there must be a way to get back to a version that did work. Changes must be made smoothly, and with a minimum of interruption to the production workflow.

2. *Production mirror.* This is a copy of production that contains clean, functional software. This environment enables rolling back to a working production copy in the event that defective software is installed in production. The production mirror only gets updated after an update to production has been installed, and is proven to work.

3. *Quality Assurance (QA).* This is a true test environment for applications that are believed to be production-ready. Quality assurance is the last stop for code before it goes live. Changes made to this environment should be as well-controlled as changes made to production or to the production mirror.

4. *Development.* Clearly this environment is for works in progress. Change need not be monitored very closely, but at the same time, the environment must be maintained for developers to work. In development, code can be installed and run that may not work 100 percent. It may be genuinely buggy. That's okay here, as long as the software running in development and its bugginess does not affect the other environments in any way.

5. *Laboratory.* The laboratory is a true playground. This is where SAs get to play with new hardware, new technologies, and whatever else that comes along. An interesting side benefit of a good lab environment is that it works as a change of pace for your system administrators. With all the automation and procedures that are in place on many production systems, it's healthy to allow the bored or burned-out SA to have a place to go where the rules aren't so strict. The lab may contain new cutting-edge equipment, or be used to set up and solve duplicated thorny production problems in a nonproduction environment. Labs can be a wonderful opportunity for your SAs to develop some real hands-on experience.

6. *Disaster recovery/business contingency site.* This site is located some distance, possibly thousands of miles, away from the main production site. In the event that some major catastrophe takes out the production site, a reasonably quick switchover can be made and production can resume from the disaster recovery site.

Not every company will need, or can afford, all six environments. If no code is developed in-house, then you don't need a development environment, and the test environment becomes less important. You do still want to test out externally developed applications before implementing them, but that integration function may be combined with a QA environment in a single "staging area." In some cases, the production mirror and disaster recovery sites could be the same, but the rules for handling them would be somewhat different. Changes would have to be applied to the mirror first, but would have to be easily rolled out. Combining these two environments does introduce some risk. Just like everything else, you need to determine how much risk is acceptable in your environment.

#9: Invest in Failure Isolation

Failure isolation means that a problem in one area won't be able to bubble over and affect something else. You're able to contain failures close to where they occurred so that they can be identified and resolved before they spread. This means that applications check data before committing it to databases, and that hardware components are separated from each other by management systems that check for and correct failures.

One example of well-implemented failure isolation is found in the separation of hardware RAID from software-based volume management (as described in detail in Chapter 4). Consider when a disk fails. If hardware RAID is in place, then the disk will be automatically replaced via the hot-sparing ability of the array. In that case, the volume management software will never know that a disk has failed and been replaced. If the disks do not have hardware hot sparing, then the responsibility for recovering from the failure bubbles up to the volume management software, which then replaces the failed disk with a hot spare. If there's no hot sparing, the database or filesystem riding on top of the volume will fail.

#8: Examine the History of the System

In order to see what changes to make on your systems to make your system more resilient, you need to look at the recent history of the systems. Why does your system go down? What are the most common causes? Don't just rely on anecdotal information. ("Well, it sure seems to go down a lot on Thursdays.") Keep real records. Check them often. Look for patterns. (Maybe the system really does go down a lot on Thursdays. Now you need to figure out why!) Maintain availability statistics over time.

Account for every incident that causes downtime. Understand the root cause of the failure, and the steps needed to fix it. If you've invested in failure isolation you should have an easier time finding root causes. Look closely at the MTTR, and see if something can be done to improve it. Did it take two days for key parts to arrive? Was there a single person whose expertise was critical to the repair process—and he was unavailable?

Use the evaluations to identify your most common problems, and attack them first. Don't waste your time replacing the CPU if the most common cause of downtime is an application bug. The old 80/20 rule of thumb works here. Eighty percent of your downtime is probably caused by 20 percent of the potential problems. Fix the 20 percent and you should see a tremendous improvement in availability. Then you should be able to reapply the 80/20 rule on the next 80 percent of downtime.

#7: Build for Growth

Boyle's Law states that the volume of a gas will expand to fill all of the available space. Boyle's Law also applies to computing system resources. System use always expands to fill system capacity. This means that the 2TB of disk you just bought for that server will be all used up in a few months. For that matter, so will that server's CPUs and memory. That's just the way of the world.

So, when you design a computer system, do so with Boyle's Law (as applied to computing resources) in mind. Make the systems easy to expand. If you need 8 CPUs in your server, buy a 16-CPU server, and only put 8 CPUs in it. Leave room for growth. If you buy and fill an 8-CPU server, when it's time to add more CPUs, you may have to purchase a whole new server to obtain the additional capacity. If you buy a large disk array completely full of disks, to expand your disk capacity you will need to buy another array, and if you find that you don't have enough I/O slots in the server, you're in trouble. When you find you need to add entire servers, you have to worry about workload distribution and dividing up the applications across the new server base.

#6: Choose Mature Software

Let's say that you have a choice between two Relational Database Management Systems (RDBMS); for our purposes, we'll say the choices are Oracle8 and Joe's

Database v1.0. (We are not endorsing Oracle; the same rules would apply to any mature software product. As far as we know, Joe has not yet released a database.) Perhaps for your purposes, Joe's product has a couple of features that make it a little easier to use, and it comes in a *lot* cheaper than Oracle does. You like Oracle, but Joe's sales rep took you to the World Series last year.

No offense to Joe or his sales rep, but in the end, you will almost certainly be better served by going with the product from a large company like Oracle (or Sybase or Informix or IBM). The large-company product has benefits that you simply cannot get from a small-company product like Joe's. Established RDBMSs have web sites, user groups, user conferences, and other mature support structures. A small company like Joe's is unlikely to have any of those things. These established support structures mean that it is easy to get help from many different sources. You can find users with whom you can discuss various implementation options, performance optimization, problems you may have encountered, and all sorts of other interesting issues. You can also more easily find reference sites that are willing to show you what they have accomplished with their product. When designing for availability, sometimes you'll have to sacrifice the latest-and-greatest technology for something established because you know you'll have to fix it when it breaks.

There's an intermediate ground, however, in the area of publicly available software. Software that has large user bases and many developers working on fixes and improvements is likely to be easily obtained, fixed, and managed, because you'll find a reference model for its use in your application. Windows utilities, Winsock utilities, Unix tools, cross-platform languages like Perl, browsers, and even authoring tools can be obtained by looking and evaluating carefully.

You should have reservations about dot-zero, or first major revisions of software. Not that you shouldn't put these releases into your test bed or laboratory environments, and evaluate the new features and their integration with your world. But hesitate to put them in production until you've done the shakedown. When dealing with Internet software and startup companies, sometimes you need the latest killer application. The enabling technology may only be a year old, forcing you to deal with version 1.0 products. In that case, refer back to Key Design Principle 11 repeatedly.

#5: Select Reliable and Serviceable Hardware

Mean time between failures information can be difficult to obtain, and is often considered proprietary, but when purchasing new hardware make an effort to secure and compare this data. Get an idea of how often the various pieces of hardware will fail. Obviously, using more reliable hardware components will result in more reliable systems.

Building for easy repair is more a matter of selecting hardware that is easy to fix, and easy to access. It is much easier to swap out a client computer if its disks are located outside the box, rather than inside. If they are outside, then you need only swap out the computer and plug everything back in to get the client's user back in business. If the disks are inside the client computer, then the old computer must be opened and the disks removed. Then the new client computer must be opened and its disks removed, and the old computer's disks inserted. All the while, the user is unable to work at his desk.

BURIED TREASURE

My very first car was a used 1974 Camaro. For the most part, it ran just fine. One day, though, it began leaking oil. I brought it in for service and was told that the cause was a faulty engine gasket, a 79-cent part. The only problem was that to get to the gasket, they would have to take apart the whole engine. The end result was that I lost the car for a week, and it cost me (okay, my Dad) about $800. By providing an easier access point for the gasket, the manufacturer could have saved us time and money, and the MTTR would have been much shorter. The same lesson applies to computer system design.

—Evan

Another way to cut down MTTRs is to manage your spare parts properly. Know what spares you are likely to need, and determine how long it will take your vendor to supply them. Also consider what will happen if the vendor is out of the parts: Are there alternate suppliers? Or do you have to wait for the part to be back ordered? Does it make sense for you to inventory certain key spare parts? Balance the extra cost of the parts and the space and inventory overhead with the convenience and the potential reduction in MTTR.

#4: Reuse Configurations

In the words of an old friend of mine, "Plagiarize, plagiarize; never let another's work evade your eyes. But always call it research." Of course, he stole that line from the wonderful satirist, Tom Lehrer.

If you have success with a particular system configuration, reuse it everywhere! Replicate it throughout your enterprise. We recommend picking three or four configurations for different situations (small, medium, and large) and no more. Of course, as technology changes, these base configurations will need to be revisited from time to time, but by limiting the number of different models, there are fewer elements to revisit, and overall, fewer configurations are running in your enterprise.

The advantages of replicated configurations include:

Ease of support. Fewer configurations means fewer permutations of hardware and software, less stuff to learn, and fewer things that can go wrong.

Configurations are pretested. If the same exact configuration works in 20 other places, how much additional testing is required before rolling it out the 21st time? And if some elements actually have changed, only those changed elements need significant testing.

High degree of confidence for new rollouts. If you know that a particular configuration has worked in other rollouts, it makes it much easier to justify using it for future rollouts.

Bulk purchasing. It is often easier (and cheaper) to purchase large quantities of a single component then to purchase smaller quantities of many different components. This is especially true when multiple vendors are involved.

Spare parts. Fewer different components mean fewer spare parts to stock (if you choose to stock them at all). This lowers the overall cost of the spare parts, decreases the storage space required to stock them, and simplifies the inventorying process.

Less to learn. Perhaps the biggest benefit of replicating configurations is in how much less there is for incoming system administrators to learn. Giving your SAs less to learn means that they can come up to speed on the way your company does things much faster, and as a result, they can be productive much sooner.

#3: Exploit External Resources

Most likely, whatever problem you are trying to solve, or whatever product you are trying to implement, someone has done it before you. The vendor probably has a consulting or professional services organization who, for a fee, will visit your site and implement your critical solutions for you, or at least offer advice on how to architect and implement your plans.

Arrange for on-site consultation from vendor resources or independent contractors, and be sure a transfer-of-information or technical exchange is part of the planned work. If vendors offer training classes on a product, take them, so that you learn the pitfalls and issues before you start implementation. Rely on documentation, user groups, published conference proceedings, web sites, and anything else that looks like it might make a good case study.

#2: One Problem, One Solution

Someone once said that a good tool is one that has applications that even its inventor did not foresee. While that's true, most tools are designed for a single purpose. You wouldn't use a butter knife as a screwdriver and expect the same good results you get from using a screwdriver. The same holds true for software.

Don't take a single solution and shoehorn it into solving two problems. Don't try to make a solution fit if the designers did not intend it to be used in the way you propose. Complex problems have many aspects (subproblems) to them, and may require more than one solution. Examine one subproblem at a time, and solve it. If your solution happens to help solve another subproblem, that's serendipity. But don't expect it to happen every time. In fact, one solution may create other unforeseen problems, such as incompatibility with other products.

BE CAREFUL WHAT YOU ASK FOR

A prospective customer of mine wanted to replicate a database from a site in New Jersey to a remote site in Kansas. My company offered a perfectly satisfactory solution to implement this replication. However, he also wanted the replication software to hold the replicated data for four hours before applying the updates to the remote site. This way if a database administrator accidentally corrupted the database by, say, deleting a table, he wanted to have his worldwide user base switch its access point to the delayed copy in Kansas.

Even though my company offered three other products through which he could achieve his goals, he insisted that we provide the solution through the replication software. He did not want to hear about the issues associated with reinitializing the New Jersey copy of the database after switching to Kansas, nor in considering our detailed alternate proposals.

In the end, after a lot of custom work to the replicator, he did not select our product. He felt that the solution was cobbled together. It was. In the end, his chosen solution could not do the job adequately either. If he been willing to consider a different approach, his problems could have easily and quickly been solved.

—Evan

#1: KISS: Keep It Simple . . .

Simplicity is key to availability design because you're building something complex to begin with. When you factor in networks, disks, systems, applications, and management, you have many points of control and many places where things can get unnecessarily complicated. Simplicity means eliminating extraneous hardware on critical systems, slimming down servers so that they run only critical applications, choosing host names that are easy to remember and easy to communicate on the telephone, and generally removing ambiguity from the environment. If it's not clear who you should call when something breaks, or who has authority to take a network down, the wrong thing will happen.

The bottom line is that you want to minimize the points of control and contention, and the introduction of variables.

Why is simplicity so important? Because it is easy to make mistakes on complex systems, and mistakes (even honest ones) lead to downtime. By making systems simpler in every possible way, you give your administrators (and your users) less opportunity to make the kinds of mistakes that lead to downtime.

Late jazz bass musician Charles Mingus said that "anybody can take something simple and make it complex; making something complex simple is real creativity." What we're recommending is that you find the simple but powerful ways to solve problems. They'll last longer, be more resilient in the face of new and increasing demands, and generally make your life easier. And it's a creative process to get there, not one filled with rejection of anything interesting or new. As we get into our discussions of system and application design, we'll focus on those creative aspects that lead you to a simpler, more manageable approach to availability.

CHAPTER

4

Highly Available Data Management

Disks, and the data stored on them, are the most critical part of just about any computer system. In this chapter, we will discuss many of the options you have for storing data on these disks, and ways of protecting the data against inevitable failures of disks, cables, interface cards, and so forth. We spend a lot of time defining terms in this chapter, but the definitions act as a framework for the availability and design lessons.

To that end, in this chapter we will discuss:

- Various types of disk hardware
- RAID levels
- Data redundancy
- Disk space
- Filesystems

Fundamental Truths

There are four fundamental truths that relate disk storage to overall system availability.

1. *Disks are the most likely component to fail.* Most systems have more physical disks than any other component. If your system has 100 disks in it, with an MTBF of 200,000 hours (almost 23 years) for each disk, that doesn't mean that you'll be error-free for two decades and then suddenly all 100 disks will fail at once. Each disk has the same probability distribution of errors, but with many more disks, the probability of no disk showing an error goes down exponentially. Calculating the actual MTBF for a system with that many disks can be done using a simulation or by combining the probability distributions and determining the new mean and standard deviation for the system with 100 components in it. Both approaches are beyond the scope of this book. Instead we propose a very rough, and very conservative, rule of thumb: Divide the MTBF for a specific component by the number of those components in the system, and you have something of a worst-case "time for first failures." With a 200,000-hour MTBF, you should expect a 50 percent chance of failure in the first 200,000 hours, but over 90 percent of those failures fall within one standard deviation of the mean. Using our simple math, that figure gets reduced to 200,000/100, or about 83 days for a 50/50 chance of at least one disk going south.

   Power supplies tend to have the worst MTBF figures for any component in the system, but since you only have a few of them, the overall frequency of failures will be lower than for disks. Even in the 30,000 hour range, you may only have 6 power supplies, giving you a good shot at a failure in just over 200 days, using the same voodoo math approximation just described.

2. *Disks contain data.* This incredibly obvious statement transfers the value of data, which in most companies is their single most important asset, to the associated disks, the medium on which the data is stored. Disks themselves have very little intrinsic value; their value comes from the data that is stored on them.

3. *The data must be protected.* If you lose the hardware components of your system, they can be replaced pretty easily. If you lose your data, however, it could take years to recover, if it can be recovered at all. If a company's key data is truly lost, the company may never recover from that loss. Probably the single most important action you can perform to protect your systems, and therefore your data, and therefore your job, is making backups. That means backups that are successful, that are tested, and that are done with the regularity of breathing.

4. *Data accessibility must be ensured.* If the data is critical, and it has been backed up, then your next-most-important job is to ensure that the data can actually be reached by the user community. Data that cannot be read

is not doing anyone any good. This calls for data redundancy via RAID, data path redundancy via multiple pathways and the appropriate management software, and storage management software that notifies you when a component has failed or is failing.

The model to use when deciding precisely how to manage your data storage is diagrammed in Figure 4.1:

1. *Physical disks.* These are the physical commodity items where data is actually read and written.

2. *Hardware RAID.* This is the management layer that may be present within your disk array. Usually it is associated with its own management tool. Although the RAID management interface that manages these disks may be accessed from the system console (some RAID vendors use specialized consoles), the actual management of these disks falls outside the realm of the operating system, and is instead performed within the disk array.

3. *Software RAID/volume management.* This is the management layer that runs within or very near to the operating system. Management is performed purely on the server with no other hardware (apart from the disks themselves) involved, from the operating system and the server's CPU.

4. *Filesystem or raw device.* This is the layer that the application speaks to. The file system has its own level of managing the layout of files and data on the disk. A raw device is a piece of disk without a file system on it. Its use requires that another application, usually a database, manages the space. Some applications, notably image processing and data collection, use a raw disk for pure speed, treating it like a tape drive that has no real formatting and is a continuous stream of bytes from beginning to end.

5. *Application or database.* The most visible and obvious layer to users is how they use the data. Generally, users access data through an application such as a database or some sort of development tool.

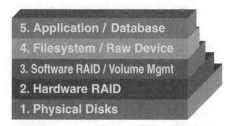

Figure 4.1 Storage management layers.

Each of these layers is independent of the others. The application could access data directly on raw physical disks without a filesystem, or any sort of RAID or other management involved. Further, the application should not care, or require a change in any way if the contents of one of the other layers change. The presence of a particular kind of file system should not, from a technical viewpoint, influence the choice of volume management tool.

Disk Hardware and Connectivity Terminology

In this section we introduce some disk hardware terminology.

SCSI (Small Computer Systems Interface)

SCSIs come in many varieties; for example, there are narrow, wide, and ultra SCSIs. Each of these refers to the amount of data that can be sent across the bus (data cable or transport) in parallel. Narrow is 8 bits, wide is 16 bits, and ultra is 32 bits. The wider the bus, the faster the data can get across it. Theoretical maximum speed for narrow is 10 megabytes per second, for wide is 20 megabytes per second, and for ultrawide is 40 megabytes per second; in reality, top speeds will usually run 10 to 15 percent slower because you have to add in the overhead of the SCSI data transport protocol.

There are at least three different levels of SCSI: SCSI-1, SCSI-2, and SCSI-3. There are differential and single-ended SCSI varieties, and there are ultra, fast, fast narrow, and fast wide SCSI varieties:

SCSI-1. This is the original SCSI technology, developed in the early 1980s. It only supports 3–5MB/second transfer rates, and only allows one disk and one system on a bus. You'd be hard-pressed to find SCSI-1 hardware on production systems today.

SCSI-2. Work started on this update in 1986. It is faster and more reliable than SCSI-1, comes in several varieties, typically has an 8-bit-wide data path, and uses a 50-pin connector. The theoretical maximum throughput of SCSI-2 is 10 megabytes per second.

Single-ended SCSI-2. This is the "regular" version of SCSI (so identified to separate it from Differential SCSI). Due to line noise, transfer speeds rarely exceed 5 megabytes per second.

Differential SCSI-2. This uses a more complex method of transmitting signals, which results in longer supported cabling distances (up to 25 meters), easier termination, and faster transmission speeds (up to 10 megabytes per second) because differential SCSI puts less noise on its data cables. Not all SCSI devices are compatible with differential SCSI.

Fast/Narrow SCSI-2 (also called Fast SCSI-2). Cable lengths are limited to 6 meters. A 10-megabyte per second throughput is possible in some cases.

Fast/Wide SCSI-2. Fast/Wide SCSI-2 doubles the 8-bit width to 16 bits, doubling throughput to 20 megabytes per second at the same time. Fast/Wide can come in either differential or single-ended varieties. Since 16-bit Fast/Wide uses a 68-pin connector, it is easy to recognize.

SCSI-3. This is also called Ultra-SCSI. At 8 bits wide, SCSI-3 can transmit data at 20 megabytes per second. Once again, SCSI-3 is available in differential or single-ended varieties.

Wide Ultra-SCSI. This takes the 8-bit SCSI-3 bus and doubles it to 16 bits, with 40 megabytes per second throughput.

Ultra-2 SCSI. Ultra-2 offers 40 megabytes per second at 8-bit widths, and 80 megabytes per second at 16-bit widths. It no longer comes in a single-ended variety.

Ultra-3. This once again doubles throughput, potentially to 160 megabytes per second. Ultra-3 devices are expected to begin shipping in volume in the year 2000.

A SCSI bus is an electrical circuit that requires a terminator on both ends. A system generally acts as the terminator on one end. If there is only one system on the bus, then a terminator device is required on the other end. Since a SCSI bus is a circuit, it should never be broken (unplugged) while in use. If it is, data loss can—and almost certainly will—occur.

There are two kinds of devices that can sit on a SCSI bus: *initiators* and *targets*. Generally, initiators are computers; they place commands onto the bus that targets respond to with data. Targets are usually disks and tape drives, although other devices are possible. Every device on the bus must have a unique address. The range of valid addresses is from zero to the width in bits, minus 1. On a narrow bus, the address range is zero to 7. On a wide bus, it is zero to 15.

SCSI resets can occur when an initiator ID is changed, when a system connected to the bus reboots, or when an operation in progress is interrupted. SCSI resets can, in some cases, result in the loss of data in transit. It is generally best not to mess with an active SCSI bus.

Traditionally, host adapters on servers have a default address of 7. When more than one initiator ("multi-initiated SCSI") is placed on a single SCSI bus (as in Figure 4.2), one of the initiators must change its address. This is usually a manual operation.

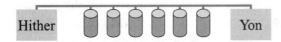

Figure 4.2   Multi-initiated SCSI.

From one terminator to the other, a differential SCSI bus cannot exceed 25 meters or 82 feet in length, including the short runs of cable within enclosures. Single-ended SCSI buses cannot exceed 6 meters, or about 20 feet in length. At the higher data rates of Fast/Narrow SCSI, long single-ended SCSI bus chains can introduce reliability problems due to noise. Electrical and noise requirements constraining the length of a SCSI bus put a serious limit on the maximum distance between a server and its storage.

Without going into a lot of dull detail, in addition to defining an electrical standard, SCSI also defines a command set for moving data across the bus.

Fibrechannel

Fibrechannel is a newer technology for connecting servers to disks. At this writing, Fibrechannel supports speeds up to 100 megabytes per second, but since it is usually deployed in dual-attach style, the capacity is doubled to 200 megabytes per second in most implementations. The 100-megabytes-per-second throughput is expected to grow to, and probably exceed, 1 gigabyte per second (GB/sec) over time. Up to 126 devices can be deployed on an FCAL "network."

FCAL supports much greater distances for disk connectivity than does SCSI. A single straight cable run of 2 kilometers can be supported in FCAL, and through the use of repeaters, distances exceeding 10 kilometers are possible. Moreover, differential SCSI's 82 feet is the limit for the *total distance* of a SCSI bus; while in a FCAL environment, the 2-kilometer limit is between *any two* devices. Therefore the total distance of the FCAL can be much greater, as long as no segment is longer than 2 kilometers (10 kilometers with repeaters).

FCAL also supports all of the networking hardware normally associated with LANs, such as routers, hubs, and switches. A FCAL that includes these devices is often called a *fibre fabric*. Fibrechannel cables are thin and light because they do not need the 50 to 67 separate wires running in them that SCSI cables require. Fibrechannel also offers complete electrical independence of its devices, allowing them to be unplugged or plugged in without affecting the other devices on the bus.

In spite of all the physical differences between SCSI and Fibrechannel (see Table 4.1), Fibrechannel uses SCSI's mature and well-known interdevice communication protocol, thus easing the transition and acceptance period.

Table 4.1   SCSI versus Fibrechannel

TECHNOLOGY	THROUGHPUT	SUPPORTED NUMBER OF DEVICES	MAXIMUM DISTANCE
Ultra SCSI	40MB/sec	31	82 feet total
Fibrechannel	200MB/sec	126	2km between any 2 devices

Multihosting

This means connecting one set of disks to two or more servers at the same time. Both servers can see and access the disks, but generally not at the same time. Multihosting is most commonly used in a failover environment, enabling the takeover server to get data that is as up to date as possible.

Multipathing

This means connecting a single host to a single disk array with more than one data path. This technology requires multiple interface cards in the host, and a disk array that has sufficient inputs to support all the connections.

Data transfer rates can be increased linearly (i.e., two 20MB/sec connections yield an effective 40MB/sec transfer rate) if both connections are active all the time. If one of the connections fails, the other should be able to take over the full data transfer load without interruption.

Connections may fail due to a cable breaking or being removed, or because an interface card or controller in either the disk array or in the host has failed. All of these failures will be transparent in a properly configured multipathed environment.

Disk Array

A disk array is a single enclosure or cabinet, containing slots for many disks. The array may use SCSI or Fibrechannel internally to address its disks, and may use SCSI or Fibrechannel to connect to its host(s). The same array may have SCSI disks internally, while connecting to its host(s) via Fibrechannel.

JBOD (Just a Bunch of Disks)

"JBOD" refers to a collection of disks without any sort of hardware intelligence or real organization. Usually JBODs are literally a stack of small disk cabinets that each contain a disk or two. On a critical system, these disks will absolutely require some sort of logical volume management capability.

Hot-Pluggable Disks

In a disk array, disks are hot pluggable if they can be added or removed from the cabinet without any downtime or other impact on the other disks or on the host(s) to which they are connected. Hot pluggability is very important on systems that require high levels of availability.

Warm-Pluggable Disks

Warm pluggability, hot pluggability's poor cousin, is the ability to add or remove disks from a disk array or cabinet while only impacting some of the disks in the cabinet. For example, a disk array with three disk trays in it, that requires pulling out one tray to change a disk in the tray, while allowing the other disks to remain active, is warm pluggable. Proper mirroring can limit the impact of warm pluggability to nothing more than inconvenience.

Hot Spares

A hot spare is a disk that sits in reserve, waiting for a critical disk to fail. The hot-sparing software agent migrates the data that was on the failed disk to the hot spare. Hot spares require some sort of RAID, so that the contents of the failed disk can be recreated on the replacement. Hot sparing can be performed by either the disk array or by logical volume management software.

Write Cache

Many disk arrays contain some specialized memory which acts as a staging area for disk writes. Since memory is much faster than disk, writes to this cache can complete many times faster than writes to disk. Write cache can increase the cost of a disk array, and unless the disk array has a reliable battery backup, can cause data loss if the data written to the cache never makes it to disk.

Storage Area Network (SAN)

A storage area network is a new model for organizing storage and computing systems. The best short definition for a SAN is a storage pool that many hosts can access. In this way, the storage resources can be accessed by any or all of the hosts.

At this writing, SANs are an up-and-coming technology, which is expected by industry analysts to become prevalent around the years 2001–2003. The enabling technology for SANs is FCAL.

We offer a very simple depiction of a SAN in Figure 4.3. We have left out the hubs, routers, switches, and other hardware that are almost always present in a SAN. We have also left out any mention of disk mirroring or other form of RAID for clarity, although you'll need to add that functionality to a SAN for data reliability.

Storage area networks solve many of the problems associated with the traditional one-to-one relationship between hosts and storage. By putting newly purchased storage into the storage pool, it can be allocated as needed between the hosts in the SAN, and storage purchases become much more efficient. When you request a disk purchase, and management complains that "you just bought 2 terabytes of storage," you don't have to say, "Yes, but we put that 2 terabytes on that server over there; now I need disks for this server here." All the storage can be shared and easily allocated between all of the servers on the SAN.

Other SAN advantages include:

Centralized management and allocation. The storage pool and its allocation can be centrally managed from one host in the SAN. This means that a single collection of disks can be allocated in whatever chunks are required, and can easily be reallocated among hosts as needs change.

Intrinsic resilience and high availability. Disks can be centrally RAIDed, and will usually have dual connections to the SAN, so that the loss of a single controller or connector will not cause a failure.

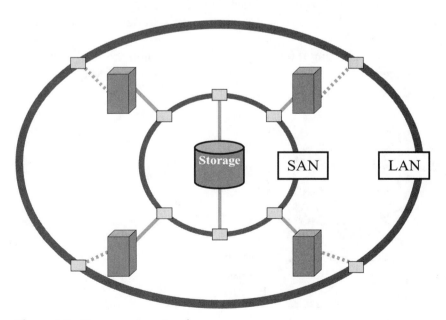

Figure 4.3 Storage area network.

Disks need not be colocated. The 2-kilometer FCAL distance limit means that disks can be located some distance away from their associated servers. In fact, servers on the same SAN need not be in the same room or even in the same building. Whether servers are next to each other or 2 kilometers (or more) apart, they function exactly the same way.

Smart and more efficient failover. More complex failover configurations, such as N-to-1, N-to-N, cascading, and service level failovers are much more practical in a SAN environment. We will discuss this in much more detail in Chapter 6.

Efficient resource deployment. The resources on a SAN are visible to all the members of the SAN, so a tape silo or other expensive backup device can be shared all across the SAN. This makes the purchase of high-speed backup devices much more practical and justifiable.

LAN-free backups. With a tape drive on the SAN and some SAN-aware backup software, it will be possible to back up your server directly to tape, by putting the data on the SAN, rather than on the LAN, thus reducing the impact of backups on your user community.

As SANs mature, more features will develop, and costs will drop. It will be practical for parallel applications to be developed. A parallel application will support more than one server in a SAN reading and writing to the same disk data at the same time, resulting in increased performance and reliability. Currently, a single SAN hub or router can cost hundreds of thousands of dollars. It is not hard to predict that prices will have to drop significantly before wider acceptance can begin.

Perhaps the most exciting future feature has been called the "Holy Grail" of SANs—heterogeneous access to data. If a common data storage format (per-

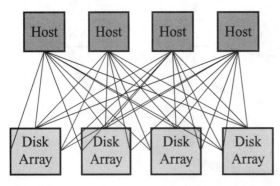

Figure 4.4   Four hosts connected to four disk arrays via SCSI.

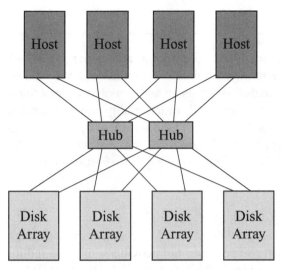

Figure 4.5　Four hosts connected to four disk arrays via Fibrechannel.

haps a cross-platform filesystem) can be developed, there is no reason why parallel access from Windows, Solaris, and HP/UX servers could not be achieved, thus eliminating some portion of the operating system wars.

SCSI versus Fibrechannel

Let's look at two configurations (Figures 4.4 and 4.5) that provide the same functionality. In both examples, we have four disk arrays and four hosts. Each host has two distinct data paths to each array, and each array has two distinct data paths out of it, for maximum availability and performance.

The first diagram (Figure 4.4) shows this configuration built using standard SCSI technology. The second diagram (Figure 4.5) shows this configuration built with Fibrechannel technology.

The data in Table 4.2 indicates the reasons why fibrechannel is emerging as the winner in disk interconnects: It's simpler, cheaper and more reliable.

Table 4.2　SCSI versus Fibrechannel

COMPONENT	CABLES	TERMINATORS	HOST BUS ADAPTERS
SCSI	32	0–8	32
Fibrechannel	16	None	8

RAID Technology

The RAID standard describes several ways to combine and manage a set of independent disks so that the resultant combination provides a level of disk redundancy. Five levels of RAID are defined, plus an additional loosely defined level that does not provide any redundancy. RAID functionality can be provided from within a disk array or on a disk controller (hardware RAID) or from the host system (software RAID). In general, software RAID requires work from the host system CPU; hardware RAID is performed on a separate dedicated CPU.

RAID Levels

There are five levels of RAID that provide various levels of increased disk redundancy, and one more (RAID-0), which does not provide additional redundancy. The RAID levels are numbered from RAID-0 to RAID-5. Other RAID levels (apart from RAID 0+1 and 1+0, which result from combining RAID-0 and RAID-1) are not officially recognized RAID levels, and are usually marketing names for slight variations on the standard levels.

RAID functionality is totally independent of the data stored on the disks. The data could be stored in a file system or in raw format (non-filesystem-based); it could be user data, application data, source code, or any other sort of data. RAID simply manages where and how many times the data is written.

RAID-0: Striping

RAID-0 is another name for disk striping. In a striping model, each chunk of data to be written to disk is broken up into smaller segments, with each segment written to a separate disk. Since each disk can complete the smaller writes at the same time, write performance is improved over writes to a single disk. Performance can be enhanced even further by striping the writes between separate controllers, too.

The size of each segment is called the *stripe width*. In general, the optimal size of a stripe width is the average size of a disk write, divided by the number of disks in the stripe. However, if the disk array has its own cache, the rules may change.

The first and most important thing to know about RAID-0 is that, unlike all the other levels of RAID, RAID-0 does not increase your system or data availability. In fact, when used by itself, RAID-0 *decreases* availability. In order for a stripe set to function, all of its member disks must be available. If any disk in a stripe fails, the entire stripe fails and cannot be read or written. Consider a 2GB filesystem, and disks with a 200,000-hour MTBF. If the filesystem lives on a single 2GB disk, the MTBF in is simply 200,000 hours. If the filesystem is striped across 4 disks, with 500MB of data on each disk, the MTBF is reduced significantly due to the increased probability that *at least one* of the disks will fail.

Please note that when we use the term RAID throughout the book as a generalized way of adding disk redundancy, we are specifically excluding RAID-0 from that discussion, since RAID-0 *reduces* overall system availability, and all other levels *increase* it.

RAID-1: Mirroring

RAID-1, or mirroring, is a model where a copy of every byte on a disk is kept on a second disk. The copy is (normally) 100 percent in sync. In this model, if one disk fails, the other disk continues to operate without interruption.

A common misconception of disk mirroring is that a master/slave relationship exists between the disks, and if one disk fails, the other takes over. This is not the case: Both copies in a mirror act as peers. A better way to think about this relationship is to imagine a logical disk that sits above the mirror copies, and sends all read and write requests to both disks at the same time. If a disk fails, the logical layer is not affected; it continues reading and writing to the surviving disk. Reads are usually requested of both underlying copies, and the logical layer returns the data that comes from the first physical disk to reply.

In fact, mirrors are not limited to two copies. Many users will keep three or four copies of their data, and split one off from time to time for backups, or to provide production-like data to their development, QA, or disaster recovery environments.

Another, slightly less common misconception about mirroring is that if your disks are mirrored you don't need to take backups. This is not true. Mirrors will absolutely protect your users from hardware failure, but they will not protect you from the careless or malicious deletion or corruption of critical files or data. All mirrored copies will be affected by the deletion. Point-in-time copies or checkpoints will protect your users from such a deletion; we will discuss those in Chapter 12.

The primary advantage of RAID-1 is data protection when the inevitable loss of a disk occurs. A secondary advantage is that read performance is a little faster under RAID-1 than it is without because more than one disk is servicing a read request in parallel, and the first disk to respond completes the request. Some of the time, the single disk that would have been used without mirroring will be the slower one.

There are definite disadvantages to RAID-1 as well. The primary disadvantage is in the added expense. Each mirror requires 100 percent disk overhead. It takes another 10GB to mirror 10GB. There are no economies of scale possible with RAID-1. The other disadvantages are performance related. Resyncing a failed or new RAID-1 disk requires a block-for-block complete copy of the contents of the original disk. This takes time, and it also requires a tremendous amount of I/O, which can slow down the service times for regular requests that have nothing to do with the resync. Write performance will generally also suffer a little with RAID-1; just as read performance improves because one disk will return data faster than the other, write performance suffers because all disks must be written to, and the write request will not complete until the slowest disk has finished writing. "Slowest" in this regard doesn't only refer to the transfer rate of the disk but rather to the average rotational and seek latencies incurred in setting up the write head to move the data. Obviously, when the disks are in a disk array with a large write cache, performance will not be affected in this way, and write performance will be much better than it would have been without the cache.

Combining RAID-0 and RAID-1

Unlike in the world of mathematics, addition of RAID levels is not commutative. RAID 0+1 is significantly different from RAID 1+0. RAID 1+0 (sometimes inappropriately called RAID-10) is a superior method of combining these technologies, but it is often harder for vendors to implement, or to implement well, and as a result many vendors have allowed the confusion between 0+1 and 1+0 to stand uncorrected.

The difference between the two models depends on which combining method is employed first. As shown in Figure 4.6, in RAID 0+1 (or mirrored stripes), one side of the mirror is built first and then mirrored to the other copy. Figure 4.7 shows RAID 1+0 (or striped mirrors); the mirrors are built separately first, and the mirrors are striped together as if they were separate disks.

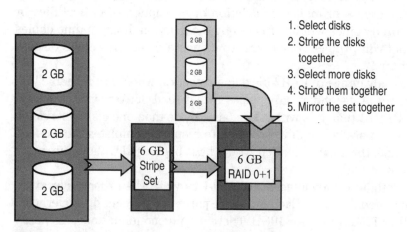

1. Select disks
2. Stripe the disks together
3. Select more disks
4. Stripe them together
5. Mirror the set together

Figure 4.6 Building RAID 0+1: mirrored stripes.

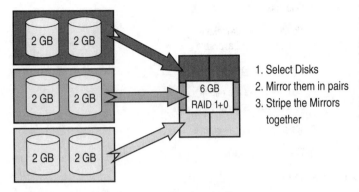

Figure 4.7 Building RAID 1+0: striped mirrors.

The differences between 0+1 and 1+0 are not particularly apparent in the description of how they are built. But when you look at how they handle failures, and how they recover from those failures, the differences become much more obvious.

As shown in the RAID 0+1 example, the loss of any member of a stripe causes the loss of the entire stripe. In Figure 4.8, if disk A, B, or C fails, all of stripe 1 is lost. If disks D, E, or F fail before the first failed disk can be recovered, the entire data set is lost.

In the RAID 1+0 example in Figure 4.9, if A or B fails, there is no data loss. If C or D fails, there is no data loss. If E or F fails, there is no data loss. However, if A and B fail at the same time (or C and D, or E and F), then and only then, the entire RAID device is lost.

One might note that either RAID composition could sustain the loss of one-half of its disk members and still survive. However, the odds for surviving are

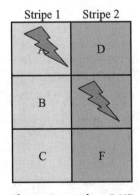

Figure 4.8 When RAID 0+1 disks fail.

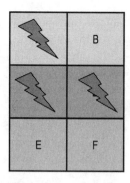

1. One disk fails

2. No other disks are taken
   off-line; data still available

3. Another disk fails

4. No other disks are taken
   off-line; data still available

5. *Matching* disk goes off-line

6. Then data is lost.

Figure 4.9 When RAID 1+0 disks fail.

very much in favor of 1+0. If disk A fails in either figure, both compositions will survive. In the RAID 1+0 example, of the five disks that remain after disk A fails, only one of them (B) could cause a catastrophic failure. In the RAID 0+1 example, if A fails, then a catastrophic failure will result if D, E, or F fail. So, in our examples, the chance that a second disk failure will cause a catastrophe in RAID 1+0 is only 20 percent (1 in 5), while in 0+1 the chance is 60 percent (3 in 5). And since B and C are not actually in use once A fails, the chances for catastrophe are even greater.

The other issue when comparing the two combined RAID levels is recovery. Once disk A has failed in RAID 0+1 (Figure 4.8), and the entire stripe is lost, all three disks in the stripe (A, B, and C) must be synced with D, E, and F in order to bring stripe 1 back on line. To recover from the loss of disk A in the RAID 1+0 example (Figure 4.9), only disk A needs to be resynced.

The reliability advantage of 1+0 over 0+1 is clear. The only real downside to 1+0 is that each of the stripe components needs to be the same size. That can be inconvenient when designing the layout. RAID 0+1 does not have that requirement, and only requires that all sides of the mirror be the same size.

RAID-2: Hamming Encoding

We include this RAID level purely to be thorough. RAID-2 uses the same Hamming encoding method for checking the correctness of disk data as is used by ECC memory. We have been unable to find even one commercial implementation that uses RAID-2.

RAID-3, 4, and 5: Parity RAID

RAID levels 3, 4, and 5 are all called *parity* RAID, because they do not involve maintaining a complete copy of the original data on a second set of disks. Instead, each RAID volume requires space equivalent to one extra disk. This additional disk's blocks contain calculated parity values, which are generated by taking XORs (eXclusive ORs) of the contents of the corresponding data blocks on all the other disks in the RAID volume. If any one disk (including the parity disk) in the RAID set is lost, its contents can be calculated based on the contents of all the other disks in the set. If two disks are lost at the same time, or a second disk is lost while the first disk is being rebuilt, all the data on the RAID stripe is lost and must be restored from a backup. The overhead in a parity RAID model is generally only about 20 to 25 percent, depending on the number of disks in the stripe.

Parity RAID requires that each member disk in the RAID volume be the same size.

When writing to a parity RAID set, not only do the writes have to complete, but there are serious performance penalties when the parity must be recalculated; data has be read from otherwise unaffected disks in the set so that the correct parity value can be written to the parity disk region. Therefore, RAID writing, especially when the writes are small, is generally pretty slow. RAID read performance is unaffected by parity calculations, since none needs to be performed.

Because a rebuild requires reading every block on every disk in the volume, and performing calculations on it, rebuilds are very time consuming, and unless hardware RAID is involved, rebuilds will put a significant load on the server CPU, slowing down all other work.

The performance of a RAID set is also dependent on the number of disks in the set. Once you exceed six or seven disks in a RAID set, performance will really fall off.

The differences between RAID-3, RAID-4, and RAID-5 are in exactly how they use the extra space provided by the additional disk.

RAID-3: Virtual Disk Blocks

In RAID-3, virtual disk blocks are created that are striped across all the disks in the RAID-3 volume. Every disk operation touches all the disks, regardless of the size of the write. The RAID volume can only process one disk I/O at a time.

RAID-3 performance depends on the nature of the writes. If the I/Os are small, and random (all over the volume, rather than sequential,), performance will be poor. If the I/Os are large and sequential, performance will be fast.

Commercial implementations of RAID-3 are generally in hardware, rather than software. Storage Technologies (Storage Tek) and Baydel are two disk array vendors that implement RAID-3 in hardware. For the most part, the hardware disk array vendors ease any performance issues with the use of disk cache.

RAID-4: Dedicated Parity Disk

In RAID-4, one entire disk is devoted to RAID volume parity, as shown in Figure 4.10. Whenever a write is performed to any data disk in the RAID set, the parity

Figure 4.10   RAID-4 dedicated parity disk.

disk is also written to, so that its parity data can be updated. On a write-intensive system that makes the parity disk a performance bottleneck.

In a manner similar to that for RAID-3, small writes are especially poorly performing on RAID-4. Larger writes aren't quite as bad, but since parity must be recalculated whenever any write occurs, performance will suffer.

Commercial examples of RAID-4 are also generally limited to hardware RAID vendors, and can be found in EMC's RAID-S implementation, and in Network Appliance storage devices. As with RAID-3, most hardware vendors ease any performance issues by placing a battery-backed-up memory-based disk cache logically in front of the disks. The memory cache takes the writes from the system at a high speed, and delivers them to the disk in the background.

RAID-5: Striped Parity Region

RAID-5 works almost identically to RAID-4, except that the bottleneck imposed by the presence of a single parity disk is eliminated. As shown in Figure 4.11, the parity disk is striped across all the disks in the RAID set. Because RAID-5 is a little better suited to general applications than RAID-3 or RAID-4, you will see software implementations of RAID-5. However, software implementations of RAID-5 will generally still be slow for any sort of write-intensive application.

The rule of thumb is that for applications with more than 15 to 20 percent writes, RAID-5 performance will probably not be acceptable.

Since recovery from a disk failure requires a complete read of all the surviving disks in the stripe set, plus XORing them together, recovery from the loss of a RAID-5 disk can be very time consuming. During that time, system performance will suffer noticeably, and if another disk fails (more likely than average since the disks are so busy) all of the data in the stripe will be lost, and it will be necessary to restore it from backups.

Hardware RAID

The difference between hardware and software RAID is where the disk management is performed. Hardware RAID functions are performed, as the name implies, within the disk hardware. The disk array has dedicated internal CPU,

Figure 4.11 RAID-5 striped parity.

I/O, and memory, and performs these functions without impacting the host computer. Management of hardware RAID is performed through an interface program that runs on the host computer; but any management work that is to be performed is done within the disk array.

Taking another look back at Figure 4.1, you'll see that hardware RAID performs its functions independently from the operating system, and independently of any software-based disk management. The output of a hardware RAID function is a *logical unit* (LUN). A LUN looks exactly like a disk to the host system, regardless of whether its underlying configuration is a 9-disk RAID-0 stripe, a 14-way RAID-1 mirrored set, a 6-way RAID-5 stripe with cache in front, or something else entirely.

In general, users need not be concerned with the RAID level that is used on a hardware RAID array. The assumption that data is being properly managed should be adequate for most situations. Of course, your mileage may vary.

Some of the advantages of hardware RAID are:

Performance. Parity RAID becomes more acceptable in a hardware RAID configuration than in a software RAID configuration. The CPU overhead is offloaded from the host system to the dedicated outboard CPU.

Disk cache. Many disk array vendors put cache memory in their arrays. This cache will greatly improve write performance, and can improve read performance when the data that is being searched for remains in the write cache. Other enhancements, such as read-ahead, where the array prereads data from the disk it expects will be requested soon, will also generally improve read performance. Putting disk cache in front of a slower parity RAID model usually counteracts the performance disadvantages they impose.

Advanced features. Some hardware RAID manufacturers offer features like wide-area data replication, or the ability to share disk hardware between multiple hosts.

There are also disadvantages to Hardware RAID. Depending on the vendor you choose, some or all of these may be present. They are all conditions to ask your vendor about.

Some of the disadvantages of Hardware RAID are:

Limited to one disk array. Since Hardware RAID cannot combine disks that are in different arrays, the disk array itself can introduce a single point of failure.

Difficult to resize or reconfigure LUNs. If a LUN is full, the only solution is to dump its contents to tape (or to another LUN), destroy and rebuild the original one larger, and restore the data to it. The associated downtime can be considerable, especially for a large LUN. Some hardware RAID vendors are close to overcoming this rather significant problem.

No management interface standard. Every hardware RAID vendor has its own management interface. Learning to use one is no guarantee that you will be able to use another.

May limit the number or size of LUNs. Hardware limitations may exist on one array or another, forcing implementers to make design and configuration choices that achieve less than the original intent. Some hardware RAID vendors are starting to overcome this limitation.

May lock you into a single vendor. Adding a new hardware RAID vendor to your configuration will introduce a new management interface, with an associated learning curve. By adding more of the same kind of hardware to your environment, management will be simpler, but you may lock yourself out of another vendor's new hardware or management features.

Potential single points of failure. Not every disk array will have all of these points of failure, but when deciding which disk array vendor to purchase from, here are some more items to consider:

- *Power supply.* A single power supply can fail over time. A good array will have more than one power supply, with elements powerful enough to assume the full load if one supply fails.

- *Cooling.* The failure of a fan can be very subtle. Overheating equipment does not usually fail in obvious (or even in predictable) ways. Ensure that if a fan fails, its companions can take over for it, and that you will be notified of the failure.

- *Power cord.* Cord security is important: If a clumsy system administrator, a member of the cleaning crew, or a visitor on a data center tour trips on your disk array power cord and pulls it out, your array goes down, without warning.

- *Fuses.* These are not generally a problem, but if an internal fuse blows, resolution can be quite confounding.

- *Internal disk controllers.* These provide internal connectivity and some of the intelligence that makes the array function. If they fail, what are the consequences? Are there backups if one board fails?

- *Cache memory battery power.* We have seen some disk arrays fail without warning because the battery on the cache dies, even when ample electric power is being supplied to the array.

- *Backplane.* Virtually every piece of computing equipment has an internal central pathway over which its data moves. Generally these pathways do not fail, but they can. What are the implications if yours does?

- *Easy-to-lean-on power switch.* Where is the power switch located? Is it protected by a door or a lock? Can it be accidentally kicked, leaned on, or backed into? What happens if someone hits the switch; is there any sort of user-level confirmation? These switches are especially vulnerable to data center tours.

- *The enclosure itself.* Cabinets of all varieties can topple over. They can be moved, forcing cables to be pulled out or broken. Something external can fall onto or into the cabinet. Look for strong, well-constructed cabinets that will stand up to disasters.

Disk Arrays

Hardware RAID, when it is present, is usually only one feature that a disk array might offer. As has been discussed, many disk arrays offer cache memory for performance improvements, often mitigating the performance impact of underlying hardware parity RAID protection.

Other disk arrays may offer the following additional features:

Wide area data replication. Data is copied across a WAN to a remote site, where it can be read (usually not written to) by another application, or maintained off-line for use in a disaster.

Intelligent disk buses. If two hosts are connected to the same disk array, it is critical that only one host access a particular disk at a time; otherwise data corruption can result. Intelligent disk buses can lock out one host when the other is actively working on a disk or a bus.

Parallel buses. A single host can be connected to the same set of disks via more than one connection. In some cases, this means increased throughput since all of the buses can be active at the same time. On other arrays, only one bus is active, and the other remains passive until the active one fails.

Connections to many hosts at the same time. Often combined with intelligent disk buses, some disk arrays allow connections from several servers at the same time, enabling disks to be shared among several hosts. This can result in major savings when compared to purchasing a disk array for each host. This capability essentially makes your environment into a SAN.

Hot pluggable disks. If a disk fails, it can be removed and replaced without affecting the function of the other disks in the array.

Hot spares. If a disk fails, its data can be automatically moved to another disk in the array without affecting the function of the other disks in the array.

Read-ahead buffers. Performance gains can be achieved when a smart disk array reads more than the data requested. Statistics demonstrate that a high percentage of reads are sequential, so by reading the next block of data, and storing it in memory, when that next block is requested, it can be returned at memory speed, not at disk speed. (Memory speed can be thousands of times faster than disk speed.)

Internal data copies. Though doing so will impose serious hardware overhead costs, some disk arrays support making internal copies of active data. The copy can then be used for backups, feeding data to development or QA, for disaster recovery, or for handing off to another server.

Storage administration. Some disk array vendors bundle complete and total array management services with their arrays. These may manage the array for you from afar, and simply show up on-site when a problem requiring hands-on access occurs.

Phone-home capabilities. Your disk array may be smart enough to pick up the phone and call its manufacturer's support center when it detects that it has a problem.

Many of these features have additional costs associated with them, and not all are available from all vendors.

Software RAID

Software RAID moves the disk management functions off of the disk array, allowing more flexibility in the choice of disk hardware. However, since the functions are performed on the host computer, additional load is added to that system. If parity RAID is involved, then significant CPU overhead will result. Regardless, though, there will be some additional I/O and limited CPU and memory load on the server.

Disk management is often packaged with logical volume management for additional features. Just as the output of hardware RAID operations is a LUN, the output of software RAID operations is a *volume*. A volume is the object on which filesystems are written, or on which databases write their data. The filesystem and database don't care how a volume is organized.

The advantages of software RAID include:

Flexibility. You can mix and match vendor disk hardware. You can combine LUNs when one fills up.

Removal of hardware limitations. You can combine disks from different arrays into logical volumes, and resize and rearrange LUNs without restriction.

Costs scale better. When buying additional disks, you are not limited to potentially expensive hardware RAID capable hardware. Any disks will do. Therefore, as a system's storage capacity grows, the additional storage hardware you need to purchase is much less expensive; it need not include the hardware RAID intelligence.

The only real downside to software RAID is reduced performance, but this does not occur in all cases. If you must do parity RAID, then it is probably best to do so with hardware RAID. Writing in software-based RAID-5 is generally too slow for most high-volume, insert- or update-intensive production environments. When software RAID-1 is used, the performance is generally fine for most applications.

Logical Volume Management

Software RAID is often just one feature of logical volume management (LVM) software. LVM offers many other features besides software RAID. While each LVM product is different, here are some of the more useful features:

Online reconfiguration. This feature includes the ability to add and remove mirrors, to expand and, in some cases, shrink a volume or filesystem, and rearrange the disk layout of data, and to do so without interrupting user service.

Removing OS-imposed limitations. For example, in Sun's Solaris operating system, a disk cannot be divided into more than seven "slices." A good LVM would remove that restriction, allowing whatever slicing is required.

Hooks into system management tools. When the LVM detects failures or performance issues in monitored devices, the information should be automatically shared with system monitoring tools. The LVM might even offer suggestions on how to better layout data for improved performance.

Hot sparing. If one disk fails, a dedicated spare disk can be automatically moved into its place, transparent to the users.

Some commercial examples of LVMs are: Sun's Solstice Disk Suite (SDS), Microsoft Windows Logical Disk Manager (LDM) and Disk Administrator, Hewlett Packard's Logical Volume Manager (LVM), and VERITAS Software's Volume Manager (VxVM), which runs on all three platforms.

The Right Answer

The best solution, of course, is a combination of Hardware RAID, Software RAID, and LVM. Ideally, you would mirror in hardware (parity RAID to save money on disks), stripe between hardware arrays in software for performance, and use LVM to manage the whole thing. Or you might choose to mirror between your disk arrays for availability and stripe within each array in hardware.

There are, however, two downsides to this approach. One is the cost. As we have discussed, you always need to balance the costs against the value of the systems and data being protected. For most systems, however, this is an area where it makes sense to spend the money.

The other disadvantage is the complexity of managing all those layers. The same advice about cost applies; when designing a system, you must balance the complexity against the advantages being provided. The advantages here are clear, and they greatly outweigh the complexity issues.

Disk Space and FileSystems

When designing a system, subscribe to Boyle's Law as applied to disks: Disk usage will always expand to consume all available resources. Extra disk capacity, especially disks kept off-line, are vital to stave off disaster. Remember that a full filesystem is just as much an availability issue as a down system. If a user needs to save a file and cannot, then the system may as well be down. In fact, the inability to save critical work after it has been performed may be worse than the system being down. It is certainly more frustrating to the average user.

So, when you purchase system resources, look toward optimal disk performance, not storage capacity. Once you have determined the optimal performance, buy another 25 to 40 percent of disk capacity for growth and availability. A clever system administrator will keep a certain percentage of unused disk space off-line, so that in the event of an unexpected critical disk space shortage he will still be assured of an adequate reserve. Realize that to handle the extremes of read or write requests, you should optimize the number of disk units, which may give you more disk space in bytes than you would assume, gauging from the total size of the data and expected growth. You may find you "waste" disk space because you need the disk spindle count to keep up with the I/O demand. In this case, having sufficient disk unit overhang is critical for ensuring continued smooth system operation.

When you arrange the physical layout of your disks, there are a number of factors to consider.

Hot pluggable disks. If you have to bring your system down whenever a disk fails or new disks are added to the system, your overall system availability will be seriously impacted. Hot pluggable disks will allow your system to continue running while maintenance is being performed.

Physical capacity. How much data can you store on each disk? How many disks can you fit on each controller? How many disks can you fit in each disk cabinet? If you use RAID, you will lose a significant portion of that disk capacity, and you must purchase additional disks to make up for the shortfall.

Performance. Just because you can put six disks on that controller, should you? What will the impact be to system performance? If the disks are busy, will that overflow the capacity of the disk bus?

Cabinet space. If there are no empty slots for new disks in your disk cabinet, then as soon as you need to buy more disks you will have to buy a new cabinet. The incremental costs will stun your purchasing agent. By providing extra space for expansion, the large incremental cost can be better planned for sometime down the road.

Data center floor space. The new cabinet will also require a chunk of floor space in your data center; be sure you have it available, and that it is physically located within the distance limitations for the technology you are using. If not, there may be serious ramifications.

Cable runs and conduits. Make sure that your cable conduits have the necessary space for the additional cables that will be required.

Power requirements. More hardware means more power. Be sure that your data center (or other physical location) has sufficient power for all of the incoming hardware.

Backplane slots. Make sure that if you add more disks you will have slots for the cards to connect the disks to the host.

Cooling capacity. While it is unlikely that one more disk will be the straw that breaks your cooling system's back, it is definitely better to make sure that the air conditioning can handle the extra load.

Planning for costs. Be sure to build all the costs, both short- and long-term, into your growth plan.

What Happens When a LUN Fills Up?

If you fill up a hardware RAID LUN, your fate will be decided by how you've planned for such an eventuality. If you have a good LVM and hot pluggable disks, things won't be so bad. If you don't, then plan on spending the weekend on the job.

If you don't have a good LVM and hot pluggable disks, then you will probably have to follow these steps:

- Get your users off the system.
- Halt the system.
- Add your new disks to the disk array.
- Reboot.
- Take a full, clean backup. (You might choose to verify the backup, but that can be incredibly time consuming.) Good backup software will allow you to take your backups on-line, of course, and so you could take your back-ups as the first step. See Chapter 12.
- Wipe out the old LUN.
- Build a new LUN with the appropriate amount of disk space.
- (If appropriate) build a new filesystem on the new LUN.
- Restore the contents of your backup.
- Check that everything works okay. Note that if you're using this LUN as part of a filesystem exported via NFS, you've just rendered the volume unusable by clients until they unmount and remount it, or until they reboot. We discuss this case in Chapter 11.
- Make the new LUN accessible to your users, and let your users back on the system.

If you have users who use disk space other than the affected LUN, then they will only be interrupted by the reboot. But the users whose data is on the LUN in question will be down for the entire period.

However, if you have taken our advice and have a logical volume manager, you can save yourself a lot of effort and downtime:

- Plug your new hot-pluggable disks into your disk array.
- Create a new LUN on these new disks.
- Use your LVM to combine the old and new LUNs into a resized LUN.
- (If appropriate) grow your filesystem into the space on the resized LUN.

All of this work can be done during the day, without downtime or any adverse impact on your users. Life is good.

Managing Disk and Volume Availability

As evidenced in the previous section, there is no substitute for good planning. With that in mind, we offer some more suggestions for maximizing the avail-ability of your disks, volumes, and data:

Redundant data paths and controllers. Use at least two data paths and controllers. In order for this to work, your disk array, operating system, and LVM must support alternative paths to the same disk.

Redundant disk array hardware. Due to all the potential single points of failure in any cabinet, it is always best to mirror between two or more disk arrays.

Cabinets and racks. Never put all of the disks from one volume in the same rack. Mirror between separate racks and cabinets. Racks and cabinets are not failure-proof. They can collapse or topple; shelves can come loose and fall; liquids can spill down them; power cords can be pulled (most cabinets run on just one power cord); circuits controlling a cabinet can blow; they can be moved (most of them are on wheels, after all), pulling or breaking cables; ceilings can fall on them. And what happens if the doors on your cabinet get locked, and you cannot find the key?

Cables. Always run two sets of cables along separate and distinct paths. Never run them in the same conduit. Beware of electrical or magnetic interference. If pairs of cables are being run outside, never, ever, put them in the same conduit: Backhoe problems are a real possibility. Always leave slack in your cables, and tie them down so that if they are pulled, the pressure point is the tie-down, not the connection to the system. And, of course, always use the screw-ins to fasten your cables securely into their connectors. Neatness in cable runs is good (but don't be a maniac about it).

Power management. Don't plug mirrored devices into the same power source or the same circuit. Be sure that your disk arrays have redundant power supplies, and that the array can switch from one power supply to another without interrupting its service, or that if a power supply fails, the remaining ones provide enough juice to keep the array running without interruption.

FileSystem Recovery

Windows and Unix filesystems do a lot of their work in memory. This work gets written to the disk periodically, but most of the time there are filesystem changes in memory that have not yet made it to the disk. If the system crashes, these changes never do make it to the disk. If a disk operation had begun and did not complete, filesystem corruption can result. Normally if corruption does occur, it is minor and correctable, but it must be corrected. If a running filesystem stumbles onto a corrupt region, unpredictable results can occur, including a total system panic and crash. (The original design decision to perform so much of the filesystem's work in memory was made for performance reasons;

it is much more efficient to save up small disk writes in memory, and make a bunch of writes in a group. The downside to this design is the potential loss of data that was in memory and never written to disk.)

The likeliest time for corruption to occur is when the system is brought down abruptly. Therefore at boot time, the system must check its filesystems for corruption. Any corruption that is found must be repaired. To handle this task, Windows provides the *scandisk* utility, while Unix provides *fsck* (File System ChecK). Both utilities read every data block in the filesystem, and check it for consistency. Even though more than 99 percent of the filesystem is just fine, all blocks must be examined. There are no shortcuts. These checks can take hours on a system with many large filesystems. Even a small filesystem can take an inconvenient amount of time to regain consistency. One rule of thumb is that fsck takes about a minute per gigabyte of disk space. During this period, the system is unusable.

Fortunately, there is a technology that can overcome this loss of availability. A *Journaled FileSystem* (JFS) can reduce disk check times by better than 99 percent. A journaled filesystem reserves a small chunk of disk space for a journal or intent log. When a write occurs that would cause corruption if only partially completed, an entry is written to the journal before the write is performed. The journal entry contains enough information for the filesystem to recreate the transaction. If the system crashes after the journal entry is written, but before the actual data write is performed, the fsck or scandisk will read the journal and recreate the data write. If the system crashes before the journal entry is written, then the transaction is lost. The parts of the disk where no transactions were occurring are simply not touched by the filesystem checker.

The size of the filesystem has no bearing at all on the duration of the filesystem check. With a journaled filesystem, the log consistency check can be completed in a few seconds. The end result is a great increase in overall system availability.

▶Key Points

- Disks contain data, probably the most important asset of your entire business.

- Before you work to protect any other component of your system, protect the data.

- Backups (see Chapter 12) are the first line of protection for your data.

- Mirroring (RAID-1) is the best way to protect your data from hardware failure online.

- It is better to mirror disks across controllers and between disk arrays then not to.

CHAPTER

5

Redundant Server Design

The most complex component of any computer system is the host. The host consists of dozens of components: CPUs, disks, memory, power supplies, fans, backplane, motherboard, and expansion slots; most of these in turn consist of many subcomponents. Any of these subcomponents can fail, leading to the failure of a larger component, which will in turn contribute to the failure of the host. If parts are required to fix a failed component, it could take days for the parts to arrive. By having a second server as a backup for the first, an extended outage of your main server will not have nearly as serious an impact.

In this chapter we will look at ways to protect your users against the failure of your servers, including things you can do to a single server and how to put two servers together to enable them to back each other up.

Server Failures and Failover

It can take hours, or in some cases days, to diagnose a failure, especially if this failure is of the intermittent variety (which can be almost impossible to nail down). Once a failure is conclusively diagnosed, if the problem is in hardware, a replacement for the failed part must be obtained, and then someone who is capable must be called upon to replace it. If the problem is software, then a patch to the application or to the operating system must be obtained. Assuming the fix works, the host must be rebooted, and recovery must be initiated from any damage that the failure may have caused.

If the server is a critical one, this sort of hours- or days-long outage is simply unacceptable. You could put your applications on a skillfully designed and implemented multimillion-dollar fault-tolerant server, which may still not offer adequate protection. A more practical solution is to take two or more servers and tie them together, so that if one server fails, the other server can take over. Besides, even on a fault-tolerant server, the operating system or other software could still cause a system outage.

To guarantee data consistency and rapid recovery, the servers should be connected to the same shared disks. The discussions in this chapter assume that the servers are located within the same site, and generally in the same room. Failover to a remote site, or wide-area failover, is a disaster recovery issue, and while it seems similar to local failover, actually introduces many new variables and complexities. We will discuss disaster recovery issues in Chapter 14.

The migration of services from one server to another is called *failover*. At minimum, the migration of services during a failover should meet the following criteria:

Transparent. The failover should be no more intrusive to the clients who access the server's services than a simple reboot. This intrusiveness may not be reflected in the duration of the outage, but rather in what the clients must do to get back to work once services have been restored. It may be necessary for the user to log back into his application, but only in some cases (primarily databases). Non-authenticated web and file services should not require logging back in.

Quick. Failover should take no more than five minutes, and ideally less than two minutes. The best way to achieve this goal is for the takeover server to already be booted up, and running as many of the underlying system processes as possible. If a full reboot is required in order to failover, failover times will go way up, and can take an hour or more. When the time required to failover is roughly the same as doing a "cold start" by rebooting the original failed server, the appeal of having a redundant machine is reduced to having a readily available supply of parts to repair hardware failures. Often, much of the time required for failover with shared disk is spent checking filesystems.

Minimal manual intervention. Ideally, no human intervention at all should be required; the entire process should be automated. Some sites or applications may require manual initiation for a failover, but that is not preferable. Under no circumstances should the host receiving a failover require a reboot.

Guaranteed data access. After a failover, the receiving host should see the same copy of the critical data as the original host. Replicating data to another host when disks are not shared adds unnecessary risk and complexity, and is not advised for hosts that are located near to each other.

The systems in a failover configuration should also communicate with each other continuously, so that each system knows the state of its partner. This communication is called a heartbeat. Later in this chapter we will discuss the implications when the servers lose their heartbeats.

When a failover occurs, three critical elements must be moved from the failed server to the takeover server:

1. *Network identity.* In an Ethernet environment that means the IP address, and in some cases the MAC (or hardware) address.

2. *Access to shared disks.* Operating system (and in particular filesystem) technology essentially prohibits multiple servers from accessing the same disks at the same time for any reason. In a shared disk configuration, logical access must be restricted to one server at a time. Whatever restricts the second machine from accessing the disks must reverse itself and lock out the original server, while granting access only to the takeover server.

3. *Set of processes.* Once the disks have migrated to the takeover server, all the processes associated with the data must be restarted. Data consistency must be ensured from the application's perspective.

The collection of these elements is commonly called a *service group*. If your servers have multiple service groups, the groups must be totally independent of each other so that they can live on any machine in the cluster, regardless of what the other service groups might be doing.

Logical, Application-Centric Thinking

One of the more interesting aspects of working with systems that failover is the new way you must think about the server pair and its services and resources. Normally, you think of a computer system as a single box, with a single network identity (though it may have more than one network address), that runs one or more applications on its local or perhaps network-attached storage.

A collection of servers that failover among themselves must be thought of in a nontraditional way. The bottom-line component is no longer the server, but rather the application. Applications are associated with network identities, storage, and computing resources. The computer is merely an application, or network, service delivery mechanism. Just as a disk is subsumed under a host when you enable data redundancy, the server is subsumed under the service when you add in host redundancy. It's just another term in the overall delivery equation.

The computer itself is the least interesting component of an application-service delivery mechanism. Any computer that runs the right operating system and is made up of the same basic hardware components can deliver this service (albeit not always optimally). The computing hardware itself is an interchangeable commodity. If a computer dies, you should be able to swap out the computer itself, replace it with another, and continue operating as before. An FMS (failover management system; i.e., software that automates the failover process) gives you the same ability, only it does this swap automatically, to a second computer that has been designated for this function and that is configured and waiting to assume the responsibility.

In this environment, an IP address does not connect you with a particular named computer, but rather a particular service using that name at that point in time. The name, and the IP address, might reside on either machine in a redundant pair. It should not matter to your users which computer is running the application—only that the application is running, and that they can obtain the services that the application provides.

Consider what happens when you move from one house to another and take your phone number with you. A caller does not know which house he called, only that he has reached his desired service (you). In this example, the phone lines represent the network, your phone number is the network address, and your house is the server. Since the same phone number can be used at your new home, you still live at the same IP address (or network name). Despite your change in physical location, the very same logical network service is still being provided.

Disks and storage devices, similarly, may not be associated with a particular server. The data, and possibly the application code itself, can move between servers.

The unit that performs a particular service is no longer a single computer, but rather the failover pair or cluster, on whose computers the application may be running at a particular moment. It should not matter which computer runs the service, as long as the service runs.

Consider that the cluster acts as a black box providing a particular service. Your users connect to a network address, present data to that address, and get back responses. Assuming the speed at which the responses come is adequate, it doesn't matter to the user what is providing the service. The server could be a Unix computer, an NT computer, a mainframe computer, or even a fast-typing monkey with a keyboard. As long as the service is being provided, the users should, at least in theory, be happy.

Failover Requirements

A failover pair or cluster requires more than simply having two servers placed near each other. Let's examine the various components that are required to turn the two servers into a failover pair. (We will elaborate on each of these required components in the next section, and we'll discuss larger and more complex combinations of servers later on.) The necessary components include the following:

Servers. You need two servers—a *primary server*, and a *takeover server*. We'll refer to the takeover server as the "secondary server" in some cases, but it's the same idea. A critical application that ran and later failed on the primary server migrates to the takeover server in a process called *failover*. The servers should be running the same operating system version, have the same patches installed, support the same binary executables, and as much as possible, be configured identically.

Network connections. There are two different types of network connections that are required to implement failover, and a third that is strongly recommended. A pair of *heartbeat* networks, which run directly from one server to the other but which are totally independent of each other, is a basic requirement. The heartbeat networks allow the servers to communicate with and monitor each other, so that each knows immediately if something has happened to its partner that requires action, without fear of outside interference. The second required network connection is the *public*, or *service*, network. This is the network that carries your user and client data. The third type of network connection is the administrative network, which allows the system administrators a guaranteed network path into each server, even after a failover has occurred.

Disks. There are two different types of disks required for failover. The *internal, unshared* disks contain the operating system and other files that are required for the operation of each system in the pair when they are not the active server, including any software required to initiate and maintain the failover process. The other kind of disks is the *shared* disks, where the critical application data resides. These are the disks that migrate back and forth between servers when a failover occurs; they must be accessible by both servers in the pair, even though under normal circumstances they will only be accessed one at a time. All disks on a failover pair should have some sort of redundancy; mirroring is always preferred over parity RAID. Shared disks are known as *public disks*, because they move with the publicly available network service, and the internal, unshared disks are called *private disks*.

Some FMSs (see Chapter 6) use a configuration called "shared nothing" rather than shared disks. In a *shared nothing* configuration, the data on one server are replicated via some sort of network to the other server. This is a less desirable configuration because of the added complexity and dependency on another network that are introduced. Shared nothing configurations are fine for wide-area failover, but for local failover, where the systems in question are located close enough together that SCSI and/or Fibrechannel specs are not exceeded, shared disks are a far superior and more reliable solution.

Application portability. A vitally important but often overlooked element of failover pair design is the requirement that the critical application(s) can be run on both servers in the pair, one server at a time. Most often, the bugaboo is licensing. If your application won't run on both servers, one at a time, you do not have high availability. Speak to your application vendor; many vendors will provide a discounted license to run on a backup server. (Your mileage may vary.) But it may be necessary to purchase two complete, full-price licenses to permit your application to run on either server as necessary. If it does, then it does. Nobody said that achieving HA was going to be cheap or easy!

No single point of failure. This is a very general component that refers to every element in the pair. If there is a component of your failover pair whose failure will cause both servers to become down or otherwise unavailable, then you do not have high availability. We discuss the notion of single points of failure (SPOFs) throughout the book.

Servers

The fundamental requirement when designing a failover pair is that there be two servers. The servers must be the same platform (i.e., the same processor type), and should be running the same operating system release with the same patch releases. The servers should offer similar performance, via identical memory and processor speed. Ideally, the servers in the failover pair are completely identical.

Similar or identical hardware also works to keep the configuration simple, conferring all the benefits of simple systems—ease of management, brief learning curve, fewer parts to break, and so forth.

If Server A is noticeably faster than Server B, then after A fails to B, users may complain about the loss in performance. This may lead the administrator to fail back to A before the problem that caused A to fail is fixed, or at a time when the brief outage will inconvenience the user community.

Some vendors release variations of their CPUs that have subtle differences. Each generation may have unique instructions that allow for different optimizations in applications, or may require operating system support in terms of a "kernel architecture." Sun's earlier SPARC chip families, for example, had several kernel architectures, requiring minor variations in the SunOS or Solaris operating system. When a processor supports special memory access modes or fast block copying, and an application such as a database takes advantage of them, you must be certain you have identical processors in each server—or you'll need differently optimized versions of the database on each node. While these differences are hard to detect, there are no guarantees that these differences won't, at some point in the future, make two machines incompatible in the same failover pair. This unlikely incompatibility becomes virtually impossible if you select matching hardware.

In the Microsoft world, there may be similarly subtle differences between the various Intel architecture CPUs that run Windows operating systems. Processors made by Intel and AMD are supposed to be perfectly compatible, but it is not hard to imagine that there could be minor differences that won't appear for years after their initial implementation. Not all Windows NT systems are binary compatible: Compaq's Alpha chip is not capable of running the same code that runs on an Intel Pentium processor, for example. The same vendor may have several chip lines running different operating systems, or the same operating system on multiple chips. You need consistency at combination of the chip and operating system to be sure you're getting a consistent applications platform on all nodes in your failover configuration.

Vendors may have dozens of different system models. It is unlikely that any vendor has tested every single combination of systems that can possibly be built into a failover pair. Never be the first to do anything, when production machines are involved. Stick with simple configurations; use combinations that are well-known and well-tested.

Failing Over between Incompatible Servers

It is amazing how often system administrators suggest creating failover pairs using incompatible systems, such as an NT server and an HP/UX server. Why? There is an apparent cost savings if you can combine two systems that are already in hand. After all, little or no additional hardware must be purchased.

However, people who want to failover between incompatible servers just don't get it. In order to successfully failover between incompatible hardware, a number of issues would need to be addressed:

Failover software. Both systems would need to be able to run compatible versions of the failover management system that could communicate with each other. The FMS would have to handle a multitude of combinations of hardware. Each server type has many variations (kernel architectures, as just described, are just one example), and when you add another whole class of server, the permutations increase dramatically.

Applications and data formats. The application would need to function identically on both servers, despite differences in hardware architecture. It would also need to read data written by the other server, on a potentially incompatible filesystem, or in an incompatible format or style (word size, big versus little endian, and so forth). An application vendor who is willing to give a discount for a failover server license may be less willing to do so when the failover server is from a different vendor.

Network interfaces. The heartbeat networks become much more complicated when the NIC cards on each server are of drastically different types. If the network technologies are incompatible, then a network bridge or other hardware may be required.

Disks. In addition to all the other disk requirements, now disks must be physically compatible with both servers. While interface cards don't need to be the same for both servers, they must be able to operate in a dual-hosted environment, with the other card on the same bus.

Administration. This would be a very difficult situation for a system administrator, who would need to be proficient in the administration of both operating systems and hardware environments. Work performed on one server would need to be translated to the operating environment of the other before it could be applied there. It is safe to say that this environment would more than double the amount of day-to-day tinkering required to keep the systems operating properly.

Support. When there are problems, which vendor do you call? It is not hard to imagine that one server might cause some sort of subtle problem on the other; then what? If, as we previously noted, it is unlikely that a vendor has tested every possible combination of its own servers in a failover environment, what are the chances that two competing vendors have tested every combination of their servers working together?

Despite all the negatives, it is likely that the introduction and widespread acceptance of storage area networks will turn out to be the first steps down the long path to make incompatible system failover a reality. SANs solve the shared disk problem, and open the door to vendor partnerships that will solve the other problems, enabling incompatible system failover in limited combinations.

Heterogeneous system failover will likely be available by around the year 2002. Whether it is practical and actually usable at that time is an entirely separate issue.

Networks

Three different types of networks are normally found in a failover configuration: the *heartbeats*, the *production* or *service* network, and the *administration* network. For more detail on networks, please see Chapter 8.

Some operating systems support virtual network interfaces, where more than one IP address can be placed on the same network interface card (NIC). While virtual IPs can be used in some failover scenarios, beware of introducing a single point of failure.

Heartbeat Networks

The heartbeat networks are the medium over which the systems in a failover pair communicate with each other. Fundamentally, the systems simply exchange "Hi, how are you?" and "I'm fine, and you?" over the heartbeat links. In reality, of course, the heartbeat packets can be much more complex, containing state information about each server or commands from one server directing the other to change states or execute some other function.

Heartbeat networks can be implemented over any reliable network link. Most often, simple 10 Base-T Ethernet is the medium of choice for heartbeats, since 10 Base-T is inexpensive and does not require any specialized hardware or cabling. Using a faster or more complicated network medium for your heartbeats will add absolutely no value to your system, so why spend the money? Fast networks are ideal when sending large streams of data, but heartbeat messages are short and relatively far apart (on a network traffic time scale). You don't want to go all the way down to a serial line, if possible, because you want low latency for sending the heartbeats.

A server learns of the demise of its partner when the heartbeats stop. However, there are many possible reasons why the heartbeats might stop. We will discuss them, and what can be done to prevent this occurrence from being mistaken as a down server:

Primary server really is down. This is the case that we are looking for, and we hope that this is the case. However, there are other events that might cause the same loss of heartbeats.

Heartbeat NIC has failed. This might occur on either side of the connection. To combat this likely eventuality, use two separate networks for heartbeats, in separate network cards. This means that if you have multiport NIC cards, you should never put both heartbeats in the same card.

Heartbeat cable is broken, or has been pulled out. The use of two separate networks will keep this from being a problem.

Heartbeat network storm. Restrict the number of machines that have access to a heartbeat network—ideally, only the servers in a particular failover pair (or cluster) have access to the network. Running parallel networks will also help to protect your servers in this situation.

Network hub fails. In a two-host configuration, don't use hubs. A simple crossover network cable (the Ethernet equivalent of a null-modem serial cable) plugged directly from one machine's NIC to the other will suffice to create a simple two-node heartbeat network. Again, parallel networks will also protect you, especially if there are more than two members in your cluster. Of course, if there are more than two members in your cluster, hubs will be required.

Heartbeat process has failed. If the process that sends the heartbeats fails, heartbeats will stop, regardless of how many networks are monitored. The process that sends the heartbeats must, therefore, be monitored and/or made redundant. If it stops, it should be automatically restarted by another process.

Remote server is running too slowly. This is a trickier case. If Box A is running too slowly to report heartbeats to Box B in a timely manner, Box B may mistakenly assume that A has failed. To reliably fix this, B must leave enough time for A to send heartbeats, thus slowing down detection. In return, A must make sending heartbeats its highest priority, so that even if A can only squeeze off one extra compute cycle, it goes to sending heartbeats. Again, minimizing the latency on the heartbeat network helps, as it gives B more time to receive and process the heartbeat before A starts wondering what happened to its partner.

Low-level system problem takes all networks off-line. If a server cannot see any of its networks, it is not serving any useful function at all. A good FMS package should shut a system down that cannot see any of its networks. Should this system decide to access its shared disks after another server has accepted a failover from it, data corruption is almost certain to result.

Copper no longer conducts electricity. If this occurs, you have bigger problems. Like electricity. Like the laws of physics.

ELEVATOR TO NOWHERE

Some people find our closing worry about copper and electricity a bit facetious, but it has a real dark side as well. Large magnets and moving wires can cause copper to *induct* electricity—when you move a magnetic field around, you can create an unexpected electrical charge in an electrical conductor like copper wiring. Not everyone keeps large magnets around, unless you happen to be near a large motor, such as one used to power an elevator. One customer site complained of intermittent failures that seemed to occur late in the afternoon nearly every weekday. After traces of power, network, system, and disk cabling, eventually the root cause was found to be noise inducted into various poorly shielded cables by an elevator that ran in a shaft outside one wall of the machine room. (And you thought we forget everything from freshman physics.)

—Hal

Of course, the ultimate protection against a false positive condition is human intervention. When an alert goes off, a knowledgeable human being can easily log in to the servers, evaluate their conditions, and decide what action to take. This is not always a workable option, as failures can occur at all hours of the day or night, any day of the week. The human intervention may also introduce delays that are unacceptable in a critical production environment. It may not be practical (or desirable) to wake up your system administrator at 4:00 A.M. Sunday morning to have him log in to a server and check its condition.

We assume that the heartbeats and the assumptions taken when a failure is indicated must be as reliable as possible. Most environments do not have the resources necessary to monitor their servers in person (or nearly in person) 7 days a week, 24 hours a day. And even if your environment does have sufficient resources, if heartbeats are employed, you do not want unnecessary alerts going off.

There is a viable alternative to network-based heartbeats, which is well-suited for two-node clusters, and could be adapted for larger clusters. Instead of sending heartbeats on a network, the functionality of heartbeats can be achieved through the use of carefully managed shared disks. A disk, or disk slice, can be dedicated to the exchanging of disk-based heartbeats. If well-implemented, disk heartbeats make an excellent addition to a network-based heartbeat. Many commercial FMS products offer optional disk-based heartbeats.

When the Heartbeat Stops

What happens when the heartbeat between systems stops? There are basically two options. You can assume that if the heartbeat has stopped the other system is really down, or you can require manual intervention to make sure that it really is.

Nearly every site that uses FMS has it configured for automatic failover. Some sites choose to require human intervention when a failover is necessary. These people are particularly concerned about the systems getting into a state called *split brain*, where both servers believe that they should be the primary one, and try to write to the shared disks at the same time. Good FMS takes extreme measures to make sure that split brain does not occur. In reality, it almost never does. When planning your systems, make sure that you have some manual intervention to handle the rare case when split-brain syndrome occurs. (For more information, see the section on split-brain syndrome in Chapter 7.)

One extra level of protection against split brain would be for systems in a failover configuration to automatically shut themselves down if they lose *all* network connectivity, including heartbeats. Depending on its configuration, a host that cannot talk to any networks at all isn't doing anyone any good by staying up. While this might be seen as a drastic step, it would add a level of protection that would be hard to beat.

We will discuss the steps that are required for manual failover in detail in Chapter 6.

Running Heartbeat Networks

Heartbeats should be run across two parallel, inexpensive dedicated networks. In a simple two-node configuration, the networks should be nothing more than two crossover twisted pair Ethernet cables. Ten Mbit per second is plenty for heartbeat applications; heartbeat packets tend to be small and relatively infrequent. If you've standardized on 100 Mbit/second interfaces, you can use a crossover Fast Ethernet cable as well. The speed of the link doesn't really matter once you're up into Ethernet speeds; you get low latency and a sufficiently fast wire to pass small packets.

A small network appropriate for heartbeats can also be run with regular (not crossover) network cables and network hubs. Network hubs overcome the one downside to using crossover cables: When one system is powered down, the surviving system will report annoying network errors, which may cause a performance degradation, or other minor ill effects. However, network hubs (even low-end workgroup hubs) add expense, hardware that can fail, and power requirements to an otherwise simple element of the overall configuration. So, even though network hubs work just fine, we recommend against single ones in two-node networks, since they add complexity. If you're going to use redundant hubs on redundant heartbeat networks, and can afford to hook up the hub monitoring ports to your network management software that will let you detect heartbeat network failures within the hub, you may find the approach beneficial. In clusters with more than two nodes, network hubs are required to build heartbeat networks.

There are, of course, other options for the physical network layer of heartbeat networks. A heartbeat network can also be constructed using a serial line, and by running PPP (point-to-point protocol) or SLIP (serial line internet protocol) across it. Vendor implementations of PPP and SLIP networks tend to require significantly more configuration and care and feeding than Ethernet links, and are therefore less appropriate for use in a critical environment. If you don't have any more ports to connect Ethernet to on a particular server, then a serial-based network is alright as a fallback, but definitely less desirable than Ethernet. Think of it this way: Do you want to go through the equivalent effort of installing a modem for outbound dialing simply to spare the expense of buying another network interface card? If you're out of I/O slots, however, you must have missed the key design principle about planning for growth.

Sometimes the easiest way to configure dual heartbeats may be by putting both heartbeat networks (from the same host) on the same multiport NIC (network interface card). But if that NIC card fails, both heartbeats will be lost, and the value of having two of them in the first place is lost. Be sure to configure your heartbeats on separate NIC cards.

Similarly, some operating systems support putting more than one IP address on a single NIC. When that IP address is on a different IP network, you have two logical IP networks on the same physical wire. These virtual IP addresses are useful for moving logical host names around, but not at all appropriate for heartbeat networks. You want unique identities, and redundancy in the heartbeat networks. Running both logical heartbeat networks over the same physical wire defeats the purpose of having two networks. It should never, ever be done in a production configuration, although you may find using virtual IP addresses useful for testing heartbeat configurations in limited-equipment test labs.

Again, for a more detailed discussion of networking and virtual IP addresses, see Chapter 8.

Public Networks

In order to provide the service for which it was deployed, the server pair needs to be connected to at least one public service network. This network should also be the home of the client workstations who get their critical applications from these servers, or at least be connected to a router that gets to those client workstations. The public network is the "visible face" of the server pair. Of course, the servers may serve more than one public network to their clients.

Redundant Network Connectivity

NIC cards do fail from time to time. Ideally, the most critical NICs will have backup network cards to which their services can be migrated in the event that they fail. It may not be necessary to have one spare card per NIC, but certainly one spare card per subnet served is a good goal. Good failover management software will take the networks served by one NIC and migrate them to another NIC on the same server without requiring a full failover. You can also configure redundant public networks and move all traffic from one network to another. We discuss network interface redundancy and public network redundancy in Chapter 8.

In a failover configuration, since both servers must be configured identically, both servers must be physically connected to the same networks, whether stand-alone or redundant. Otherwise it will be impossible for one server's services to be failed to the other.

Moving Network Identities

When a failover occurs, the IP address and logical host name used by the primary server need to migrate to the takeover server. Normally, this is done by reconfiguring the public network interfaces on the takeover server to use the "public" IP address. Simple on the surface, the process is made more complicated by the mapping of hardware or MAC addresses to network or IP addresses.

Every machine has a unique MAC address, a 48-bit value that can be used by all interfaces on that machine. Every network interface has a unique 32-bit IP address. The Address Resolution Protocol (ARP) is used to determine the mappings between IP addresses and MAC addresses; when a host wants to send data to a particular IP address it uses ARP to find the MAC address that goes into the packet header indicating the right network hardware destination. It's possible for all interfaces on the same host to share the same MAC address but answer to different IP addresses (one per interface); this is the way many Sun systems are configured and is a source of confusion for someone looking at the network interface configuration tables. When a client sends an ARP request and gets a MAC address matching the known IP address as a reply, that MAC address is cached on the client for anywhere from 30 seconds to several hours, eliminating the need to "ask before speaking" repeatedly on the network.

What happens when a failover occurs, and the IP address associated with a data service moves to another machine with a different MAC address? At that point, the clients that had cached the IP-MAC address mapping have stale information. There are several ways around this problem:

- When the secondary machine configures the public network interfaces with the public IP address, it may send out a "gratuitous ARP." A gratuitous ARP is an ARP request for a system's own IP address, meant to inform other listening network members that a new IP-MAC address mapping has been created. Hosts that hear the gratuitous ARP and cache it will update their tables and be able to find the secondary server using the same IP address as before. Their IP-MAC address mappings are different, but the client and client applications see no impact. However, not all machines or operating systems send gratuitous ARP requests, and not all network clients pick them up and do the right updates with their information.

■ You can move the MAC address from the primary to the secondary node. In this case, it's best to create your own MAC address on the public network interface; when the primary configures its public network interface, it uses this MAC address and after the failover, the secondary machine configures its public network with the same MAC address. There are two ways to choose a private, new MAC address. The first is to change one of the first six 4-bit values in the address. MAC address prefixes are assigned in blocks to vendors, so all equipment with the 8:0:20 prefix is from Sun Microsystems. If you choose 8:0:21 as a prefix for a private MAC address (keeping the same, existing 24-bit suffix), and verify that you have no other equipment using that address, you should be safe. The second solution is to follow some of the guidelines for locally assigned numbers in Internet RFC 1597, which is already a bit dated. You'll need to be sure that the primary recognizes that a takeover has occurred, and goes back to its default or built-in MAC address; you also want to be sure that if the primary reboots and comes back as the secondary node, it also uses its built-in default MAC address rather than the locally created, public one. The advantage of moving the MAC address is that clients don't have to do a thing. The IP-to-MAC address mapping stays the same, since you move both the logical IP address and MAC address to the secondary host.

■ Wait for the clients to realize that the host formerly listening on that MAC address has gone away, and have clients send new ARP requests for the public IP address. If ARP entries are only cached for 30 seconds, this means that there's a 30-second MTTR before a new ARP request is sent, and the clients see a short pause (probably no longer than that required to get the secondary machine up and running anyway). You'll need to be sure that the client application can tolerate this delay, and that your ARP cache entries time out quickly. Many system administrators tune the ARP cache expiration period up to over two hours, reducing the volume of ARP traffic on the network, but making it impossible for clients to recover from an IP address migration quickly. In short, you want to keep

ARP cache time-outs at their minimum levels on all clients of HA systems, because you want to be sure they'll find the new server after a takeover, even if the client misses (or ignores) a gratuitous ARP sent by the secondary server.

There are other side effects of moving MAC addresses between hosts. Switches and hubs that track MAC addresses for selective forwarding need to handle the migration; not all equipment does this well. You want to be sure that moving a MAC address doesn't trigger a spanning tree algorithm that splits the network at a switch that believes a loop has been created through improper connections or cabling. We'll look at redundant networks, moving IP addresses, and the use of virtual addresses for ease of management in great detail in Chapter 8.

IP Addresses and Names

There are three different kinds of hostnames that a system might have in a failover configuration. One is its *private name*. This is the name found in system configuration files, and the one that shows up if you ask the host for its name. Depending on how the network is configured, that name may or may not be resolved on the network. If your machine's private name is *shirley*, that does not necessarily mean that other hosts on the same network know about *shirley*.

The second kind of name is the *public name*. This is the name that maps to IP addresses that other systems on the network know about. In a failover configuration, this name and IP address do not necessarily map to a particular machine, but rather to whichever machine that is running the services associated with that address.

The third kind of name is the *administrative interface name*. That name may or may not match the system's private name. It's probably best if it does, but it does not have to. For example, in a configuration with an administrative network, one public network, two heartbeat networks, and an NFS server, a pair of servers might use the following host names:

- *laverne* and *shirley* are the "real" host names. They are the names assigned to the administrative network interfaces. Only the system administrators will access the systems using these names, because they refer to physical machines and not logical services.

- *milwaukee-nfs* is the "logical" hostname. It doesn't correspond precisely to one interface, but will instead be bound to the primary server's (*shirley's*) public network interface by default, and migrate to the takeover server's (*laverne's*) public network link during a failover.

- *shirley-net1* is the actual hostname assigned to the public network on the primary server. Similarly, *laverne-net1* is the hostname on the secondary server.

- *shirley-hb1*, *shirley-hb2*, *laverne-hb1*, and *laverne-hb2* are the hostnames for the interfaces connected to the redundant heartbeat networks.

Moral of the story: You're going to use an awful lot of hostnames and IP addresses. Make sure that you have a sufficient number of subnets available and IP address space to allocate for each server pair. Also, keep the names obvious, and use suffixes indicating what net, what kind of network, and what number the interface is on a net if required. Refer to our key design principle about simplicity: It counts when you're sorting through 14 network interfaces, trying to figure out why a secondary server can't send NFS replies back to clients connected through a router.

Selecting Logical Hostnames

Hostnames like *halp56v4* or *ibencqa1* can be very confusing. It's easy to mix up two similarly named machines or to misspell one, especially when the names are of this sort. Consider a crisis situation, where a system administrator is sent off to the data center, after being told that the down machine is *ibencqa1*. Upon hearing the name, he rushes off to reboot the system. By the time he gets to the data center, he's asking himself if that was a "b" or a "p". Was it "qa1" or "aq1"? Over the phone, it can be even worse. N's sound like m's. C's sound like t's, which can sound like p's.

Recognizable names selected within a theme—such as cartoon characters or Greek mythology—are much easier to deal with, to remember, and to spell. (Okay, so maybe "Sisyphus" and "Odysseus" aren't that easy to spell!) A good rule of thumb is: If you have to verbally spell out more than 3 or 4 of the characters in a machine name in order to tell it to someone else, you've probably picked a bad name.

When selecting a naming theme, be sure that you don't choose one that has an automatic limit built in. Avoid a theme like Snow White's dwarfs; after you've named your seventh machine, where do you go? (Okay, the eighth is named *snowwhite*. But then what?) If you like children's stories, then pick machine names from across all children's stories. Allow your users and administrators to be creative within the theme. As long as the names are generally short and easy to spell and remember, and the universe of possible names is fairly large, you'll probably be okay.

This is yet another area where you can allow simplicity to rule the day.

KILLER HOSTNAMES

A long time ago, I visited one user whose hosts were all named after serial killers and mass murderers. They had *jdahmer, jripper, ahun,* and like that. Kind of sick, but easy to remember. And the scheme gave each host its own personality.

In Solaris, the ping command is used to determine whether a host is functioning. If the system you have pinged is on the network, you get a response of "<machine> is alive." For that reason alone, we had systems at one company called *elvis* and *paul.* Management had a problem with our attempts to name machines after various religious figures.

At a different user site, the customer agreed with the value of giving their systems memorable names, although they had never done it before. The problem was that they had 250 systems, and wanted a theme that would be large enough to handle that many, and then to grow further. That afternoon, we sat down and came up with over 300 cartoon and comic strip characters, from every corner of the genre; everything from *snoopy* and *blondie* to *AdamAnt* and *QuickDraw.*

—Evan

When we got our first real dedicated VAXen in the Princeton Computer Science department, they were named after different ways they could misbehave: *quirky, flaky, down, panic,* and so on. The running joke was that we could call each other and ask "Is it *down?*" "No, it's *flaky.*" "You mean is the machine named *flaky* not working?" "Yes, it's down right now." Six machines and a few system managers made this both fun and manageable, and there wasn't any large money riding on our ability to quickly identify a troublemaking machine.

—Hal

Administrative Networks

In some failover configurations, the backup server will boot up with no network connectivity, apart from the heartbeat connections to its partner server. The side effects of this lack of public network connectivity at boot time can be seriously detrimental to the server. Naming services will fail, as will e-mail, network printing, and other network services. If a public network interface is not present, the initial implementation of the FMS will be greatly complicated because those services will need to be disabled at boot time, only coming to life when the server receives a failover.

It is best to configure failover servers with an additional interface connected to the public network. We call this network connection the *administrative interface*, because it is used solely for administrative purposes. Besides providing basic network connectivity and services, this connection allows system administrators a guaranteed connection to a particular server, rather than to an "anonymous" server providing a particular service. The administrative interface allows an administrator to log in to a failed server and investigate the cause of a failover before the server is put back into public use.

This interface should not be publicized to users, as it is not highly available, and does not provide them a guaranteed route to their applications. Instead, it provides a route to a particular host.

Disks

There are two kinds of disks in any failover configuration. There are the disks containing the boot information, operating system information, and other private system information. These disks are dedicated to one, and only one, server. They should be electrically independent from the *shared* disks, which can be accessed by both servers in the pair. The shared disks contain the critical data that is needed by the applications for which the servers were made highly available in the first place.

To maximize system availability, disks must have a level of redundancy, as discussed in Chapter 4. Ideally, all disks should be mirrored from one disk controller to another, and from one disk cabinet to another. If the system is important enough to make highly available, then the system is important enough to have its disks mirrored.

Private Disks

These disks are generally located inside each server, although that is absolutely not a requirement. In fact, it is better that the private (or system) disks be physically located external to a server. This way, if a server fails, no surgery to extract the disks from one server and to install them in the other will be required, thereby delivering a quicker MTTR.

These disks contain the operating system, the system identity, swap space, and particularly the failover management software. In order to start this software at boot time, it must be located on the private disks.

Private disks, by definition, cannot be dual-hosted. Only one server can ever see the data on these disks.

The entire contents of the private disks should be mirrored. Some may argue that swap space need not be mirrored. This is simply not true. If the disk containing critical application data in swap fails, then at the very least, the application will stop working. Most likely, though, the server will stop working and possibly crash, resulting in a failover and causing some downtime.

The requirement of private disks calls attention to a serious bit of administrative overhead associated with systems that failover. Many administrative files on the two systems must be kept in perfect synchronization. There are no tools to help with the synchronization; it must be maintained automatically. Unix files like /etc/system must be the same on both sides; when you change one, it is vital that you change the other. Failure to do so will result in failovers that do not work properly.

Shared Disks

Shared disks are the disks that contain the critical data. Both systems need physical access to these disks, although it is critical that only one system at a time access them. (At this writing, the technology needed for more than one server to access data at the same time, at least in NT or Unix, does not exist. It will someday, though, and then the rules will change.) If both servers try to write to shared disks at the same time, data corruption is inevitable.

There are two ways to achieve shared disks. One is commonly called *dual hosting*. In this model, both servers are physically connected to the same disks at the same time. Access is arbitrated by external software that runs on both (all) servers. When a failover occurs, and access to the shared disks migrates from one server to another, all the data successfully written by one server is guaranteed to be accessible by the other.

The other method of achieving shared disks is through a technology called *shared nothing*. In this model, data is replicated across a network (possibly the heartbeat network, or another parallel private network) between the servers. Shared nothing is a more complicated model, since it requires a functional network, and a functional host on the other side to assure that the writes actually succeed.

Dual hosting is a superior method for sharing disk data, although it requires specific hardware that permits this dual hosting. Not all disk or controller hardware does, especially in the NT world. Check with your vendors before you make blind assumptions.

Besides mirroring or RAID-5, another way to increase the overall availability of your data access is through the use of multipathing. Multipathing allows the access path to the data to shift from one SCSI or Fibrechannel card to another, in the event that the first fails.

A *disk cache* is a chunk of memory that is used to hold disk data before it is written to disk, or to hold data that is read from the disk before it is actually needed. Since memory access can be 1000 times (or more) faster than disk, there are tremendous performance implications by using disk cache. From an availability perspective, prereading (or prefetching) disk data has no implications. However, writing can.

Normally, when an application writes to a disk, the disk tells the operating system that the write is completed, and when it is the application moves on to its next task. When a disk-write cache is employed, the disk reports successful completion of the data write when it is written to the cache. Since a cache is nothing more than memory, it is volatile; if power is lost to the cache, its contents are lost with it, regardless of whether they made it to the disk.

Write caches can live in the disk array, or on the system's disk controller. Caches in the disk array are fine, as long as they have battery backups. Caches without battery backups will lose their cached data if power to the disk array is lost. A write cache on the system controller board is not acceptable in a failover environment. When a failover takes place, the cached data is locked inside the cache, and the other system has no way to access it, or even to be aware of its existence. Prestoserve is one example of system-based disk-write cache boards. Those boards are completely unacceptable and unsupportable in failover configurations.

Placing Critical Applications on Disks

One of the more interesting questions in designing HA systems is where to place the critical application executables. There are two choices: You can place them on the private disks, along with the boot and system information, or you can place them on the shared disks along with their associated data.

If you install the applications on the shared disks, the good news is that you only need to maintain one copy of the executables and of the associated configuration files. If you need to make a change in the application configuration, you only need to make it in one place.

If you install the applications on the private disks, then you must maintain two copies of the executables and of their configuration files. Changes must be made twice; otherwise a failover will not guarantee an identical environment on the other side.

However, with just one copy of the applications, it is almost impossible to install an upgrade to the application safely, and with the ability to rollback. With two copies of the application, and system A active, you can install the upgrade on system B, and failover to B. If the upgrade was successful, then B should take over, running the upgraded application correctly; you can then upgrade system A, and move on. If the upgrade fails, however, then you need only fail back to System A, and try the upgrade again on B.

This is one of those questions for which there is no single correct answer. It depends on your environment, the frequency with which you perform upgrades, and your willingness to deal with the complexity of managing parallel environments.

▶Key Points

- Since everything fails eventually, the most important components of your system must be duplicated.

- To maximize application availability, you need a second system that can take over the application if the first system fails.

- Be sure your application can actually run on the takeover server.

- Think of your computer as a service-delivery mechanism. Your applications need not run on any one particular system.

- Plan out your IP address space and host-naming conventions carefully. You're going to use quite a few of them, and you want to be sure you can easily identify hosts and host-network connections.

CHAPTER 6

Failover Management

So far, we have discussed building systems that have appropriate levels of redundancy, and the concept of failing over from one system to another. In this chapter, we will look at the methods for actually enabling the failover. We'll build on this foundation in the next chapter, where we talk about failover configurations and variations on them.

All failover management methods start from the same point; they require some degree of component monitoring. The quality of each solution can be determined by the variety of components that are monitored, and the method chosen to monitor them.

Component Monitoring

The easiest components to monitor are those that comprise the system hardware. Are the disks functioning? Is there network connectivity? Is the system up and running at all? There are relatively easy tests for monitoring the current state of each of the hardware components that can be performed by the system itself, or by a separate monitoring computer. The monitoring computer can either be the system that takes over for the primary host when it fails, or there can be a centralized monitoring system (which needs to be made highly available itself).

More difficult to monitor are software components. There are several ways to monitor the health of an application. The easiest (and the weakest) monitoring method is to examine the system's *process table*. The process table is a list of the programs that are running on a system at a particular point in time. It offers information such as the amount of memory and CPU the process is consuming, when the process began running, and so forth. The process table does not provide any indication, however, that the process is running properly. There is no way to tell from the process table if the application will respond to a query, or if it is hung or in some other way operating improperly. All the process table will tell you is whether the process runs.

If the process table is unreliable, there must be a better way to find out if an application is running properly. There is—but it is much harder to implement. You must query the application itself, and see that you get a response. For some applications a query is easy; for others it can be almost impossible. It is easy to query a database server; accepting queries is a fundamental part of what database servers do. If you have an application that sends a simple SQL query to a database and watches for a response, you have a simple monitor for that database. If the database doesn't respond to the test query, it won't respond to genuine user requests.

Unfortunately, it's even a little more complicated than that. You must be sure that you are testing the right things. If the test query asks for the exact same data on each query, then perhaps the database has cached the answer in memory (databases do that to improve performance). The database will provide the right answer, but the test is not properly or completely exercising the database or the hardware behind it. A good test query will exercise the disk. If the disk has failed, the database will not receive a response. Does the query originate on the same system that the database runs on? If so, then you may not be adequately testing network connectivity.

So, your test query must exercise the disk, the network, and the database application itself. Then it is a reliable test.

What makes this sort of application testing especially complicated is that every application type will require its own specialized test method. Databases must be queried. Web servers must download a small web page. File servers must provide file data. And all of these tests must exercise all of the components that any user's use of the application will exercise.

And there are other issues:

- When a test fails, does it hang, or does it time-out quickly and report the failure to its application? If it hangs, or causes other problems, then the test is unacceptable. Tests must be totally unobtrusive.

- What if the time-out value is set too low, and you time-out before the application has a chance to respond to the query? On the other hand, setting the time-out value too high adds unnecessary delays to the identification of a problem.

- How often do you run the test? Running it too often can put an unwelcome and extraneous load on the systems and networks being tested. But running the test too infrequently could result in a failure going undetected for an extended period.

- Some applications simply do not invite easy and non-intrusive testing. For those applications, process table examination may be required as a last resort. Otherwise it may be necessary to monitor a process that is dependent upon the one that cannot be monitored.

- What happens if the test itself is broken? How do you determine that? What monitors the monitor? And what if the monitor's monitor fails? What monitors the monitor monitor? And what if that fails . . .

When Component Tests Fail

Once your test has found what it believes is a problem, then what happens? The first thing that must happen is that the test gets rerun. If the first failure is a fluke, it is certainly better to know that and not to overreact than it is to act hastily upon failure detection.

Let's assume that the failure detection is genuine; a key component has actually failed. The next hurdle to clear is to decide upon the appropriate action to take. The correct action will vary based on your environment, as well as on the component that has failed, and on the way your system is configured. (Of course, with an automated FMS, these decisions have been made long before the failure occurs. They are usually made at installation and configuration time.)

If the failure is in an application, then the choices are to:

- Ignore the failure entirely.

- Send notifications out to key people via an appropriate method (e-mail, pager, etc.), and do nothing else.

- Initiate a failover to the secondary server without attempting any restarts.

- Attempt to automatically restart the application a particular number of times, and if the application can not be restarted, then:

    Ignore the failure.

    Send notifications.

    Initiate a failover.

For most applications, the preferred choice is to attempt to restart the application, and after a given number of failed attempts, initiate a failover. This is not always the best choice, of course. Some database applications fare much better if a database administrator is given the chance to examine the cause of the failure, and to repair it before the database is restarted.

When the monitored application is a homegrown one, the developers should be made aware of the monitoring requirement early in the development process, so that the testing can be done in as nonintrusive a way as possible.

If the failure is in a hardware component, then the choices are:

- Ignore the failure.

- Send out notification of the problem, and then ignore it.

- Initiate a failover without attempting any restarts.

- Attempt to restart the component (bring a NIC back on line, or remount a disk or file system) a given number of times, then:

     Ignore it

     Send out notification

     If the component is a NIC, attempt to migrate the network connections that were active on the NIC to another NIC with the same network access

     Initiate a failover

If the failed component is a NIC card, then the preferred choice should be failing to another NIC on the same server. If the failed component is a disk, and it is redundant (i.e. mirrored, RAID-5, etc.), then no action should be required other than notification so that the bad disk can be replaced and returned to the mirrored volume. If hot spares are in operation, then the failed disk should be replaced, and the replacement can be made the hot spare. Failover should always be the option of last resort.

Time to Manual Failover

So now we have determined that a condition exists that requires a failover. Most shops will opt for an automatic failover, so that MTTR is reduced and minimal (ideally no) human intervention is required. Other shops prefer the manual approach, so that accidental failovers never take place.

Automatic failover is generally very much preferable to manual. Let's look at the steps that are required for manual failover to work:

The system administrator must find out about the problem. He could be notified via pagers or e-mail, or his users could start screaming, or storm his desk carrying torches. Of course, for this to work, he has to be near his desk or his phone (and not using it), or have his pager on him. What if he is out of the building at lunch, or in the bathroom? What if the failure occurs at night or on a weekend?

The system administrator must get to the servers. He must get to and enter the data center, or whatever room the servers are located in. That may or may not require elevator trips or pass cards, which can cause unfortunate delays. (In several Wall Street banks and trading firms, it may be necessary to switch between two or even three elevator banks to get from the floor containing the users to the floor containing the data center.) He has to locate the server in the data center. Servers and rows of cabinets may all look the same; he has to find the right one. Finding the right server also assumes that he knows the correct name of the server that has failed; servers with non-English names, or similar names to other servers can cause confusion. If he messes up and begins working on the wrong server, he'll cause all sorts of new problems, while not fixing the ones that sent him to the data center in the first place.

The system administrator must perform the correct steps to recover from the failure. If he manages several failover pairs, one hopes that the steps are the same for each pair. If they are not, then they need to be posted on or near the servers. What is the procedure? Does it require a complete reboot? Does it just mean running a predesignated script and throwing some A-B switches? How long will it take? If he has to read the procedure it will take longer to complete. And any manual process is more prone to error than a well-tested automated process.

Manually initiated failover seems less expensive than automated failover. But it rarely is. In a shop that already has a knowledgeable operations staff that is present 24 hours a day and 7 days a week, and is located near the servers, then manual failover may be workable. But most shops cannot afford these luxuries, and so automated failover is the prevalent solution. Manual failover requires rapid response times, a reliable and quick notification system, and full-time presence. It is very difficult for even the best shops to provide all of these things, and to maintain them every day of the year (even Christmas and New Year's Eve).

When you are considering manual versus automatic failover, ask yourself the following questions. If you are satisfied with the answers, then perhaps manual failover is right for you:

- What happens when one knowledgeable operator is at lunch, and the other is in the bathroom at the moment something fails?
- What if a failure occurs at 4:00 A.M. on December 25th?

- What happens when knowledgeable operators abruptly leave the company? How quickly can they be replaced and their replacements trained?

- What happens when the satellite that relays pages to pagers gets knocked out of orbit?

- What happens when procedures are not followed properly, and as a result, systems get broken worse than before?

- What happens when your knowledgeable people cannot gain access to the servers, or cannot find the servers when a failure has occurred?

Good automatic failover addresses most of these issues. However, there *are* cases where you may want to use manual failover, particularly when you need to make several systems and several parts of those systems failover to a new set of resources in unison, and without any stragglers. This is commonly the case with failover between multiple public networks, requiring network operations and systems administration staff to coordinate their efforts. Again, we'll talk about this more in Chapter 8.

Homegrown Failover Software versus Commercial Software

Another option for implementing failover management software (FMS) is homegrown or homemade failover software. Generally this consists of code that one or two system administrators wrote in their copious spare time to manage failover for one or two pairs of servers. Since their salaries are preapproved expenses, it may seem that having them write this code is a wonderful idea. But who is left doing the job they were hired to do while they are writing and testing this code? But putting that aside, let's look at this coding effort and compare it to our key HA design principles:

Homegrown FMS is not mature code. Nobody else has tested it. You are placing your critical systems under the care of code that has never been rolled out anywhere else.

Homegrown FMS is version 1.0 code. It is new and untested; it will inevitably have bugs. The only way to discover the bugs is to use the code. Testing the code in production violates another principle.

Homegrown FMS has no reference sites. It also has no Internet newsgroups to discuss problems and issues with other users, or any user conferences, or any of the other ancillary features that mature well-installed code offers.

Homegrown FMS has little or no support. Who are you going to call for help when it doesn't work on a weekend or in the middle of the night? What happens when the author(s) leaves the company. They take the support with them, and you are left with none.

Your homegrown FMS may handle the easy cases well, but there are a load of corner cases that may not happen very often but nevertheless must be considered and provided for by any worthwhile FMS. They are the hardest ones to think of, and once thought of can be the hardest to code for. Decisions must be made regarding the best way to handle these situations. Commercial FMS solutions have examined these and have worked out ways to handle them (hopefully the *best* ways to handle them), or have given the user configuration options that he or she can choose from at install time.

Some examples of corner cases are:

- What if a host loses connectivity to the public network?
- What if a host loses all of its heartbeat links?
- What if an application is running, and can read cached data from memory, but cannot access certain disks?
- What happens if both servers in a failover pair boot at the same time? Which takes charge?
- What if the takeover server has problems, and cannot accept a failover when it needs to?
- What happens if a failover script has an error in it, and cannot run to completion?
- What if a server is too busy to send heartbeats for a while?
- What happens if a few heartbeats get corrupted on their way to the other server?
- What if the FMS daemon crashes or is manually killed?
- How do you handle extreme levels of network or system latency?

Good, mature commercial FMS has run into all of these issues and many others, and should be able to handle any of them.

Commercial Failover Management Software

Commercial FMSs offer many advantages over homegrown versions. The software is going to be mature, well-tested, and robust. It should come with support

24 hours a day, 7 days a week. It should install easily, and communicate with third-party monitoring frameworks (Tivoli, Solstice Domain Manager, HP Open-View, BMC Patrol, CA Unicenter, etc.), and it should be able to monitor many popular third-party applications, including databases, web servers, e-mail servers, and file servers. If you have unusual or homegrown production applications, the commercial FMS should be able to easily extend itself to monitor them. If you require manual intervention for failover, good FMS will offer that, too. It should be customizable for just about any configuration you may have. The vendor should offer regular enhancements and upgrades, and it should be possible to install those upgrades without incurring any downtime at all.

We offer a brief discussion of some well-known commercial FMSs (contact the specific vendors for up-to-date and complete information about each product):

VERITAS FirstWatch. Available on Solaris and Windows NT. Far and away the market leader on Solaris, FirstWatch supports all of the common networks, the major databases, and other common applications. It supports any combination of Sun servers and most third-party disks, and is easy to install and customize for new applications. The NT version supports most dual-hosted disks available on NT, and any hardware that Microsoft's Cluster Server supports.

VERITAS Cluster Server (VCS). Available on Solaris, and HP/UX, and on Windows NT by early 2000. Released in 1999, VCS does everything that FirstWatch does, but also supports SAN environments, rule-based failover, and complex failover rules in configurations of up to 32 nodes, with 64-node support due soon after as NT support.

Microsoft's Cluster Server (Wolfpack). Available on NT only. Since Microsoft gives this technology away, it is likely to become the de facto standard on its platforms. It is fairly simple to install but is limited in its scope.

Legato Fulltime HA+. Available on Solaris, NT, HP/UX, and AIX. HA+ supports all the common networks, the major databases, and other common applications. It supports any combination of Sun servers and most third-party disks. The NT version supports most dual-hosted disks on NT and any hardware Microsoft Cluster Server supports.

Sun Cluster HA. Available on Solaris only. It supports all Sun servers and Sun disk arrays, some third-party disk arrays are supported. It can be quite complex to install, and Sun recommends consulting services to be sold with it. It is produced and supported by the hardware vendor, which can simplify support in some cases.

Hewlett Packard's MC/Serviceguard. Available on HP/UX only. HP sells Serviceguard primarily on its high-end servers. It supports all networks and most critical applications. Implementation is very complex. This product essentially owns the market for FMSs on HP/UX.

IBM's HA/CMP. Available on IBM's AIX systems only, this product essentially owns the AIX FMS market. It supports all networks and most critical applications, and is very complex to implement.

Some of these products support or plan to support dynamic failover. Dynamic failover requires more servers, generally in a SAN configuration, all with access to the same storage. Before a failover actually takes places, rules are configured into the system that will help to determine which server an application will failover to, although the final decision may not be made until failover time. Rules may be based on load average (fail to the lightest loaded system), time of day (don't fail to system D between midnight and 6:00 A.M., because that server does my backups during that time), or any other customized rules that may be appropriate for your environment.

▶Key Points

- Be sure that your component tests actually test the right things, and that they emulate client processes that depend on them.

- If you decide to go with manual rather than automatic failover, be very sure that the inherent delays are tolerable in your environment.

Failover Configurations and Issues

"I think she's dead."
"No I'm not."
—Monty Python (Mary, Queen of Scots)

In this chapter we will look at some of the varied designs that have been used for building failover configurations, and then at some of the issues commonly (and not so commonly) seen when implementing them. For the sake of organization, we have broken the most commonly seen failover configurations up into three groups: two-node configurations, more complex (more than two-node) configurations, and offbeat configurations.

To simplify the discussion, we will not assume the presence of an administrative network, unless otherwise stated. An administrative network would not significantly change the configuration or the diagrams of any of these configurations.

Two-Node Failover Configurations

The simplest and most common failover configurations are the two-node kind. There are two kinds of two-node configurations, *asymmetric* and *symmetric*. In the asymmetric configuration, one node is active and doing critical work, while its partner node is a dedicated standby, ready to take over should the first node fail. In the symmetric configuration, both nodes are doing independent critical work, and should either node fail, the survivor steps in and does double duty, serving both sets of services until the first node can brought back into service.

Asymmetric 1-to-1 Configuration

Asymmetric failover (Figure 7.1) is the baseline failover configuration. Every configuration that we will discuss in this chapter is just a variation of the asymmetric model. In an asymmetric configuration, there is one master server, *rhythm*, which normally provides all of the critical services within the pair. It is connected via two dedicated networks to the dedicated backup server, *blues*. The dedicated networks are the heartbeat networks. In this configuration, the heartbeats are simple point-to-point networks, as described in an earlier chapter.

Both servers are connected to a set of dual-hosted disks. These disks are ideally divided between two separate controllers and two separate disk arrays, and the data is mirrored from one controller to the other. (Of course, the configuration works just fine if the mirrors are on a single controller or in a single cabinet. The resultant configuration is just not as resilient or as highly available as it would be with separate controllers and separate cabinets.) A particular disk or filesystem can only be accessed by one server at a time; ownership and conflicts are arbitrated by the failover management software.

Both servers are also connected to the same public network, with production clients on it. They share a single network (IP) address, which is transferred by

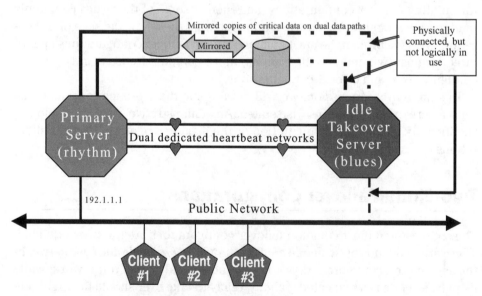

Figure 7.1   Basic asymmetric failover configuration.

the failover management software from one server to the other. We call this address a *virtual address*, as it is not permanently assigned to a particular server. Only one server in the pair actually owns the address at a time; ownership and conflicts are arbitrated by the failover management software. The other host has no identity on the public network (without the inclusion of an administrative network), and cannot be addressed by the user community. The heartbeat networks are managed separately from the public network interface, and should be configured to not support routing. Properly configured failover servers will also have administrative network interfaces, which allow system administrators to access the servers regardless of their failover state. We discussed administrative interfaces in detail in chapter 5.

After an asymmetric failover has completed (Figure 7.2), the takeover server has access to the disks, owns the virtual IP address, and is running the critical processes. No physical connections will have changed; all changes are in software.

How Can I Use the Standby Server?

Probably the most common question asked about asymmetric failover configurations is, "How can I use the standby server?" It is most difficult to justify to the people who approve technology spending that they need to buy two identical servers, thus doubling the expenditure, while only actively using one of

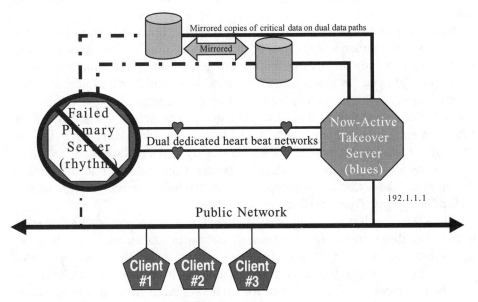

Figure 7.2 After an asymmetric failover.

them at a time. So the obvious suggestion is to find some activity that can realistically and safely be performed on these standby boxes. Probably the most common request is to put developers on the standby server. Of course, this is also probably the worst thing to do.

The key question to ask when evaluating a potential activity for its fitness to be placed on the standby server is: *How likely is it that this activity will cause the server to be unable to accept a failover?* Look at the likelihood that your standby server application will cause that server to crash, hang, freeze, or have its critical files altered. If the activity on the backup server causes a critical failover to fail, downtime will be the inevitable result. Another inevitable result will be you on the hot seat, trying to explain to your management why all the money that they spent to implement a highly available system did not do what it was designed to do.

A number of activities might be performed on the standby server. We have categorized them into four levels of advisability:

1. Bad

Probably the worst activity to put on standby server is full-blown code development. (We say *full-blown* to differentiate it from database development, which is generally constrained by the database itself, and which is subsequently discussed under "Acceptable.") By their nature, developers write untested code with bugs in it. (This is not intended to disparage any particular developers; the first pass on just about any code is going to contain bugs. If your developers do *not* write code in this way, we recommend giving them a handsome raise. They are worth it!)

Bugs can produce all sorts of effects, including but not limited to system crashes, system lockups, depletion of one or more system resources (such as memory or CPU), or leaving the standby system in a state that makes it unable to accept a failover. (Obviously, bugs can also have much less serious effects on your system, resulting in compilation errors or program failures. We are not presently concerned with them.) If your management has just spent lots of money to make your servers highly available, and just when you need to use the standby for a failover it is unavailable, everybody looks really bad.

Allowing developers on the standby server also violates one of our key design principles—that the development and production environments should be totally separate from one another.

Worse than just letting developers work on the standby box is allowing them to have privileged (administrator or root) access on the standby box. If developers have that level of access, then you may as well grant them privileged access directly on the main server. They can (either naively or maliciously) modify or delete critical configuration or executable files, and appropriate disks and other resources. This should never be permitted to happen. It is nothing less than a surefire recipe for calamity.

A similarly bad activity for the standby server is QA testing. In a QA environment, the testers are out to find bugs and other problems in the code that is being tested. If they do their job and find bugs, those bugs could lead to a similar situation, where the standby server has problems that make it unavailable at the critical time.

2. Acceptable

Unlike raw code development, database development has some constraints to it. Database development generally takes place within a mature database application, such as Oracle or SQL Server, and the actions performed by the code are more likely to be restricted to database-related activities. If your database developers are writing code that might hang or crash the standby system, then their work should be classified as "Bad."

Of course, if you do choose to put developers on the standby server, then they must be prepared to be kicked off that host at any time. And while critical services are running on their development server, they are unable to develop. That places a very limited value on their work and gives the impression that they are not particularly important to the overall operation. And, there is the additional cost that the business will incur as a direct result of their idle time. When evaluating the overall cost of rolling out the server pair, be sure to include the cost of idling developers in the event of a failover, and of keeping them idle for the entire duration.

3. Good

The first acceptable use in our list for the standby machine is as the primary server for a separate and independent critical and mature application. Even placing a critical application on the standby server, making the failover configuration into a symmetric one (discussed later in this chapter) adds a small amount of risk to the configuration. Even the most mature and well-tested applications can, on occasion, cause the same crashes and hangs that development-quality code can.

But for most critical applications, the cost savings in implementing a symmetric configuration outweighs the slight additional risk of placing a second critical application on the backup server.

4. Best

If availability is the only factor that really matters, and cost is secondary, then the very best way to configure a pair of failover servers is to dedicate the standby server as a standby server, and run absolutely no other applications on it. And for many applications, that is exactly what is done. But in many other shops, the costs of dedicating a separate server just for failover is prohibitive.

However, by dedicating the standby server, you virtually guarantee its availability when it is needed. The less the server does, the less risk there is that it will fail at an inopportune moment.

Symmetric 1-to-1 Failover

The symmetric failover model (Figure 7.3) is very similar to the asymmetric model. The main difference is that there is no dedicated idle server in the symmetric model. Instead, both servers run critical applications, and in the event that either server fails the survivor takes over its partner's application and performs double duty until the failed machine can be repaired and the applications reset.

From a cost perspective, symmetric failover is the better way to go. It makes much better use of your hardware dollar. Instead of incurring a more-than-100 percent overhead, the only extra cost is the cost of running dual-connect disks, and heartbeat networks. Those costs are much more manageable for all but the poorest organizations.

There are two fundamental downsides to symmetric configurations, but they are minor and usually acceptable. The first was just described, and is the lim-

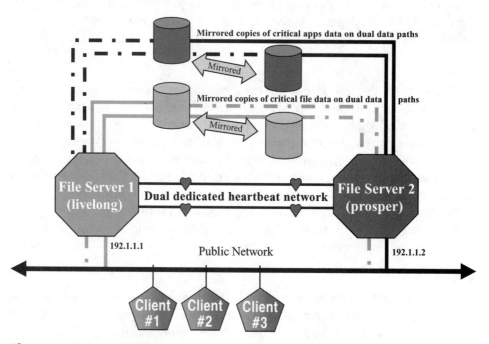

Figure 7.3   Symmetric failover.

ited risk that one critical application will render one server unable to pick up from its partner. If the applications are well-tested and mature, the risk here is negligible. The second downside is in the inevitable performance impact that will be felt on the takeover host when it begins performing double duty. If you are concerned about this performance impact, there are basically two ways to handle it: (1) buy extra CPUs and/or memory for both servers, so that they can more easily handle the additional load (but remember Boyle's Law), or (2) don't worry about it. If you buy extra hardware, it is difficult to ensure that this hardware will be dedicated for takeover time only. More likely, the additional hardware capacity will be sucked up by the resident application and will still be unavailable at failover time. When you consider that each server will likely be running in dual mode less than 1 percent of the time, you will see that concern about performance after a failover is much ado about nothing. If you can afford the extra hardware, great. If you cannot, don't worry. It's not going to be a very big deal, and it's certainly better to have two services running a little slow than it is to have one service stop running completely. Figure 7.4 shows what a symmetric pair looks like after the failover has completed.

It is important that the servers be truly independent of each other. You cannot have one server in the pair act as a file client of the other. Taking the example of NFS, if servers *livelong* and *prosper* make up a symmetric failover pair,

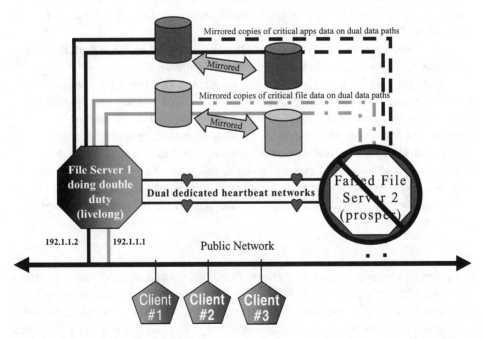

Figure 7.4 After a symmetric failover.

and *prosper* is the NFS client of *livelong*, then if *livelong* fails, *prosper* will be impacted by the failure; it will hang, and most likely not recover. The failover will fail, and downtime will result. Interdependencies like this should be avoided in either a symmetric or asymmetric configuration. We cover dependencies on network services and ways to identify these interlocking server issues in Chapter 8.

Symmetric or Asymmetric?

Bottom line: Asymmetric is better for pure availability. But it is harder to sell to management. (We did not even address the added physical space and power requirements for all those standby servers.) If you believe that asymmetric is truly the way to go, then sell it to your management the same way you might sell life insurance. Failover software and configurations *are* life insurance, after all.

FAILOVER AS LIFE INSURANCE

Every few months I send my life insurance company a check. In return for that timely payment, I receive . . . nothing! (Not even a lousy calendar.) And personally, I hope that relationship continues for a very long time. If I were to stop paying those bills, the insurance would go away, and when my family finally needs it, they won't get any of the benefits. (Personal note to my wife: I have no intention of stopping my life insurance payments. Relax.)

If your company won't invest in a standby server, then when it needs it, it won't get the benefits that a reliable standby server can provide.

Just as I (at least in theory) eat right and exercise so that I will live a long, healthy life, and I have to keep making those payments, and keep getting nothing in return, we build our computers with spare NICs, mirrored disks, mature applications, and all the other key stuff we have discussed. Someday, despite my best efforts, that life insurance policy will pay out. And despite your best efforts, someday that critical server is going to fail. When it does, you'll want the most reliable server backing it up. Otherwise, downtime will be the inevitable result. The most reliable takeover server is one that isn't doing anything, except waiting to step in.

—Evan

However, roughly four out of every five FMS installations that I have been involved with have been symmetric configurations. Realistically, they are more economical, and the risks that they bring along are acceptable for most environments. Once again, your mileage may vary. Choose the configuration that makes the most sense for you.

Service Level Failover

A variation, and complexity, that is increasingly being added to failover configurations is the concept of service level failover (SLF). We defined a *service group* as a set containing one or more IP addresses, one or more disks or volumes, and one or more critical processes. A service group is the unit that fails from one server to another.

As servers grow larger and able to handle more and more capacity, there appears to be no reason to assign only one service group to each server. As long as the resources associated with each service group are unique to their service group (i.e. not accessed by any other service group in the cluster), the various service groups may be failed over independently of one another. If there is any requirement for resources to be shared between multiple resources, then all of those resources must be joined into a single service group.

To determine the practical value of service level failover in the real world (Figure 7.5), you must first decide in what model you will be running your failover configuration. In a traditional model, where no more than two servers can physically access a set of disks, SLF is of little real value. SLF becomes very important in larger failover clusters, though.

Consider a pair of failover servers, *hope* and *crosby*. *Hope* is running four service groups; all are invocations of Oracle. We will denote each service with a

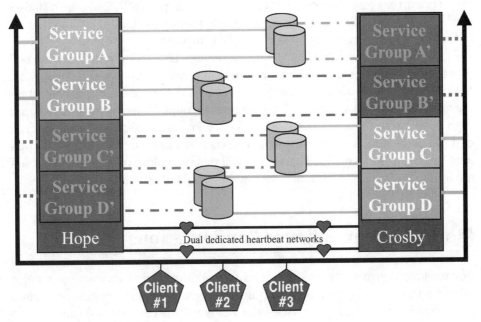

Figure 7.5 Service level failover.

letter a through d appended to the hostname. In order for one of them (*hope-a*) to fail and successfully migrate to *crosby*, several conditions must hold:

1. Whatever causes *hope-a* to fail must be totally isolated to *hope-a*, and not affect any of the other service groups on *hope*.

2. Whatever condition caused *hope-a* to fail must not exist on *crosby*, so that *hope-a* can be restarted there.

The cause of the *hope-a*'s demise cannot, therefore, be a system crash or hang. It could be a NIC failure, but that can be overcome with an agent that is smart enough to migrate a NIC's IP addresses to another NIC on the same server. The cause could be a failed disk interface card, but traffic will continue to flow over the surviving disk card, since you have properly configured your server with two. The failover could be caused by a massive disk failure that does not affect the other invocations, but since in a failover the disks migrate with the application, the failure would migrate along, too.

The only useful condition for SLF in a traditional configuration is in a maintenance configuration. Employing SLF would allow you to fail *hope-a* to *crosby*, install a patch or other upgrade to the database executables, and fail back to see if it works. Of course, if all of the database invocations are using the exact same executable, or if you choose to migrate your database executables with the data and the disks, then there is no value here either.

SLF also adds a tremendous amount of complexity. Some FMSs require multiple concurrent installations of their product to support SLF, one installation per service group. Problems become much harder to debug, as it's hard to determine which service group is causing the problems.

In a storage area network (SAN) ring, however, SLF suddenly shows some real promise. In a configuration where several hosts (say seven—*sleepy, dopey, doc, bashful, sneezy, grumpy,* and *happy*) all access the same disk farm via Fibre-channel, let's say that *doc* is running six service groups. When he crashes, a smart FMS could be configured to send each service group to a different host. Instead of a 100 percent increase in workload, each server might only see a 10 to 15 percent increase. This workload balancing will make a failure much easier to tolerate for the entire user community, and makes SLF a worthwhile FMS feature.

More Complex Failover Configurations

For reasons that usually boil down to attempts at saving money, companies often try to build failover configurations that involve several machines in complex combinations. Unless service level failover (SLF) is involved (and we are not going to combine SLF and these *N*-to-1 combinations quite yet), all of these configurations work virtually the same as 1-to-1 failover models.

An *N*-to-1 failover model is where there are *N* machines running critical applications which all fail into a single standby server. In this context, we are speaking specifically of the traditional (non-Fibrechannel) configurations. We will discuss the Fibrechannel model a little later on.

N-to-1 configurations are traditionally limited to three or four servers failing to one. And even that many requires a large server to accept failovers. The first requirement for the standby server is that it has sufficient interface cards for all the networks and disk buses that it will be required to access. In a 4-to-1 configuration that follows our basic guidelines, the standby server requires at least 10 SCSI bus connections (2 each for the four primary servers, plus 2 for the standby's local private disks), and 2 NICs for heartbeats, 1 for an administrative connection, and at least 4 for public connections for the four primaries; that's 7 NIC cards. That adds up to a minimum of 16 external interface cards to support 4-to-1 failover. Consider the size and expense of a server that will be employed as nothing more than a dedicated standby holding 16 or more interface cards.

Some operating systems support Virtual IP addressing, where multiple IP addresses can coexist on the same NIC. That feature would reduce the number of NIC cards required in our *N*-to-1 configuration. Some manufacturers make NIC cards with multiple ports on them. Fewer cards would be required if those multiple NIC cards are selected, as long as no SPOFs are introduced.

N-to-1 configurations add a tremendous amount of complexity and hardware, plus the potential for mistakes. For instance, 10 disk cables run to different disks from the standby server. Each of them supports a different service group. Accidentally pulling the wrong cable, much more likely in a complex configuration, could be catastrophic. Keeping the configurations simple gives well-meaning administrators fewer chances to make a mistake.

The more parts there are in a system, the greater the likelihood that one of them will fail. A 4-to-1 configuration has more than twice as many parts as does a simple symmetric configuration, thereby increasing the probability that any one component will fail.

N-to-1 Asymmetric

In Figure 7.6 we see the classic example of a 4-to-1 failover configuration. Each primary server in the set is connected to its own disks, which are then connected through to the standby server. The standby server takes over for any or all of the primaries that may fail. But there is no direct relationship between the four primary servers. In no way do they back each other up, or assist one another. They are totally independent of each other.

The perceived advantage of this configuration is that there are fewer idle servers than there are in a series of asymmetric pairs. But offsetting that advantage are several disadvantages. We already discussed the added complexity and how the standby server has to be a high-end server. Further, the added capacity

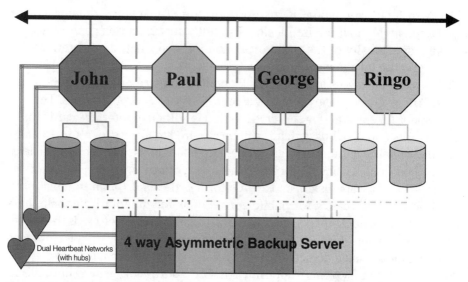

Figure 7.6 A 4-to-1 asymmetric failover configuration.

in that standby server will not be utilized the vast majority of the time. You may go months between failovers, and during that time, the standby server, with its 16 external connections, is sitting idle. The other concern with this configuration is that if the standby server itself fails, then four critical servers must operate without protection.

Some FMS software may not support these configurations right out of the box. They may be treated as consulting specials, which at some companies means that they are not given the same level of support as standard configurations.

Our advice: Don't go here. Take the four machines, and make them into two symmetric pairs. Then take the money you would have spent on the standby server and use it either to add capacity to the four servers or to give yourself a nice bonus for being so clever.

N Host, Networked

In order to build a workable multihost configuration, you need to look at a storage area network. We offer two diagrams, Figure 7.7 and Figure 7.8, that are really just different representations of the same configuration.

Both of these representations are of SAN-based failover configurations. If you decide to evaluate such a configuration, be sure that your FMS is capable of handling such a configuration. Not all of them are.

These configurations represent a much more robust model for multiple host failover than the N-to-1 configuration previously described. This configuration

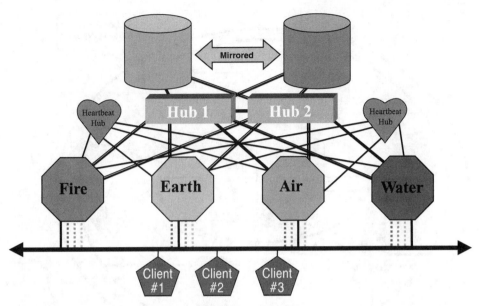

Figure 7.7 Four-host configuration, traditional representation.

is sometimes called *N*-to-*N* or *N*-to-*M*, because any host can send its services to any other. Assuming that the surviving host had sufficient capacity, and that the configuration was set up properly, you could actually lose three members of this network, and still continue to provide services on the fourth.

A smart FMS could be configured to manage multiple levels and combinations of failures, migrating services between any or all of the four servers (*fire*, *air*, *earth*, and *water*). Consider service groups *fire-a* through *fire-c*. If *fire* fails, the FMS might send *fire-a* to *air*, *fire-b* to *earth*, and *fire-c* to *water*. If *air* then fails before *fire* has been returned to service, *air-a* which normally fails to *fire* would fail to *earth*, *air-a*'s predesignated backup standby server. Or if *air* fails, and all of its services are migrated to *earth;* if *earth* then fails, all of the services it held could be migrated to *water*. The flexibility of this configuration offers is almost limitless. Confusing, but almost limitless.

Consider a parallel application that runs simultaneously on all four servers against the very same data. Assume that the application is smart enough to make this work. If *earth* fails, the only action required would be to migrate its IP addresses to another host. The remaining three servers would simply continue offering the same services as before, and hosts that were using *earth* could still access it via the same IP addresses. If this sounds arcane, it's not— it's exactly the way that large web farms work. There's one "public name" for the site, but in reality there may be tens of servers spitting out http replies. Network redirectors are used to spread an incoming workload over many hosts,

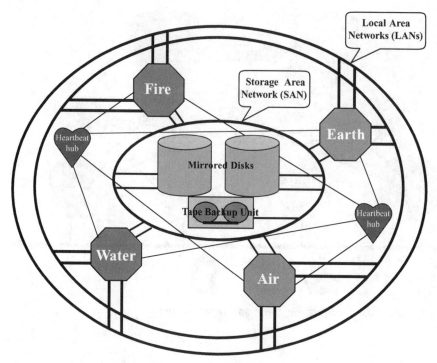

Figure 7.8 Four-host failover, SAN representation.

preserving naming conventions. They are commonly used with web servers, although there are many applications for them. We'll look at network redirectors and scalability of parallelized applications in Chapter 9.

The advantages are flexibility and efficient use of servers and disks. The main disadvantage is that these are all new technologies. The networking hardware to implement SANs is still (at this writing) new and relatively immature. The other disadvantage may be in configuring your FMS to handle these complex relationships between servers. Once SAN technology matures a bit more, and crossvendor hardware standards emerge, this model will likely carry the day.

Offbeat Failover Configurations

People can be very clever, and may suggest all sorts of seemingly clever failover configurations. In this section, we will take a quick look at three of them. The downside to cleverness is that it often breeds complexity, which violates key design principle #1. Simplicity is your friend, and creativity should be exercised cautiously.

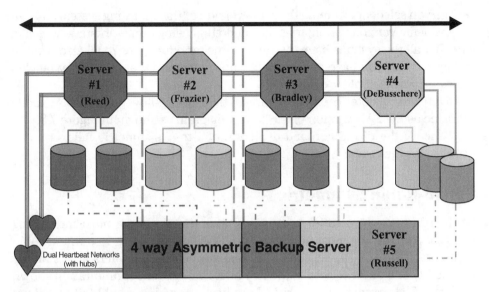

Figure 7.9 4-to-1 symmetric configuration.

N-to-1 Symmetric

An N-to-1 symmetric configuration is very similar, as you might guess, to N-to-1 asymmetric. The only real difference is that the standby server also runs a critical application, and when it fails, it migrates to a predetermined one of the N servers. Although it eliminates any idle servers from the configuration, this model carries with it all of the disadvantages of N-to-1 asymmetric.

The 4-to-1 symmetric configuration (Figure 7.9) continues to be a very complex configuration, with even more cables running between all the machines. And either the standby server is underconfigured to accept a failover, or it will remain underutilized under most conditions. Our advice: Keep away from this one. Build symmetric pairs, and simplify your life.

1-to-N (Spray) Asymmetric

This model shown in Figure 7.10 resembles N-to-1 asymmetric, turned upside down. Instead of a single server backing up many, in this configuration we run all of our critical services on a single primary server, and if that server fails, all of our service groups are migrated to several smaller machines.

This model is useful if you wish to use some old equipment as standby servers for a particular single application, rather than for the whole set of services. Once again, though, the savings will be false; they'll be eaten up in the complexity of the model. If you do choose to do this, make sure that all the servers you select are running the same version of the operating system and can run the same versions of binaries. If you do this using Sun workstations, make sure that all the systems have the same kernel architecture. You'll also want to make sure that you have enough backplane slots, and that all the newfangled hardware works in older equipment.

An interesting note: The SAN version of the 1-to-*N* failover diagram is exactly the same as the SAN version of the *N*-host diagram as shown in Figure 7.8.

(We leave the discussion and depiction of 1-to-*N* symmetric failover as an exercise for the reader.)

Round-Robin Symmetric

Of the offbeat configurations, round-robin is definitely the most interesting and probably has the most potential until SANs come along. In a round-robin configuration, each server runs a critical application and acts as a standby for exactly one other server. In the five-host round-robin configuration shown in Figure 7.11, *ginger* runs a critical application, which would fail to *baby* if necessary. *Ginger* is also the standby server for *scary*. *Ginger* has no relationship whatsoever with *posh* or *sporty*. However, if *sporty* fails, *posh* would take over.

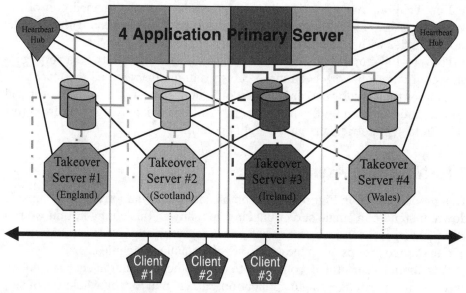

Figure 7.10 1-to-4 (spray) asymmetric configuration.

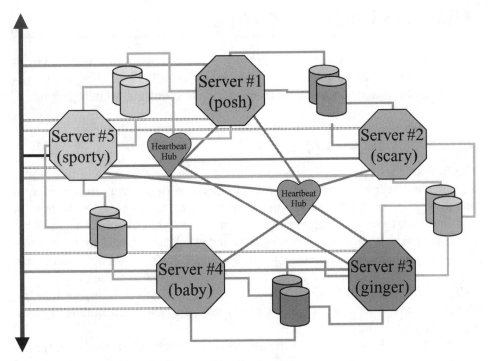

Figure 7.11   5-host round-robin configuration.

Logically, the servers in a round-robin are arranged in a ring. One of the advantages of round-robin is the scalability. Although some reconfiguration might be necessary, it would not be all that hard to add a sixth server (call it *spice*) to the picture. We would need to change *sporty* to fail to *spice* instead of *posh*, and we would need to tell *posh* to accept failover from *spice* instead of *sporty*. Round-robin also takes care of some of the disadvantages of other offbeat configurations. There is no idle machine. No host needs tremendous amounts of computing resources because no host should ever function at more than twice its normal load. And it is not terribly complicated; each server does not require much more hardware than it would in a regular symmetric configuration.

The other advantage round-robin offers is that it seems terribly clever at first blush. The disadvantage is that if you implement it, it is unlikely that anyone has actually supported one before. Speak to your vendor. You will also be hard-pressed to hire anyone who has worked with a round-robin failover configuration before. Stick with supported and mature configurations.

Once again, the SAN version of this diagram would be the same as the standard SAN drawing (Figure 7.8).

When Good Failovers Go Bad

Introducing new technology, such as failover management, into your environment can introduce new problems. These issues are all unique to failover environments; they have no parallel in the single-host, regular availability world.

Split-Brain Syndrome

The first of these phenomena is *split-brain syndrome*. The bane of failover management software, split brain can occur when the servers in a pair completely lose contact with each other. The fundamental cause of split brain is that there are two completely separate data paths. Systems communicate with each other across networks, but the actual data that flows between the systems flows on the disks. Normally the two media, and therefore the two systems, are in sync, but if they fall out of sync, that's when the trouble can begin.

If the shared disks fail and the network continues, that's all right, because the systems can continue to communicate with each other and initiate a clean failover if appropriate.

If the networks all fail while the shared disks continue to function, that is trouble. The backup server thinks the primary has failed since it has stopped replying to heartbeats, and so it takes over. The primary thinks the backup server has gone away, but that is not a fatal condition, so it continues writing its data. Today's operating systems and filesystems cannot support multiple systems writing to them at the same time. Since neither system has a clean or consistent view of the data, they will inevitably write over each other's data.

It's not the services that are the main concern; it's the shared disks. With conventional disk technology in a dual-hosted configuration, the very worst thing that can happen to your disks is for both servers to write to the disks at the same time. If one server fails, then some data will be lost. But if both servers succeed in writing to the disks at the same time, the result could be widespread data corruption, and the loss of considerable amounts of critical data.

When FMS is working properly, all hosts in the cluster are in sync and know the state of all the others. When split brain occurs, the hosts (brains) get out of sync and begin acting separately.

The first piece of advice we offer regarding split brain is that while you should be concerned about using an FMS that will detect and prevent it, you may not be able to build that guarantee into your system. Detecting split brain and forcing a recovery is nontrivial, and not all FMS packages do this. It doesn't mean that you should reject those products that don't handle split brain; just be sensitive to the causes of this problem and try to manage around them. As the old joke goes, if you tell your doctor, "It hurts when I do this," the doctor is likely to say, "So don't do that," and charge you for an office visit. We'll give you some pain-avoidance ideas at a lower price.

Causes and Remedies of Split-Brain Syndrome

There are several scenarios that could result in split brain. However, all of them are extremely rare, or could only be initiated manually. So even though we are devoting all this space to this discussion, understand that split brain hardly ever actually occurs in nature.

Multiple Heartbeat Failure

As just described, if the two hosts' heartbeating is achieved over parallel Ethernets or similar networks, and all of the heartbeat networks fail, split brain will occur. If all the heartbeats run through the same network hub, and that hub fails (e.g., loss of power, internal failure, someone hits the power switch), or if the heartbeats run through separate hubs, but all the hubs share a common power source (e.g., circuit, power outlet, power strip, electric utility company), and that power source fails, split brain will result. Network interface cards are available that have more than one network port in them. If all the heartbeats are plugged into the same NIC, and that NIC fails, then, once again, split brain could result.

In rare circumstances, it's possible for the TCP/IP stack of a system to lock up completely, possibly due to a denial of service attack (see Chapter 8) or a system memory exhaustion problem (see Chapter 11). It's unusual for the TCP/IP stack to fail on its own without the root causes of that failure first bringing down a database or web server or halting the NFS services. Another extremely unlikely event is the simultaneous failure of all of the NICs that operate the heartbeats. Solid-state components such as NIC cards very seldom fail, but of course they do fail. If a failed NIC is replaced quickly, the odds against another one failing at or near the same time are so astronomically high that you probably need not be concerned.

Fortunately, there are several remedies that can be designed into FMS and into the system hardware configuration that can keep split brain from taking hold.

First, some of the problem descriptions that can lead to a loss of network heartbeats are symptoms of poor overall system design: the presence of single points of failure. The heartbeats should never all be plugged into the same NIC or network hub; doing so creates a single point of failure. If separate hubs are used, they should not share the same power source any more than mirrored disks should use the same power source.

Of course, the loss of multiple heartbeats could be legitimate. To recognize this condition, some FMSs use the public network as a backup heartbeat medium. Often, public networks are designed to be a little more bulletproof than heartbeat networks, or at least they are designed to use different network hardware, so if the heartbeat networks do fail, there is another independent approach. Not all FMSs will do that; check with your vendor. Remember that public networks are prone to external failures, which make them less reliable as heartbeat transports. See Chapter 8 for more details.

FMSs may also permit the use of a shared disk for heartbeats. In this scenario, all of the hosts in the cluster take turns reading and writing status information to predesignated locations on a shared disk. Disk heartbeat permits heartbeats to be exchanged even if all networks fail totally. Depending on the FMS and disk management software, that disk may be limited in how it can be used beyond this heartbeating capability. Some FMSs may exchange less information when using disk heartbeat than they do when using network heartbeats, thus reducing some other aspect of the product's performance, although shared disk heartbeat may make an excellent third heartbeat medium. Again, ask your vendor.

Another protection method is enabled at the disk hardware level. Some disks, disk arrays, or software volume management products have an internal flag that indicates which server is writing to the physical disks at any particular time. When a server goes to write to the disks and finds the flag owned by the other server, it knows that the second server has initiated a takeover as the result of a split-brain syndrome failure. What happens next is a function of the FMS, and needs to be integrated with the write-access flag. Ideally, the system that sees its disks snatched away will immediately fail itself, using a device driver or other privileged, kernel-level mechanism to immediately halt the system. What you want is the equivalent of a soft power-down as soon as the (former) primary system detects its disks are no longer solely its own for writing purposes.

The FMS can introduce yet another level of protection. FMSs constantly monitor all of the system's resources and act when the resources reach a pre-determined state. If the server loses all of its network interfaces, heartbeat and public, then the server is simply not serving anyone. The only thing that a server in this state can be doing is bad—writing to its shared disks and corrupting data. So, when the FMS detects that all network interfaces have failed on a particular server, it should immediately shut down (or off) the server, and it should do so in the most direct and quick way possible. If it takes too long, writes, and therefore corruption, can still occur.

Suspending and Resuming the Operating System

In this scenario, the system administrator or operator performs an unfortunate action, and the system responds in an even more unfortunate way. In the Sun world, if the user hits the Stop key and the A key at the same time on a Sun keyboard (for you old-timers, "L1-A"), or you hit the break key on a terminal configured to be the console, the system freezes and you are dropped into the monitor. (The monitor is the operating system that runs the operating system.) On older Sun boxes, unplugging and reconnecting the keyboard has the same effect. All system processes are instantly suspended when the keyboard is plugged back in. In the Windows world, NT can be suspended from the Start menu, and restarted by turning the server back on after the suspension has completed.

In a failover configuration, there is no way for the partner system to tell the difference between a suspension and a true system crash or other failure. So, naturally, a good FMS will begin the process of taking over all the processes from the suspended system.

If the suspended system is then unsuspended (in the Sun world type "go" or "c" on really old systems), you have a problem. Both systems think that they are the masters; both systems think they own the disks; both systems think that they own the network address (two systems with the same network address can cause widespread network problems). As you can see, it gets ugly very fast. The problem is not the suspension of the OS, but rather its resumption.

The recommended fix for this particular problem is not a very technical one, but it can be as effective as any of the more technical ones for the other problems discussed above. The fix is: *Don't do that!* Make sure that anyone who has access to the keyboards of your critical systems understands the implications of resuming a suspended OS, and that they simply never do that.

Of course, simply saying "Don't do that" seems kind of glib, and we don't mean it to be glib. But, you wouldn't walk over to a critical NT server and type format C: on the keyboard, would you? Why not? Because you know better. (If you don't, then you may have other problems. . . .) That's the same reason you shouldn't resume a suspended OS in a failover configuration. Resuming a suspended OS may not be quite as obvious as typing format C:, but with appropriate education, it can be. There are more technical solutions to this problem, but in the interest of completeness, and in keeping with our design principles, we present the simplest first.

It is possible to disable or remap the Stop-A key combination on Suns. But that doesn't help the people with terminal consoles. There are also times when it is necessary to hit Stop-A and reboot a system that gets messed up. Disabling Stop-A is not the answer, since Stop-A is not the problem. The problem is in resuming the OS, so that is what should be disabled. Again on a Sun box, the NVRAM can be modified to print out a message when the OS is suspended that says something like, "This system is running in a failover configuration. Once the OS is suspended, resuming it via 'go' could have serious consequences. Please reboot." But of course, once the message scrolls off the screen, its value is lost. It is also possible to remove the "go" command from the monitor completely. That would make it impossible to resume the OS after a suspension, thus protecting the system from the uninformed. On NT systems, the Suspend menu option can be removed from the Start menu, thus removing the possibility of suspending the system; the Power-on switch cannot be removed.

The ultimate fix for split brain in two-node configurations, at least under today's technology, is to use serially controlled power switches. System A has a serial port connected to a switch that System B is plugged into. System B has one of its serial ports connected to an identical switch that System A is plugged into. When system B takes over, it takes the additional step of sending the signal to its serial port to cut off the power to system A. Ideally, this step is performed before system B actually takes control of the disks. Serially controlled power switches are not a solution for configurations with more than 2 nodes (except perhaps in round-robin configurations), though. Determining which server gets to turn off which other server and under what conditions will give you a serious headache. Of course, there are some who would suggest that this is too drastic; however, it is the heavy-handed approach to having a fail-fast driver for immediate system shutdown. Your goal, in dealing with split-brain syndrome, is to minimize the window in which data corruption can occur. A quick power-down and its associated risks are probably less risky than running with potentially two writers for the same disk set.

Most of the fixes for split brain involve the use of good design techniques and eliminating single points of failure and needless complexity. We believe that once those techniques are employed, the likelihood of split brain occurring is infinitesimal. Most FMS users will never see a single instance of split brain, but if you know how to detect and disarm it, you should be able to survive this rare occurrence.

Undesirable Failovers

There are two basic kinds of undesirable failovers, *ping-pong* failovers and *runaway* failovers, and both can be prevented by a good FMS.

A ping-pong failover can occur if there is, for instance, a massive shared disk failure. System A cannot access the disks, and so fails over and reboots. System B takes over, and also cannot reach them. So once A reboots, B fails back to it. This process continues until a human intervenes. A good FMS will support some sort of state locking, where if A fails to B, B will hold the critical resources until a human intervenes, fixes the problem, and unlocks the state. In some cases, ping-pong failovers can cause data corruption.

Ping-pong failures can also be prevented by disabling automatic reboot. If A crashes, it is best if it does not automatically reboot, but rather awaits some human intervention.

State locking will also help prevent runaway failovers. In a runaway failover, system A crashes and B takes over. In an effort to diagnose the problem with A, the system administrator reboots A. Immediately upon completion of the reboot, B sees that A is back, gives up the critical processes, and fails back to A before the system administrator has even begun trying to identify the cause of the original failure. If B automatically locks control of the critical resources after it takes over, then nothing that happens on A should cause B to fail back to A. Once the system administrator is satisfied that the problem is fixed, then, if he chooses, he can initiate a failback to A.

Verification and Testing

Designing a highly available system will lead to several sessions where you're sitting in a room, huddled with developers, managers, businesspeople, and the system administration staff, trying to decide what to do when all of your networks fail or when an application refuses to restart on a server. Performing some thought experiments during this part of the design phase will prevent you from ending up in an unknown or unmanageable state later on; it's time well-spent on verifying your decisions and implementation ideas.

State Transition Diagrams

A state transition diagram shows you how the system flows from one well-defined operational state to another, due to certain events. In the diagram, the states are shown as bubbles, while the transitions (changes) between the states are labeled with the events or failures that take you from one bubble to another. A very simple state transition diagram is shown in Figure 7.12, where a system has four operational states of being: OK, Application Recovery, Primary Network Down, and Manual Recovery. Every arrow is labeled with the event that takes you to another bubble, such as the application failing, a successful recovery of the application (via the FMS), or the failure of the primary or secondary network.

Normally, the system is in the OK state. If the primary application fails, the system starts recovery (by restarting the application on the same server, for example), and when completed, it goes back to the OK state. If the primary network fails, the system moves to the lower-right-hand state; again, an application fault and recovery loops into the Recovery state and then back to the starting point. But what if something happens during application recovery? At that point, or if the second network fails after the system is already in the Primary Network Down state, manual recovery begins. It's clear when the system

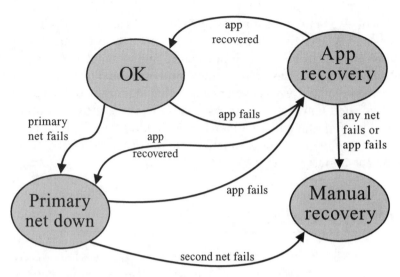

Figure 7.12   State transition diagram.

is automated, moving between states, and also clear when there have been enough failures or complex, multiple-mode failures that require a human being to make decisions.

Why would you spend the time drawing one of these? There are many motivations to develop and maintain state transitions:

- *You can get beyond the single-failure mode of most FMS packages.* What do you do if you suffer a second failure while recovering from the first? What are the kinds of failures you want to worry about handling in succession?

- *The fewer states your system can occupy, the easier it is to understand.* As you develop a transition diagram, you may find a few states that are essentially the same, or that with minor process modifications can be made to be the same. For example, in the previously described figure, there's no real reason to have "OK" and "Primary network down" be separate states; since both have essentially the same event transitions they can be merged together. When you reduce the number of possible outcomes, you make it easier to diagnose a system failure.

- *Operational and failure states are acceptable; unknown states or ambiguous states are trouble.* Are you sure that your system won't end up in the twilight zone if several things fail at the same time? Do you know that you'll end up in a state where the FMS kicks in and tries to right the boat, or that you'll be able to begin a manual intervention process that gets bodies in front of consoles quickly? If you end up doing neither, you're looking at a system that may hang for an indeterminate period of time.

- *You need to draw the line between automation and manual processes.* If you can determine those states in which your FMS will throw up its hands and cry, "Uncle! Call the SAs!" you'll know where you need strong escalation and people management processes.

- *Not all costs are apparent when the first design wave is through.* If you haven't proven that the designed system can be operated, or that it meets the operational requirements of your staff, you'll need to walk through a state diagram to show that you have all of the necessary expertise at the right locations.

Going through this process early may save you time and money later on. A design error that leaves you without a path to recovery may be more complex and more difficult to fix once developers have started. If you need the application team to accommodate certain failure cases, they're going to need to know right up front.

The other benefit to state transition diagrams is that they let you visually compare the trade-offs of different solutions. Let's say you have a 10-minute automatic failover whenever a network becomes unusable, driven by monitoring scripts that watch network traffic and communicate among themselves to time the failover (we'll talk about this case more in the next chapter). Developing and implementing this coordinated task is not easy; if you're doing it to automate a 15-minute manual process, you may decide that the extra few minutes of recovery time are worth it in the one transition that reflects an infrequent failure.

Testing the Works

Testing: You know you need it and that it's good for you, but nobody actually wants to do it. Testing is the castor oil in the design phase and the maintenance process of a highly available system. It's always the first activity that goes away (except perhaps for documentation) at crunch time. In many shops, of course, it's always crunch time, and little or no testing ever takes place.

Unfortunately, without adequate testing there is no way to tell if your procedures and safeguards are going to work. Good testing always finds holes and inefficiencies in procedures. Testing catches those quick, "Oh, I'll put together a more permanent solution next week," fixes that always work their way into all systems, even the best-run shops.

Since systems are always evolving, with applications and procedures being added and modified all the time, testing must be done on a regular basis. Failovers should be tested at least once a month. In addition, for the testing to be thorough, it must include the following:

- All documented procedures must be tested; in an emergency, it is likely that written procedures will be followed blindly. If they don't work exactly right, the result may well be chaos.

- When testing your standards implementation, make sure that systems and applications meet the documented local standards. Know what all test results should be before the test is run.

- Test your backups by restoring a couple of them. If you cannot restore your backups in a test environment, then they aren't going to be much good when you need them.

- Test any critical process whose failure may cause downtime. Try to think of the less obvious potential SPOFs, like building access scanners or locked doors.

Besides periodic procedural testing, it is also important to test applications and how they perform in high-stress situations. Always remember that long service times and failures are indistinguishable to the average user. How does your system perform as load averages increase, especially when they do so over long periods of time? What breaks first? Fix those things, and move on to second- and third-level failures. Bad assumptions made in buffer or counter sizes will often be the first things exposed.

Test the sort of problem that may not bite you for a while. The Y2K problem is an excellent example of this. Programs that were written in the 1970s, and that were believed to be temporary, are the worst culprits for Y2K. Test other unusual calendar alignments, like leap years (Remember, 2100 is *not* a leap year!). Check for assumptions that may be broken in months with six weeks in them; if August 1st falls on a Friday or Saturday, then August stretches into the beginning of a sixth week on the 29th or 30th.

Managing Failovers

As we've mentioned on other topics like security, entire good books have been developed on system management. Rather than provide a primer on system administration habits, we'll zoom in on those aspects of management that are particularly relevant to running a failover management system.

System Monitoring

Automated failovers are great to ensure that your systems recover quickly from most outages. But they are not enough. You must monitor your systems for any variety of error conditions, including system resource exhaustion (filesystems or memory fill-up), super-high CPU loads (which resemble outages), network' failures, and so forth.

Most systems have automated monitoring tools available that help trouble find your system administrators, rather than making them spend all their time looking for trouble. If the SAs don't have to spend time looking for problems, they are free to solve problems that found them, or to implement new systems properly. Products like BMC Patrol, VERITAS Nerve Center, Tivoli Global Enterprise Manager, Computer Associates' Unicenter, and Hewlett-Packard Open View will monitor your systems for a variety of potential problems, and then notify a preselected group of administrators via pagers, e-mail, telephone calls, console displays, or other alarms. Generally these applications use a protocol called SNMP (simple network management protocol) to detect and pass on information about these errors.

If your environment makes use of SNMP or a similar notification protocol, then it is vital that any third-party or homegrown applications also use the protocol, so that they seamlessly merge themselves into the existing environment without requiring the implementation of new infrastructure.

When selecting a system monitoring protocol or tool, as we said in our key design principles, be sure to select technologies that are mature, and that have reference sites and web sites as sources of good information about successful deployments.

Consoles

Every system needs to have some sort of console. A console acts as a master terminal, allowing access even when all other system resources are down. Boot messages and other critical start-up information appear on the console screen. The problem with fixed, attached consoles is that they make remote access to boot information difficult, and also complicate command entry to allow reboots from the console.

If your operating system supports a terminal server, use one to connect your consoles. GUI consoles are not practical for remote system management. Text-based consoles will enable your system administrators to access systems from anywhere in the world, at any time of the day or night. There are few things more frustrating to a system administrator than to have to get up at 3 A.M. on a Sunday morning, drive to the office, and find a down server, only to discover that a single command he or she could have given to someone over the phone would have fixed the problem. If the administrator could have logged in from home, the system would have been back on line faster, and the SA could have gone back to sleep.

Of course, if you arrange for network access to system consoles, you open up a potential security hole. Be sure to enforce good passwords on the terminal server ports to keep out intruders. Otherwise, some of these reliability measures will become massive security holes. It is best to enforce the use of tools like ssh to encrypt traffic that flows across otherwise unprotected networks.

If your server has a CD-ROM drive on it (and don't they all nowadays?), and it isn't being used for anything else, keep a copy of the operating system CD in the drive. Then, if it becomes necessary to reboot the system from the CD, nobody need visit the system to get it ready. This also helps keep track of where your operating system CDs are; lost OS CDs are a common factor in increased MTTRs.

As a final measure to protect your consoles, you should log all data that appears on the console to a system log file, and then automate the examination of these log files for notification of problems. If you decide to build your own log notification system, consider a method where console messages that do not generate alerts are written to a file, and any message that does not appear on the exclude list generates an alert. Selecting a list of messages that generates higher levels of alerts is also wise. Avoid a system where unknown or new messages are routinely overlooked.

Utilities

Most likely, whatever system problem you are trying to solve or information you are trying to collect has been previously solved or collected by someone else. Before you spend a lot of time writing a homegrown single-use application, do a web search for something like it. It is much easier to customize an existing application for your purposes than it is to write something from scratch. The customization process is also much less prone to error.

Some examples of useful public domain software include:

Perl. A very useful programming language that was designed by and for system administrators. It runs on just about every major operating system.

Tripwire. A Unix utility that watches a list of key system files, and notifies the administrators if the files are altered.

Top and wintop. These utilities return as output a list of the processes running on the local system, arranged and sorted any number of ways. Top is the Unix version; wintop is the Windows version.

Ntp. A cross-platform clock-synchronizing utility. All the systems on your network synchronize their clocks with a preconfigured time server, or with an external server such as an atomic clock located out on the web.

If you do find it necessary to create your own utilities, use the command line interface, rather than a Windows-based one. It is not hard to imagine a scenario where the person who dials into the server to fix it only has access to a slow line on a dumb terminal from very far away. A command line interface makes the repair process much simpler; no specialized hardware is required.

Time Matters

Regardless of the type of system or the method you choose, it is imperative that all systems in a cluster be time-synchronized. Applications and operating systems can get confused when a fundamental assumption is violated: that time always flows in the same direction, forward, at the same rate: one second per second. If systems are out of time-sync, then it is possible for one system to create a file on another, with a time stamp that the second system regards as being somewhere in the future. Results can be most inconsistent and confusing.

The public domain application `ntp` is the best utility we have seen to synchronize clocks between multiple systems. Unlike Unix's `rdate` command, ntp resets clocks slowly and gradually over a period of time, allowing the time to be changed without applications on the server even being aware of the change. The *rdate* command changes the date of one server to match another, but it does it all at once, often resulting in time seeming to move backward on the server whose date changes. On NT, there are similar products, such as Win-SNTP and Timeserv.

►Key Points

- The most reliable takeover server is one that isn't doing anything except waiting to step in.

- You'll have to expend more energy on management tools and management processes when you're using failover management software; if you're going to the effort to make the systems reliable you have to improve the operational management as well.

- Go through thought exercises first to determine what you need to manage, and what will happen under any operating condition.

- Be aware of issues like split-brain syndrome or undesired failovers, and have the management processes in place to identify and resolve them within the constraints of your FMS and operational tools.

8

Redundant Network Services

I live in a crumbling and defective world.
—Scott Adams, in "The Dilbert Future"

Bob Metcalfe, inventor of Ethernet and technology writer, is fond of saying that the power of networked computer systems goes up exponentially; as you connect them together their aggregate usefulness increases as the square of the number of systems. Metcalfe's Law has a dark side as well: The complexity of these systems and the number of potential failure modes also increase exponentially as they grow. Often, network failures cause the same symptoms as a server failure, and to the user sitting impatiently with an hourglass cursor on her screen, the server is simply "not there." Whether it's a failed router, a network flooded with unwanted traffic, a broken network interface card, or a server crash, the user is going to see the same client-side behavior until the problem is resolved.

In this chapter, we'll look at several ways in which networks fail and methods that you can use to engineer reliability in the face of those failures. We'll also cover key network services; how you can determine whether your network is recoverable after any type of service failure; and how to detect certain network conditions that appear to be failures. As in previous chapters, we'll start with the fundamental building blocks and demonstrate how to assemble them without single points of failure, with an eye toward management and monitoring. Using the redundant host and redundant network design rules for building platforms, the following chapters will cover application-level engineering concerns to complete our bottom-up approach to high availability design.

Network Failure Taxonomy

Network failures are difficult to detect with certainty. This is due to several factors, including the transient nature of many network overload or performance problems, the ability of IP networks to self-heal or route around single points of failure, and the tendency to equate periods of high network latency with network failures. This section covers the different types of failures that networks should tolerate in order to achieve a level of high availability, and some mechanisms for detecting these failures.

Network Reliability Challenges

On the surface, adding redundancy and reliability to a network should be no more difficult than solving the split-brain problem discussed in previous chapters. However, in the host design case, all of the resources are contained within or controlled by the system. In the network, resources are highly distributed, have multiple points of control, and are subject to outside forces. Network reliability poses several challenges to the system management team:

Network failures come and go. A period of very high traffic, followed by a lull in activity, followed by another peak, may appear to be a prolonged failure. In this case, network latency and network failure produce the same client-side symptoms. Measurement and monitoring tools must be able to distinguish between the two cases, and network segregation techniques provide isolation and protection against some forms of traffic-driven meltdowns.

It's hard to define where the network is. A typical path from a PC to a server located in a machine room on the same campus will touch a switch or LAN concentrator in a local office wiring closet, a router or two in the same building, another router entering the data center building, and one or more machine room high-speed networking switches. Add in network interface cards on PC, server, routers, and switches, and you have a dozen or more points of failure. What if the backplane on a switch fails? Or one outbound interface card on a router? Each one of these pieces of equipment may be controlled by a different operations organization, adding a people angle to the complexity.

Latency contributes to perceived network failures. A router that is overloaded or dropping packets in the middle of a long network path will greatly impact end-to-end reliability. Network design and traffic management help to reduce network latency, or at least control it, but it remains an external factor in service reliability measurement.

Denial-of-service attacks are real. Most simply, a denial-of-service attack means that a user cannot get access to a host or network service because all of the input capacity is tied up dealing with bogus requests. Here's a simple example using the ever-popular bank teller model: Five people simultaneously cash their paychecks, take the amount in pennies and unwrap them, then ask to deposit the pennies by counting them. All other bank customers queued for a teller are stuck while the bogus requests are handled. All "real work" is held pending while the annoyance requests are serviced.

Load balancing is a scalability feature, not a reliability solution. Distributing input load over several servers allows horizontal scalability of a service; that is, the service capacity can be increased by adding more hosts that perform the same function (the "horizontal" notion probably comes from the profile you see entering the machine room, as the new servers increase the width of the server skyline). When a single server in a load balancing configuration fails, or when one of the intermediate network components fails, recovery is still an issue. Reliability features can be added to load balanced configurations to improve recovery time and overall uptime, but the simple load balancing solution by itself does not improve end-to-end reliability.

Network access isn't as secure as it should be. Are all of the network interface jacks secured, or can anyone plug a random PC into the building LAN? Incorrectly configured hosts cause major network problems without any malicious intent. Network cables are also a common source of failures. Twisted pair cables are indistinguishable from telephone handset cables, and older thinnet (10base2) or coaxial (10base5) cabling is a source of constant headaches.

CLEANLINESS IS NEXT TO (NETWORK) CLEAVAGE

In a startup company, we used thinnet Ethernet to connect a few dozen workstations to our server room. We reconfigured partitions frequently to make room for new employees and ran the thinnet along the partition feet as a sort of informal cable raceway. After any minor network change, the cleaning service would, without fail (but entirely accidentally) vacuum up any cable that dangled dangerously far away from the sanctuary of the partitions. Next morning: network cleavage and some unhappy users. After the second or third time this happened, we got quite good at tracing the network segments from the repeater to successive workstations, breaking and testing the network as we went to locate the fault.

—Hal

Only end-to-end reliability counts in the networking arena. Redundant network interfaces and switches configured in pairs help to reduce the probability of a LAN failure, but without redundant routes, aggressive management and monitoring, and key service ruggedization, the overall client picture of reliability is greatly reduced. Adding this level of certainty to network services requires knowing how and why they break.

Network Failure Modes

Network failures create frustration because of the myriad failures possible when you combine host interfaces, cables, switches, routers, hubs, and network services like Dynamic Host Configuration Protocol (DHCP) or Domain Naming Service (DNS). Understanding the different possible failures for a network of systems is critical for ensuring its availability; while you may not be subject to all of the corner cases, you need to know which ones are potential traps and how you'll avoid or manage your way out of them. Some of the most common network failures are:

Local network interface. Typically on an I/O card with one or more network interfaces, the network interface represents the first point of potential failure between a host and the outside world. An I/O bus or partial backplane failure can make a network interface appear to have failed; however, these system-level failures usually cause other more easily noticed problems such as disk I/O failures or complete system crashes. In rare cases, devices on the I/O card fail, and the network interface is rendered inoperable.

Cabling. Items subject to the highest degree of physical wear and tear tend to fail the most frequently. Cables connecting hosts to hubs or switches are near the top of this category, with failures that include a broken locking clip, causing the cable to fall out of the connector; a frayed conductor in the cable; or severe physical strain resulting in damage.

Network infrastructure equipment. Hubs, switches, bridges, and other devices that sit below the IP layer are frequent contributors to network-level failures. It's not just physical failures that should give you pause; excessive load may cause packets to be dropped on the inbound side of a switch, resulting in an intermittent network outage.

Routers and route information. At the IP layer, software, configuration, and even interoperability woes are also root causes of network outages. In 1998, AT&T lost part of a frame relay network due to a misconfigured router, resulting in a multiple-hour outage for some of its FR customers. Physical failures remain a possibility; however, IP networks are typically designed with some level of redundancy to handle router failures. That redundancy, reflected in the routing tables of hosts, is yet another source of network outages.

Key network services. Even the simple act of deriving an IP address corresponding to a hostname requires talking to another host on the network, using a name service such as DHCP, NIS, or DNS. Networked filesystems like NFS, DCE/DFS, and Windows SMB services, along with naming, directory, and security services, add to complexity of network operation. A failure in any of these services, caused by any of the failures previously noted or by a failure in the system software providing the service, usually results in a network outage.

Latency. Excessive load, broadcast, address resolution protocol (ARP) storms, or a denial of service attack render a network nearly useless as the useful throughput drops precipitously. While not a network failure per se, latency creates the illusion of an outage to the nodes connected to it.

The next sections explore the physical and logical failures in more detail, providing first-level detection mechanisms. Using this basis, we describe several approaches to building reliable networks tolerant of these failure modes.

Physical Device Failures

From a networked host's perspective, it is exceptionally hard to distinguish between a broken cable, a faulty switch, or a hub. Network interface card failures tend to occur quietly, while the others may result in "No carrier" or other messages indicating a network disconnect. In some cases, the network connection merely disappears, and the host is stranded on the wire. For simplicity, it helps to lump these faults into a single class, detected by the host's inability to send or receive packets. Recovery from these failures does require knowing the exact fault location and the appropriate repair steps needed, but for initial detection and system-level recovery, a simple algorithm should suffice.

Unix hosts track the number of packets sent, received, and dropped due to errors for each network interface. The netstat -i command in both NT and Unix displays the packet counts. To detect a NIC or switch failure, look for an output packet count that isn't increasing even as you attempt to send network traffic; be wary of an input packet counter that doesn't increase; and also check for an increasing error count. Output errors are usually caused by repeated attempts to send a packet that result in a collision or can't complete because there is no network carrier.

For confirmation of a suspected network disconnect, try using ping to reach another, well-known host, or ping a router. Beware of pinging your own machine, since you may reach it via a loopback, or built-in network interface that doesn't actually send packets onto the network. Before relying on ping tests, test your operating systems to see how they transmit or don't transmit packets on the network. Also, choose your source well, using a well-run, rarely changed machine as a known, clean, starting point. One machine that tends to be very reliable in almost any network is the home machine of a system administrator. Unlike the oft-mentioned shoemaker (whose children always have the worst shoes), most system administrators make their machines the most reliable ones on the network.

In the case of a switch or router failure, attempts to manage the device will fail, giving you an additional clue as to the location of the fault. Your first responsibility, however, is to get critical hosts connected to some well-conditioned network, so it's fair to lump all of these physical failures together under the same detection umbrella. Physical failures are usually addressed by switching to a redundant network connection, and can often be handled on a host-by-host basis. One host's NIC failure does not impact others. This is, of course, the easy case. The harder problem is when you have to get several machines to change their configurations at the same time.

IP Level Failures

Once you add system administration, configuration, and network services to the mix, the complexity of network failures increases in accordance with Metcalfe's Law. Things get more complicated exponentially, and it's essential to break detection and fault repair down into well-defined tests that are as independent and isolated as possible. We'll continue our list of sniffing techniques, providing more case-by-case details.

IP Address Configuration

The simplest failure at the network level is that a host ends up with the wrong IP address or with a duplicate IP address. Duplicate IP addresses often are the result of too few checks when updating DNS or NIS tables, or overlapping DHCP address space ranges. Once "Duplicate IP address" messages begin appearing, the host borrowing another's IP address can send packets without difficulty but may not receive any input packets (since they are going to the other host with the same IP address).

From the point of view of the misconfigured host, this problem typically appears as an intermittent network failure. The failure isn't permanent or easily traced, as the exact machine that receives packets destined for the duplicated IP address is determined by a race condition in answering ARP requests on the network. When any other node needs to locate the host corresponding to an IP address, it sends an ARP request. With more than one host believing it owns that address, they all answer the request. The reply that arrives first may release an outbound packet; however, subsequent replies update the sender's ARP table with different information. In short, the host whose answer arrives last appears to own the duplicate IP address.

Incorrect IP information, such as a DNS entry that contains the wrong IP address for a hostname, typically results in one-sided traffic flows. Responses that take the misconfigured host's IP address from a request arrive without problems; however, services that look up the problem host's IP address in a name service will send their packets into the void (or to the wrong destination). Regular pings or heartbeats sent between well-known hosts should ensure that dynamic IP addressing like that provided by DHCP remains problem-free. However, the first line of protection is careful management of all network configuration services. We'll discuss change control and audit trail functions in Chapter 13, but for now note that many of these apparent "network failures" are due to system administration problems introduced by weak or unaudited processes.

Routing Information

Network connectivity is only as good as the routing information used by hosts to locate servers, clients, and service endpoints on the network. IP-routing algorithms attempt to handle redundancy and dynamic recovery from failures; however, they also introduce new complexities that result in sometimes-baffling failures. Asymmetric routes, incomplete or incorrect routing information, or networks with many hops between redundant connections also contribute to network failures.

Asymmetric routes occur when a client finds the server without problem but the server cannot send a reply back to the client because it lacks routing information. This is possible if the server is behind a firewall that blocks some routing information; if the server uses static routing information; or if a router along the path is sending incorrect route updates. Note that it's the server's return path that creates the network failure; if the client can't find the server, the client-side application will complain about an unreachable host or network.

A client sending a request on its happy way turns unhappy when the reply is discarded at the server, silently, due to an asymmetric routing configuration. NFS system administrators puzzled by `nfs_server: bad sendreply` error messages can thank asymmetric routes for their problems. This error is caused by an NFS server's inability to return a client request. Again, using the ping utility, or more prudent examination with a tool such as `traceroute`, the system administrator can locate the trouble spots and provide ongoing monitoring of the round-trip health of your network.

Technically, any host with two or more network interfaces can function as a router. This doesn't always mean that it should, however, as routing is CPU-intensive and will degrade performance for other applications. Usually, hosts that accidentally route packets do a poor job of it. Look for unwanted IP routing using `netstat -s` (in NT or Solaris).

Finally, once a router fails, the network needs to construct a redundant path to the networks on the "far side" of the failure. If there are multiple routers connecting two networks, the secondary routers will appear in hosts' routing tables during subsequent routing table updates. For example, using the Routing Information Protocol (RIP), updates are sent by active routing hosts every 30 seconds. When a router fails, it stops sending RIP updates, and hosts relying on routes through that device discard those routing entries as soon as the updates stop. It takes about 30 seconds to establish a secondary route when there are no IP address topology changes and sufficient redundancy of routers. However, if a new network number is configured, or if a new host route is created to a new IP address, then clients may wait several minutes for this updated network information to propagate through all of the intermediate routers. This is, in fact, a strong argument for cementing a network numbering scheme early on, and then leaving it static as you build redundancy around it.

Congestion-Induced Failures

Sometimes your network problems stem from a simple case of too much traffic and not enough highway. Even with a well-designed, redundant, and highly reliable hardware base, spikes in network traffic or intentional attacks create the perception of a network or host failure. When the user is looking at an hourglass cursor, she doesn't really care what broke or is overloaded; she only knows that she's not getting data from the network. Congestion-induced failures fall into two broad categories: *traffic congestion* and *denial of service attacks*.

We won't cover causes and resolution techniques in detail here as there are many good references for these topics, including the web sites of popular network hardware vendors such as Cisco and Nortel Networks. We'll look at each class of failure, give you some quick metrics to use for field identification of these beasts, and describe the general impact on reliability. Thoroughness in network reliability requires that you consider these cases, so our goal is to provide a baseline for including these failures in your operational and design processes.

Network Traffic Congestion

Network traffic overload causes reliability problems in the same way that highway traffic overload causes personal reliability problems. How many meetings or shows have you missed due to accidents, congestion, or poor planning on the road? The same constraints apply to network traffic. Unusually high traffic levels can introduce temporary or sporadic network failures as packets are dropped by switches or routers that overflow internal buffers. Excessive latency can be introduced as these pieces of network equipment struggle to keep up with the resulting load.

Break down the traffic types and try to locate root causes, or use that information to enforce filtering, partitioning, or routing schemes. Here is a short list of symptoms and problems:

Excessive point-to-point or unicast traffic. In short, too many talking at the same time, contributing to a network noise level that's not healthy. Historically, system administrators used the collision rate on a network to detect this background noise level, but switched, full-duplex networks have made collisions an anachronism. On a broadcast network using a twisted-pair hub (or thinnet/thicknet coaxial cable for history buffs) you may still find the collision rate an early warning sign. Using a network sniffer or hardware monitor will give you a more accurate reading of load. Once you start loading an Ethernet over 50 percent of its capacity on average, you run the risk of severe slowdowns during peaks or bursts of activity. On a switched network, you'll need to examine the per-port statistics on packet drops, or switch packet loss to see if you are suffering load problems. Some loss may be attributable to short bursts; however, any kind of packet loss is a warning sign.

Broadcast packets. The family of broadcast packets includes User Datagram Protocol (UDP) packets; Address Resolution Protocol (ARP) packets, used to locate the owner of an IP address on the network; and various PC file sharing and naming protocols like SMB and NetBIOS. Some examples of UDP broadcast are an NIS client looking for a server, a DHCP configuration, a boot request, and RIP information sent by routers. Look at the level of broadcast activity using `netstat -s`, breaking it down into UDP and ARP broadcasts. Too much ARP activity could indicate a network that simply has too many nodes on it, or one that suffers configuration problems causing ARP requests to be forwarded or answered incorrectly. High levels of other broadcast traffic should be addressed with routers or other filtering devices. Broadcast storms, or endless streams of broadcast traffic, can be caused by hosts using broadcast addresses as their own IP addresses, mixing old (0s) and new (1s) styles of broadcast addresses, poorly formed ARP requests, ARPs for broadcast addresses, or incorrect forwarding of broadcasts over a router or filter that should suppress them. Part of your network operations process should include the ability to detect a broadcast and break the network into subsegments to assess and repair the damage at the source.

Multicast traffic. Multicast packets are sent to a selected group of hosts. Those machines expressing an interest in the packets receive them; however, they do take up network bandwidth. Some data distribution products claim to do multicasting of data; however, they actually do serial unicasts of the same data to any subscribing clients. Watch for excessive load generated by data distributors (early versions of PointCast, for example) and multicast traffic that won't appear in broadcast packet counts. Again, a network analyzer or sniffer is your best approach to locating the head end of this problem.

Denial-of-service attacks. Rather than filling up the network with packets, a denial-of-service attack fills up a network service's input queue with bogus or invalid requests. It's possible to have a denial-of-service attack that doesn't absorb all available network bandwidth but that still brings a network service to its knees.

Design and Operations Guidelines

You don't want to experience "false positives" and perform complete network failovers simply to recover from a period of peak load or a spike in traffic caused by a poorly configured client. Network traffic nightmares tend to repeat; that is, if you bring down one network with a problem, the same hosts and same configuration on a redundant network are likely to bring that formerly clean network to a halt as well. We offer some guidelines for design and operation of networks here, as a precursor to redundancy design guidelines. Typically, network operations is a separate entity in the data center, so it's a good idea to review these "big rules" around load management with all of the operations players, just to be sure infrastructure hiccups don't bring down a distributed service.

Know your baselines. "It was faster on Tuesday" is the watchword of the underinformed system administrator. Without some knowledge of the typical packet counts, packet demographics (broadcast UDP, ARP, IP, TCP, unicast UDP, and PC protocols), or variations during various parts of the day or days in the work cycle, you'll have trouble identifying spikes or bursts as potential instigators of trouble.

Know your tools. Measuring collisions on a switched or token-based fabric like Fiber Distributed Data Interface (FDDI), or looking for output errors instead of counting switch packet drops, will ensure that you never find the needle in the haystack. Make sure that you know what your tools measure and that you can control the outputs under measurement. There's no point in taking a reading on something that can't be directly fixed by an operations person.

Routers, filters, and firewalls are good defense mechanisms. They block broadcast packets and can be used to block other kinds of unicast traffic as well. Firewalls aren't just for external defensive positions. Gaining a measure of predictability on the network means having more control over what kinds of traffic actually enter and exit the network. This requires careful coordination with applications developers and users, but it's well worth the effort.

Application-level relays. Kind of a cross between firewalls and routers, relays often help corral traffic and reduce load. Proxy cache web servers are a good example; they don't require application-level changes and improve network throughput in most cases.

Networking is not a zero-sum game. It's usually a positive-sum game. If you subdivide a network with a 60 percent utilization into three networks, don't expect to see a nice dip to the low 20 percent range on each one. Once you remove that bottleneck, nodes on each subnet will step up their activity, producing more load than before. When you stop choking someone, they tend to fight back—and the same is true for networks.

Our focus on end-to-end system reliability necessitates some discussion of network loads, latencies, and failures, but our focus will primarily be on building redundancy into the network infrastructure to tolerate physical failures. In the case of a network that goes open loop, with excessive load, broadcast storms, or other unexplained incidents that send you into an *X-Files*-like state of weirdness, treat the problem like a physical failure and resort to a redundant network while you find the truth that's out there. We'll discuss ways to build in redundancy and handle failover now that you know what you're protecting yourself against.

Building Redundant Networks

Up to this point we've concentrated on what makes networks break, and how you might detect these failures. In this section, we'll describe architectures and designs for network redundancy, ranging from multiple networks to multiple paths through multiple networks. Some of these scenarios may seem far-fetched or impractical, or you may feel that you can condense multiple failure modes into a single problem area with a well-defined recourse. Remember our key principles: You need to spend money, but be sure that you spend it the right way. When you multiply the number of nodes on a network by the cost of adding redundancy to all of the infrastructure they touch, and add in the cost of managing those points on the network, the total cost of providing network redundancy can grow large. We'll walk through the basic connectivity options and some more advanced features to fully describe the building blocks, and then look at how to ruggedize network services on top of the resilient network infrastructure.

Virtual IP Addresses

One of the most critical design rules for networked, highly available systems is to distinguish a host's network identity from the name used for a host supplying a network service. If that sentence seems like it was written by political spin-meisters, but you still understood it, skip the following list of requirements. Otherwise, here's what makes Internet protocol addressing interesting when designing for availability:

- Every host on a network must have at least one IP address. That IP address matches some hostname. We've referred to these IP/hostname pairs as *private* or *administrative* addresses in previous discussions of failover mechanics. Private addresses are useful for things like `telnet`, `rlogin`, and `rdist`, where you need to ensure that you end up at a precise physical destination.

- Any network client looking for a service uses a hostname to IP address mapping to find the required server. From the client's point of view, the IP address could correspond to a single physical location, a collection of machines, or a proxy service that forwards the request on to another server behind a firewall or redirector farm. The client doesn't really care; it only sees a logical location on the network. The converse is also true, though, in that clients want to find services at the same IP address over time. Reconfiguring clients to wander through the network looking for "available" servers isn't fast, easy, or reliable; clients should be able to rest assured that the IP addresses they use correspond to something that will be highly available.

- Services that are static or hosts that don't participate in any kind of redundancy scheme can use the same physical (private) name and logical (public) name. Your desktop machine is a good example; there's no need to give it multiple logical names.

- Services that move between hosts in an HA pair or services that correspond to one of several machines in a server farm use logical addresses that map to one or more physical addresses. Enter the concept of the *virtual IP address*.

Virtual IP addresses are redundant names given to a network interface that already has a private hostname. Most network interface cards support multiple IP addresses on each physical network connection, handling IP packets sent to any configured address for the interface. The second and successive addresses added are called virtual IP addresses and are used to create logical host names that may be moved between machines or scattered over several hosts using a redirector service.

Consider the two hosts in Figure 8.1, *norman* and *mother*. These are private names. There's also a logical, virtual IP address assigned to the single network interface on *norman* namely *psycho*. If the primary server crashes, the secondary can pick up that same logical (public) name, assign it to its single network interface as a virtual IP address, and the NFS clients using that service are none the wiser. Enabling a virtual IP address is as simple as configuring the appropriately named device with the logical IP address, here shown using the Solaris naming and configuration syntax:

```
# ifconfig hme0:1 psycho up
```

In this example, *hme0* is the physical device instance, and the *:1* notation indicates this is a virtual IP address assigned to that device. Usually, *hme0:0* and *hme0* are equivalent, and the *:0* is suppressed for consistency with other Unix commands. Some systems impose a limit on the number of virtual IP addresses per physical interface; but if you're hitting the limit you should reevaluate your network and naming architecture for overly complex designs.

Virtual IP addresses have a host of other applications in network redundancy, including virtual network numbering, which we'll cover shortly. They are also used to give a single host several names—a useful mechanism when hosting multiple services or using one machine to cohost several web sites, each with its own URL. For now, bear in mind that virtual IP addresses provide redundancy on the input side, allowing a machine to appear to have multiple personalities on any given network. Next, we'll make multiple connections to a single machine to provide reliable paths to those machines.

Redundant Network Connections

There are three fairly obvious approaches to redundant host connectivity:

1. Make multiple connections to one network.

2. Connect to more than one network.

3. Do both of the above.

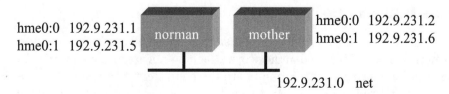

Figure 8.1 Virtual IP addresses.

You'll probably want to explore all of these options over time, so we'll proceed from the simplest redundant connection up to more complex multiple network numbering schemes.

Redundant Network Attach

Redundant network connections protect against failures in the network interface card, the I/O subsystem containing a NIC, or the cable connecting a NIC to some piece of networking hardware. To have redundant network connections, you need at least two, with only one active at a time, similar to the way asymmetric failover works. The hot-standby configuration is the simplest, involving a secondary NIC attached to the same IP network as the primary. To remove all SPOFs, the interface should be on a separate I/O bus, and even on a separate I/O card if supported by your server hardware, and definitely on a separate interface card. You want to make sure that failures in the card, the bus, or the bus-host interface don't bring down all of your redundant network connections.

Once you have the physical connectivity set, the logical configuration is a simple matter of monitoring the primary interface for failures, and then decommissioning it and bringing up the secondary:

`ifconfig le0 down` [bring down the old interface]

`ifconfig le0 unplumb` [remove system resources]

`ifconfig le1 plumb` [initialize the new NIC]

`ifconfig le1 norman up` [bring the interface up on the new NIC]

The secondary network connection retains the same hostname and IP address as the primary, so there is no impact on clients. Some operating systems and some failover management systems support this network address failover (NAFO) capability and provide configuration tools for specifying interfaces to be treated as asymmetric redundant pairs, while in others you'll have to write the scripts to monitor `netstat` output and run the `ifconfig` scripts to effect the change. Because it's simple, and does not introduce any client- or naming system configuration changes, redundant network attach is an elegant way to grant the first level of failure resiliency.

Multiple Network Attach

Multiple network attaches provide redundancy and a small measure of performance improvement. If redundant network attach points are an asymmetric HA analog, multiple network attach points are the equivalent of a symmetric HA pair. The key difference between the two network redundancy models is that in the multiple attach case, each interface has its own IP address and its own private hostname. Instead of moving the single IP address from a live to a standby interface, multiple network attach requires that you either instruct clients to use the "new" IP address or rebind a virtual IP address from the primary to the secondary interface. In this latter case, there's not a significant difference between treating the secondary interface as a hot standby or a live network connection, since it only represents the "public" name of the machine when it has the virtual, logical IP address bound to it.

Using multiple, distinct IP addresses allows you use both pipes at the same time. You can use load-balancing DNS (lbbindd) to round-robin between the different IP addresses. With lbbindd, successive requests for a hostname to IP address mapping return the different IP addresses in turn. Some vendor implementations of DNS do this when multiple IP addresses are provided for a hostname, so check your documentation and verify operation before you build the public source of lbbindd. In the event of a failure of one network interface, clients attempting to connect through the "dead" interface will timeout or find that the host is not reachable. Those clients may query DNS again, hoping to get the alternative IP address(es), but this requires fine-tuning your applications to make them aware of the server configuration. Some applications also use a list of IP addresses, allowing connection code to try them in order until they find one that appears to be live. This approach allows the application to recover from a single failure and to seek out surviving network interfaces, but again, it's a client-side implementation. Without any clear, definite way to make the clients find the alternate IP addresses, failover using multiple network attach is a bit brittle. We discuss request distribution over multiple host IP addresses in more detail in Chapter 9.

Realize that the small kick you get out of having two pipes between the network and host doesn't do much for performance. In order to gain input capacity, you'd have to be bandwidth-limited on that single network interface, in which case redundant connections to the same network get you two ways of looking at the same congestion. There are cases, however, where multiple client segments come into a switch and produce more than a single segment's worth of input for a server; using multiple switch connections in this case alleviates the bottleneck on the link between server and switch. Consider having 10 clients on a 10baseT Ethernet switch; if all of the clients are reading from an NFS server simultaneously, it's likely the server is spewing out more than 10 Mbits/second of output. Running two links between the NFS server and switch helps, provided the switch can handle the extra load on its internal bus. If the multiple attach points lead to two distinct switches and network congestion is a problem, you may see also some benefit from the multiple attachments.

Multiple network attach also raises the question of uniquely knowing a host's "real" name and IP address. Packets may be sent to any of the IP addresses, but replies will come with only one IP address in the source IP address field. Furthermore, all output to the single IP network will occur over only one interface, adding load to the output side of the pipe. The single output pipe is a result of having only one route to the outbound network—it's only one IP network, and therefore has only one current, lowest-cost route to it. In the previous NFS server example, in order for client requests to go over both switch-host legs, you'll need some of the clients to use each IP address, and some way to ensure a roughly even distribution of clients on each side. An example of multiple network interface attachments is shown in Figure 8.2.

Some operating systems fix the outbound IP address situation by "remembering" the interface and IP address over which a particular connection was built, and others allow this connection-to-IP address persistence to be enabled as an option. Solaris calls this feature "IP interface groups" and it is enabled in /etc/system.

As you can probably see, though, with input/output load distribution, client-side knowledge of IP address distribution, less-than-predictable client failover, and the need to enable interface groups, multiple network attach is less attractive as a resiliency mechanism than it first appears to be. There are variations on this theme—redundant switches, multiple networks, and IP redirectors—that skirt these issues and will be discussed in upcoming sections.

Interface Trunking

Trunking allows you to bundle several network connections together into a single virtual network interface that has roughly the aggregate capacity of the components added together. Think of trunking as the network analog of disk striping with RAID-0 to gain performance. Interface trunking combines some availability aspects with improved bandwidth between network and host, making it more attractive than multiple network attach in many respects. Trunking involves running multiple connections from a switch to a host, where both host and switch support trunking software that is interoperable. Today, that's far from a given, as there are no standards for how packets are distributed over the links in a trunk and how failures are tolerated. However, most server vendors

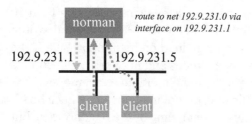

Figure 8.2   Redundant network interface attach.

have trunking software that will talk to the dominant switch vendor products—you have to do the research.

A host that is trunked to a switch has a single IP address, much like the redundant NIC case. The switch and host handle the scatter and gather of packets distributed over the multiple network links, doing their own round-robin of data on each end. Because all of the links are active, trunking increases the bandwidth between switch and host. Furthermore, trunking software handles failures of the links transparently, so any NIC or cable breakdown is hidden.

A caution with trunking is that frequently it requires devices that have several network connections on the same card. This card then becomes a single point of failure. Of course, you can combine methods and trunk over two cards to two different switches, using the multiple network attach approach described in the previous section. Given that SPOF caveat, though, trunking is an excellent choice for alleviating server input bottlenecks while gaining protection from the most common network failures—cables and connectors that are subject to physical wear and tear.

Configuring Multiple Networks

Up to this point, we've looked at single failures between switches and hubs and servers. Aside from cable damage, network failures tend to fall into the excessive load, configuration error, or denial of service categories, where protection requires separate, redundant networks. When the primary network is deemed unusable for any reason, all traffic switches to the secondary network. If you're suffering from inconsistencies in configuration or severe load problems, turning on the clean network may be the best and most expedient way to restore order among the network citizens. A word of warning: Load-related problems simply move to the redundant network and cause headaches there; configuration problems can be resolved by going to a "clean area" where they don't exist and then taking the time to diagnose the sick network.

Redundant networks are commonly called *rails* (borrowing from the AC power distribution vernacular). When wiring a data center, independent power rails bring AC to the machine room from different circuits, and possibly from different sources as well. Similar design considerations are used in data center equipment with hot swap and redundant power supplies. "Rail switching" within power supplies allows a server to switch to an alternate source of line current without interruption. The same notion of "rail switching" applies to taking all IP traffic off of one network and sending it over the redundant set of network rails.

The most difficult part of multiple network configuration is sorting out the IP addressing on each network. The simplest approach to multiple networks is to use multiple switches, with each switch connected to every server. In an asymmetric configuration, one set of switches acts as hot standby for the active set, and in the event of a failure, all interfaces on all servers failover to the second set of switches. This is essentially the redundant network attach on steroids, and it may prove more efficient to insist that all hosts failover together. If the problem is in the switch, or is a load issue, all of the hosts are going to attempt to fail to redundant connections anyway, so forcing the issue ensures a shorter MTTR. The downside to redundant switches is connecting a router to the network. The router will have to be made aware of redundancy and configured to route traffic over either interface as required. We're starting to bump into the "keep it simple" key design principle as we add complexity, and it requires that you step back at some point, look at the number of moving parts and things you need to manage, and balance that against the extra level of protection you get by investing in various network redundancy designs.

You can also run the network rails in parallel, with distinct IP network numbers on each. In this case, servers connected to both networks are merely multi-homed, and have multiple IP addresses on multiple networks, a common situation that is easily handled by routers, switches, and clients. To effect a failover, however, you'll need to make sure that all client traffic gets sent over the correct network, usually requiring some of the client-side host searching tricks previously described. You can mix in virtual IP addresses and create an entire "virtual IP network," using a third IP network number as the logical network and allocating an IP address for each host on this virtual network. This configuration is shown in Figure 8.3. For the hosts to "see" the logical network, they'll need a route to it, built using a metric of zero in the route command:

```
# route add net 192.9.235.0 norman-net1 0
```

This zero-cost route tells the host that it can reach all of the hosts on 192.9.235.0 via the interface for its primary hostname *norman-net1*. The cost of zero indicates that the network is directly attached to the host, and not on the

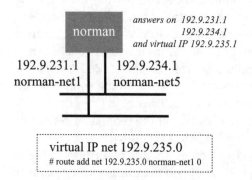

Figure 8.3   Multiple networks.

far side of a router. Usually, the cost metric indicates the number of router hops taken to get to a destination; lower numbers indicate better or closer routes. Zero-cost routes tell you there are no routers along the way; the network is directly attached and the route merely enables an alternate numbering scheme for the same physical connection.

When the primary network is taken down, all of the virtual IP addresses are assigned to the secondary network, and new routing information is added to each host to redirect outbound traffic to the correct rail. If your routers are capable of switching a network from one interface to another with a minimum of manual intervention, the virtual network approach works well. Delete the old zero-cost routes and add new ones, using the hostnames for the second network rail, to complete the failover for each host.

There's no hard requirement that all network interfaces failover in unison when using symmetric dual network rails. If you have a small number of servers, routers on each of the redundant rails, and a fairly small number of clients, it's easy to accomplish network failover merely by creating host routes and pointing them at the appropriate network side as shown in Figure 8.4. Using a virtual IP address of 192.9.231.1 for the first host, and network numbers 192.9.231.0 and 192.9.232.0 for the dual rails, clients can choose one rail or the other by adding a host route:

```
C> route add host 192.9.232.1 router-net2 1
```

This route command tells the client that it can reach the host at 192.9.232.1 via *router-net2*, which is connected to the 192.9.232.0 network. In the event of a failure, the client can redirect this host route to use the alternate router to network 192.9.231.0 with

```
C> route add host 192.9.231.1 router-net1 1
```

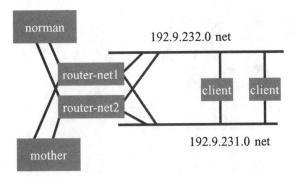

Figure 8.4 Host route configuration.

Host routes are suitable for small client-server computing groups, because they grow linearly in size as more clients and servers are added to the mix. Host routes have the advantage of putting the client in control of its path to the server, and they don't require any router reconfiguration. They support multiple routers and can be easily automated on the client side by testing connectivity, making them resistant to a variety of configuration and naming errors. The downside, again, is complexity. For larger computing groups, use redundant routers and fully redundant networks and avoid making changes on a per-client basis.

In all cases, redundant network rails consume a large number of IP addresses, so ensure that you have enough network numbers or subnets and a sufficiently large number of free network addresses to accommodate your numbering and failover system. You can conserve IP addresses by using host routes to connect servers directly to routers, eliminating networks of two or three servers. Since clients match the longest portion of an IP address possible when looking for a route, they'll find host routes to servers first in their search. In Figure 8.5, the two routers connect four servers to the client network, using only one IP network with four host routes. Without the host routes, two IP network numbers would be needed, one for each group of servers, creating a configuration that scales poorly as additional servers are brought online.

IP Routing Redundancy

Any Internet historian will tell you that IP was designed to help the ARPAnet survive a nuclear attack that might take out major portions of it. Internet protocol remains a best-effort, hop-by-hop network protocol that implements redundancy through routing choices. Getting hosts onto multiple networks requires careful engineering of IP addresses and network numbers, but routing traffic between IP networks is relatively easy once you build in a level of router redundancy.

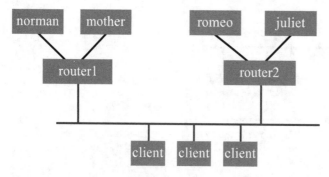

Figure 8.5 Host routes versus IP networks.

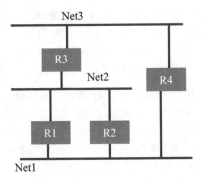

Figure 8.6 Redundant routing.

Figure 8.6 shows a typical redundant router configuration. Network net3 is accessible directly via router r4 from network net1, and through either r1 or r2 and r3. The default behavior is to use the lowest-cost route as measured by the number of router hops between the networks, so packets going to net3 from net1 will use router r4. If r4 crashes or loses its routing information, packets can be sent via the higher-cost but equally good redundant route. IP once again proves its strength as a repairman of broken networks, but the time required to accomplish the repair isn't easy to determine.

Hosts using the route through r4 will notice that r4 stopped sending routing updates within a minute of its crash. Routing Information Protocol (RIP) updates normally are sent once every 30 seconds, so allowing for the time required to recognize an update was missed and for the time needed to update routing tables, 60 to 90 seconds go by before the routing information from r2 or r1 is used to set up an alternate route to net3. Transmission Control Protocol (TCP) sockets connected between hosts on net1 and net3 are oblivious to the change, since IP handles the packet shuffle and updates. However, it's possible for application failures to result during the time required to build the second route:

- TCP sockets set a timer that detects failure of either endpoint. The default value for this keep-alive timer can be as long as two hours, depending on your operating system; however, many network managers tune it down to several minutes to allow rapid cleanup of broken connections. As a result, a network that takes two minutes to reconfigure may result in broken socket connections.

- Applications don't always wait patiently for initial connections to a service. If an application was attempting to contact a network service on net3 when r4 failed, it's possible that the application will timeout and complain. A subsequent attempt should result in a success, but the user sees a temporary failure.

- Hosts on net3 may not know about a return path to net1 via router r3. If they were using router r4 as a default route and were not receiving RIP updates, then incoming traffic will reach net3, but responses will be undeliverable because no path exists back to the source on net1.

When you lose end-to-end connectivity, in either direction, applications on either side believe the other side has failed. Errors that occur during connection setup are easily traced back, but intermediate failures, once connections are established, generate calls to the help desk. To make your network infrastructure more tolerant of routing problems, make sure that you combine routing techniques to aid recovery and early warning of problems:

Avoid single-outlet networks. A network connected to the world through only one router has a single point of failure. Even using a host as a router only for emergency purposes leaves you a fallback position. Severe router problems may require several hours to trace and repair, leaving your network partitioned without the redundancy.

Default routes are good—as long as there's more than one. Using a default route means you don't need to accept routing updates and can turn off the somewhat noisy RIP protocol on your routers. If you do this, however, make sure that you have multiple default routes (one for each possible outlet from the network). Sending packets to a default router that isn't listening is as good as being without any redundancy. While it sounds counter-intuitive to have more than one default, realize that "default" is only used to designate the route used when no better match can be found in the routing tables. Multiple default routes means that you have several choices of last resort, and can select the route with the best availability or capacity.

Dynamic redirection is also good. Ensure that your router sends ICMP redirect messages if it's asked to forward a packet better handled by another router. Without dynamic redirection, you'll clutter your network with reforwarded packets, possibly hurting performance.

Scripted intervention cuts down the time to repair. Aggressively monitor end-to-end connectivity, using ping or more advanced tools like traceroute that show you the path taken by a packet. You'll even find asymmetry in your routing tables using traceroute. Rather than waiting for a client to recognize a router failure and update its routing tables, use the route command to proactively flush the stale information and construct a new route. You can trim recovery times into the tens of seconds with aggressive monitoring, and also collect data to help locate the root causes of repeated router outages or problems.

We've covered a few cases in which scripts or system administrator help is necessary to keep the network chugging along with its packets. Unlike system-level failover involving disks, network reconnection involves multiple points of control and many moving parts. There are several configurations that make the case for manual failover as opposed to fully automated but very complex operations.

Choosing the Failover Mechanism

We've assumed automated failover as the default mode of operation through most of this book. However, network failover requires careful coordination of all hosts that need to be reconfigured, and partial failovers are often harder to sort out than complete shutdowns of a single network. We'll use this rule of thumb: If there's one point of control and one set of resources, automation is your friend. Multiple points of control, coordination of multiple resources, and multiple steps that have to coordinate with each other, and occur in order, argue for manual intervention. Some of the network redundancy techniques that rely on router information or route changes are ideal for automated care and feeding; others that require changing host routes, or ensuring that all hosts have switched to an alternate rail, are best handled by the network operations staff.

The key question to address is the MTTR. With active, aggressive monitoring and an on-call network staff, you can limit your failover time to the window in which the staff is alerted, problems found, and repairs made. With a 24 hours a day, 7 days a week staff, this window gets smaller, and with well-documented failover processes you can be reasonably sure that the failovers will happen the right way the first time.

Partial failovers are to be expected in the automated network management world. Some hosts end up stuck on the primary network, because not all of them noticed the failure, or because scripts that triggered the failover failed on the dying network. If you account for the typical time required to dig through these failure modes, you can argue for manual intervention in the case of a complete network meltdown. To repeat a bit of our management dogma, aggressive, active network monitoring will aid early detection and repair, possibly eliminating the corner cases that require interruption of someone's beauty sleep.

Network Service Reliability

With your network plumbing in good order, it's time to actually launch something down those pipes, so building reliability into the key network services is the next step.

Doing something interesting with a computer requires actually moving some data around on the network. The most interesting data tends to be that which is dynamic in nature (such as web pages with stock quotes) or valuable and persistent (such as payroll records in a database). Our discussion of failover management systems and data service reliability cover these data-moving services in detail. Underneath the interesting services are a chorus of supporting network services, such as naming, directory, security, and network management, all of which provide vital information to the higher-level data management service. Want to connect to a database to start perusing those most interesting payroll records? You're going to need to find the database first, and that means looking up a hostname in a name service and possibly finding the TCP port number corresponding to a network service name. And if you want access to your home directory so that your database extract has a place to land, you'll need another trip through the naming service and RPC binding service to find the NFS server on the other end.

We characterize network services as more informational than transactional in nature. If a name service answers a request twice, no harm is done. Replication tends to be a feature of configuration or built-in to the service, not an application level issue. While these services are hidden, they can't be taken for granted, and they need to be made as reliable as the data services above them.

TRAITORS TO TRADERS

Several years ago, one very prominent trading floor lost the use of its portfolio management application on a day when the fixed-income (bond) markets were particularly volatile. Interest rates moved, making traders froth at the mouth, and the network services felt the traders' pain. A router failure caused a naming service to become inaccessible, making the application fail without the ability to resolve key host names into IP addresses or the ability to allow users to log in. From the traders' point of view, the system administrators were traitors, having let them down in their moment of need, but the real root cause was buried several layers below the obvious failure point. The SAs have since put in redundant naming and fallback services, but it was an expensive lesson.

—Hal

Network Service Dependencies

To get a good feeling for the dependencies that exist in a typical environment, we're going to trace the average Unix login sequence and point out network service interactions. If you've ever wondered why it takes minutes to fire up your desktop, stop cursing the window system developers and look instead at what's happening on your own wires.

When you login and start your first shell, the following events occur:

- Your username and password are compared to the values provided by the naming system. If you're not using the local `/etc/passwd` file, that means going over the network to an LDAP, NIS, NIS+ or other network database to look up the right entry. Your group number is pulled from your password record, and is used to look up all group memberships in either `/etc/group` or another network database.

- Any authentication service, such as Kerberos, is contacted to generate session keys for your new log in session. Note that this is why `klogin` is required instead of `rlogin` or `telnet` when using Kerberos services; the log in process needs to pass your authenticated credentials off to the ticket-granting server to set up your Kerberos session.

- The home directory listed in your password entry is checked for *.cshrc* and *.login* files, which are executed in that order. If your home directory is accessed via NFS using an automounter, this first access completes the NFS mount. Quotas on your home directory are checked, if enabled. NFS servers and name servers needed by NFS on the client side to determine IP addresses are now brought into play. If you're using an automounter, it may use NIS for its maps or for hostname resolution.

- The shell builds its hash table of executable commands by walking every directory listed in the PATH variable, checking for executable files. This speeds up response time at the command line; however, if you have a long path that contains several directories that are automounted, starting a shell sets off an automounter storm.

- As your *.cshrc* and *.login* files complete execution, any other local commands you have added may touch other network services.

There are an awful lot of dependencies in something as simple as logging in. And we haven't even connected to a database or fired up a browser to check the market's opening yet. To make the higher level services like NFS and databases reliable, you need to make sure that you have a clean, well-ordered, and reliable set of underlying network services. One of the better ways to map out your reliability issues is to build a dependency graph of all of the services required, starting with the service you're putting on an HA pair. Figure 8.7 shows a typical dependency graph.

In this example, a web server gets its HTML files from an NFS server, and its forms rely on a user database. The database, fileserver, and network management applications all rely on a name service. Furthermore, the database requires

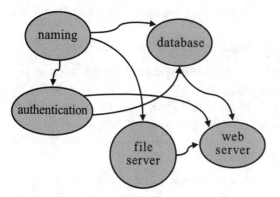

Figure 8.7 Service dependency graph.

help from an authentication service, which is also called by the web server. This example is oversimplified; we lump all file server access into a single bubble, when in reality most web sites are driven by multiple servers. We also left out routers, configuration tables, and other software-driven services that could affect reliability.

These dependency diagrams should be *directed, acyclic* graphs. By directed, we mean that the relationship between the dependent and independent service is clear; an arrow points to the item that is dependent on something else. Acyclic refers to the property that there are no "circle tours" through the graph; if you start at any node you can never get back to that same node simply by following the directed arrows. There are well-known algorithms for proving that graphs are without cycles; however, for the dozen or so dependencies you'll find, you can trace the possible paths out by hand. If you encounter a cycle, as shown in Figure 8.8, you have a deadly embrace between network services. If one goes down, it may crash another, leading to a deadlock condition that can't be broken through normal, automated methods. The example shows a pair of fileservers that cross-mount each other; when one crashes the other is taken out as well.

Look at the number of graph nodes that have no incident arrows; these are the "root" or independent services. Typically, it's naming, DNS and LDAP, and occasionally an authentication server. There are many design points to be drawn from these types of graphs:

- Make sure the root services are highly replicated and available, because failures will trickle through to appear in the applications that are at the end of the dependency graph.

- Nodes with many arrows coming into them are highly dependent on other services, and are deserving of extra redundancy engineering and aggressive monitoring. Spend the engineering effort and money to make

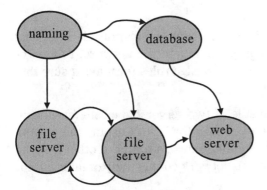

Figure 8.8 Cyclic dependency graph.

these services reliable, as they're likely to affect many users or many other services.

- Routers introduce dependencies when there's only one path between services. If you find a router in the middle of a graph, remove it by adding a redundant routing device.

- Your monitoring tools may have network dependencies as well. Something as simple as `netstat -r`, which checks routing tables, uses NIS to look up hostnames for gateways and network names. Stick with the `netstat -rn` form, using numeric representation of IP addresses, to make `netstat` a standalone management tool.

- A dependency graph with cycles represents a network that cannot boot itself. During the process of starting up, you'll hit a race condition in which some service may be waiting on another one, which is waiting on some other host that forms a dependency loop. Consider a host that issues a route command during booting to find a network service on the far side of a router. The route utility uses a hostname, which is resolved via DNS. If your only authoritative DNS server is also on the far side of the router, there's no way that host is coming up all the way. Remember, after a major reboot, your DNS cache servers may not be useful. Just because it worked fine right up until the failure doesn't mean you can boot your way out of trouble. Break the cycles and make your network more resilient to massive failures or recovery efforts such as blackouts or disaster recovery processes.

Naming and directory services are almost invariably at the top of the dependency charts, so we'll look at ways of hardening them and providing adequate capacity to prevent them from starting a Chernobyl-scale chain reaction on the network.

Hardening Core Services

NIS, NIS+, and DNS have built-in resiliency through replication. Each naming service allows multiple servers, at multiple points in the network, to answer requests with authority. Here are some basic design rules for making sure that these core services are well-behaved:

- Never have just one server. Use at least two servers, in master/slave configuration or in primary/secondary modes for DNS. Keeping the servers close to their clients, ideally on the same side of a router or other filtering device, will prevent problems due to network connectivity or intermittent routing issues.

- Make sure you list more than one DNS server in DNS client's resolv.conf files. Have a fallback position of some high-level, well-known server that can be consulted when all else fails.

- Design a fallback plan, so that a catastrophic failure in the name service can be worked around using local files if required. This means making a master password file that is consistent with the NIS maps, and an /etc/hosts file derived from DNS zone information. This data probably exists already where the NIS and DNS maps are built, so putting it into a form in which it can be used to popular critical servers is not a major task. The fallback plan should be manual, as it requires changing several machine configurations, and it should detail the failure modes under which naming service priorities are changed or other key network services are bypassed in the interests of recovering from a network failure.

- Invest in change management and operational processes that leave audit trails and do consistency checks of generated configuration files. Being process-weak is a sure way to introduce a failure at the root of your graph.

- Watch for network topology issues that can lead to a partitioning or breakdown of the network services. Keeping NIS and DNS servers close to their clients helps, but also watch for web/proxy servers, authentication (when feasible), and directory servers. The number of services calling your NIS servers, for example, should give you an indication of how to scale these servers and what kind of load they experience at peak times.

Armed with network graphs, redundant rails, and solid processes, you're ready to make data management services available. Before leaving this chapter, though, we'll briefly visit some denial of service attacks and fit them into the broader picture of network level reliability.

Denial-of-Service Attacks

A well-engineered network can be taken out by a malicious user that floods it with bogus requests, or a broken application that repeatedly sends a failed request to the server. Denial-of-service attacks that are the result of poor application design have the same impact on overall reliability as the highly publicized attacks discussed at security conferences.

Denial-of-service attacks fit into several categories:

- Traffic flooding, such as the Smurf and Fraggle attacks based on the UDP echo protocol. You'll find these described in detail on the CERT web site www.cert.org. These attacks attempt to overwhelm a system by presenting it with a never-ending input stream.

- Attempts to crash the application or its network stack, such as the Ping of Death, which attempts to overflow the network stack of PCs with excessively long packets that require reassembly on the receiving end.

- Connection attempts that fill up a service's queue and render the service inaccessible to other clients. The well-known SYN attacks that take down TCP-based services do so by flooding the input queue with bogus connection requests.

Denial-of-service attacks that fit into the malicious category are best handed off to the security team for evaluation. You can buy a measure of protection by increasing your headroom for connection requests, or by filtering more cautiously on protocols like UDP echo that are not used in the normal sequence of events. This is another topic we touch on for completeness, and to paint a picture of complete responsibility. Even well-designed services suffer when extreme conditions are presented to them; if you can quickly diagnose and recover from these corner cases you'll present a more reliable face to the world.

THE BIG SECRET

Stories surrounding the online debut of Victoria's Secret catalog are now Internet apocrypha, used by vendors to sell more hardware and bandwidth by playing on the hope or fear that another customer will enjoy the same massive audience.

Supposedly, the Victoria's Secret web site with streaming video, launched via ads during the Super Bowl, was swamped by user requests as soon as it came on line. It wasn't just the Victoria's Secret site that suffered, though: ISPs passing streaming video to those who managed to get through had excessively high loads. All intermediate networks felt the brunt of the user crush.

—Hal

Assuming that incoming load doesn't contain any unwelcome surprises, and that the key network services are well-behaved, you're ready to make your main network data services reliable.

▶Key Points

- Network redundancy can be achieved using multiple connections to the same network, multiple networks in an asymmetric configuration, or multiple live networks.

- Balance complexity and cost against benefits when choosing a network redundancy scheme because you're affecting every client and server in the end-to-end system.

- Manual failover is a realistic and practical approach to shuffling multiple hosts between networks.

- Network services such as naming need to be among the most reliable you have, if you use them, because many other higher-level services and management utilities depend on them.

CHAPTER

9

Data Service Reliability

The repairs [that Big Ben's resident engineer] oversaw were intended to give
the clock two centuries of reliable service before the next major overhaul.
—Stewart Brand, in The Clock of the Long Now

Reading Stewart Brand's description of his tour of Big Ben, you can't help but be
struck by how our computing time scales pale in comparison to those used to
measure "availability" of physical structures. At this point you should feel like an
architecture student who has studied material strength and wind shear until all
hours, but still hasn't built a *building*. Starting with our discussion of hardware
component reliability and system failover, and adding in network services, we've
described the foundation on which a data service rests. A *data service*, in our
context, is precisely what it sounds like: a network service that moves data from
one point on the network to another, reliably and predictably. Now it's time to
build that first skyscraper and layer a data service on top of an HA pair.

In this chapter we'll examine what happens to NFS, database, and web
servers when the underlying platform crashes. We'll also provide some guidelines for determining when you want to use large, multiprocessing servers and
when you want to buy a rack of low-end servers to provide redundancy. Interactions between failover systems and the data services will be covered, along
with tips and tricks for avoiding some common failover hiccups that can prevent your data services from being restored to their full capabilities. This chapter focuses only on the core data services; we'll look at application reactions to
failure on both server and client side later on.

Network FileSystem Services

Sun's network filesystem (NFS) was introduced in 1985 as a way to share disks over a network. With several million networked computers now using NFS to share data, it's become a de facto standard, and in many cases NFS uptime determines web server uptime. Famous Unix guy Rob Pike once said, while describing parts of his Plan 9 operating system, that "everything is a file, and if it isn't, it should be." If files dominate your world, whether they be user home directories for developers or HTML files served up by dozens of web servers, you need to make your NFS service as reliable as possible. We'll start by figuring out how to detect an NFS server failure.

Detecting RPC Failures

The network file system was designed so that network failures and server failures appear the same to an NFS client. The client continues merrily (or somewhat merrily) resending requests until a reply arrives, oblivious to whether the request or reply was lost on the network, damaged in transit and discarded, or simply reached a server that has gone faceplate-up. As a result, it's difficult to tell whether an NFS server has actually crashed without trying to talk to the server itself.

NFS relies on the *Remote Procedure Call* (RPC) framework to send requests from client to server. As its name implies, RPC makes a remote system appear to be part of the local one, completing the request and returning results (in this case, data) to the calling process or system. The NFS system uses multiple RPC programs:

- The NFS mount protocol, or `rpc.mountd`, used to locate filesystems available for clients and to check permissions. If the *mountd* daemon disappears, clients will not be able to complete any new mounts, although existing mounts will continue to function normally. If you're using the automounter or amd, and the *mountd* daemon freezes or dies, the server is essentially dead to you.

- The NFS data server, called `nfsd`, usually run as a set of threads in the server's kernel. It's possible for all of these threads to block or get hung, making the NFS server unresponsive. Since the NFS code lives inside the kernel, a "crash" of the NFS server-side code brings down the operating system in a hard crash or panic.

- Network locking services used for carrying file lock information between clients and servers. The `rpc.lockd` daemon and its supporting cast of processes (described shortly) need to be functional for network locking activities.

- The server's RPC *port-binding daemon*, or `rpcbind` (once called the *portmapper*). Rpcbind's job is to assign TCP or UDP port numbers to RPC programs, and to return those registrations to inquiring applications looking for a particular service by its RPC program number.

If any of these daemons suffers a failure, or locks up and stops responding to requests, NFS is dead in the water. There are two simple ways to check up on the health of your NFS server: Call the RPC server and verify that it answers trivial requests, or actually try to move data through the NFS server.

Every RPC server, regardless of its platform, implements a *null procedure*, or *nullproc*, that does absolutely nothing useful but returns upon successful receipt of a request (it's extremely tempting to call this the *management procedure*). RPC registrations and null procedures can be verified using the `rpcinfo` utility. Start with `rpcinfo -p host`, and look for the registrations of all required RPC services. Using the RPC procedure name and number, use `rpcinfo -T tcp host prognum` to ping the null procedure of the service. Use `rpcinfo -p host` to determine the program numbers of registered services, and use `rpcinfo -T tcp` and `rpcinfo -T udp` to ping the actual service daemons. If you get a response, the server is at least listening to requests. This simple round-trip ping is used by the NFS automounter when multiple servers are listed for a mount point to measure "fastest" response time.

What if your NFS failure is due to a disk problem or a bad interaction between NFS and the local filesystem? The NFS service null procedure doesn't test anything deeper than the RPC and TCP/IP stacks and the most top-level RPC service code. You have two choices. First, you can hope that disk-related problems are detected by your RAID or disk array configuration, and are handled automatically. Second, you can attempt to test all of the interactions between filesystem, NFS, and the disk system, which requires that you try reading or writing some well-known file. To make the test conclusive, be sure that you're really moving data to or from a disk, and not just the local client's disk cache.

One way to be certain that you're sending data through to the server's disk is to create a new file and write a timestamp or some other easily verified contents into it. Read the file back on another machine or on the server, since it is cached on the client that created it. If you're a purist and want to test the whole chain, write a simple program to create a file, obtain an advisory file lock on it, write some data into it, close the file, open it for reading with a new lock, and read the data back. File locking turns off all NFS data caching, and ensures that you write the data through to the server and read back the file from the server's disks. Involving the ever-popular network locking service makes sure all of the RPC daemons are in full operation. Yes, this is complex, which is why there are commercial failover management systems to test NFS data services for you.

If you're going to write your own failure-monitoring agents, make sure they don't block (i.e., prevent the monitoring application from continuing to execute until the completion of a system call). A crashed NFS server won't respond to your monitor requests, leaving the monitor hung in a noninterruptible disk-wait state. If you're running the monitor from the secondary server, avoid testing file reads and writes as you can hang the monitoring script on the machine that is about to become the primary, creating a deadlock or at least a complicated failover scenario.

When your NFS server goes down, and you're sure of that, your thoughts immediately turn to its resuscitation. Making sure the failover server takes over, quickly, requires some additional design work on your part.

NFS Server Constraints

NFS presents the best case for a failover management system because the client-side work is baked right in by design. Clients silently and cleanly rebind to the secondary server after a failure, provided it retains the same filesystems and IP address/hostname pairs as the failed primary. Not only can NFS clients not distinguish a failed server from a broken network, they generally can't differentiate one server from another that presents the same filesystem and host naming conventions.

Inside an NFS Failover

To better understand how to improve NFS failover times, it helps to have a rough idea of what happens when a secondary machine seizes the day (or disks) and assumes the role of primary NFS server. On the server side, there are only a few important steps. First, the secondary machine grabs the IP address and hostname of the primary, using some of the tricks described in the last chapter. Next, it checks each imported filesystem for consistency, mounts each one, and NFS exports the mount points. If there were outstanding file locks, the secondary server will attempt to recover them, and from that point on, it's off to serving files.

Clients see a slightly harsher reality from the time the server stops responding until the newly exported filesystems are accessible on the secondary:

They hang. Processes accessing files or directories on the failed server are stuck in disk-waits, and cannot be killed. Even something as innocuous as starting a new shell can hang the client, since the shell walks its directory and command paths.

They repeat themselves. Clients will retransmit requests to the server, after waiting for a time-out period. The time-out period doubles after each unanswered request, and after the fifth attempt, you see the "NFS server not responding" message on the client.

They eventually get turned upright. When the secondary server comes back to life, the client's requests are answered and it continues where it was previously stuck. This assumes you're using hard NFS mounts on your clients. In our chapter on client-side reliability we'll discuss the scourge of soft mounts and why you don't want to use them.

Failovers that happen quickly may fly under the radar of the dreaded "NFS server not responding" messages that signal problems to even the most naive users. A server has to stop responding for the better part of two minutes for client-side messages to appear; if you can complete the failover faster than that, few, if any, users will notice.

Optimizing NFS Recovery

How do you achieve a nirvana in a world dominated by a relatively old network protocol? Here are some rules:

1. *NFS is the only application on the server.* NFS is an application, even though it runs in the kernel. Don't mix IP routing or name services or the occasional small database with NFS. First, multiple services make failover much more complex, and second, you want your servers concentrated on spitting files out onto the network. Performance is a reliability factor, and you should focus on optimizing each server for its intended purpose.

2. *NIS, NIS+, DHCP, NT domain, and DNS servers belong on other machines.* Yes, this is a rehash of the previous point, but it's one that is skirted so often that it bears repeating. If you're relying on an NIS server running side-by-side with the NFS server, and you need to fail the NFS service to a secondary machine, you're going to have some temporarily unhappy NIS clients waiting to rebind to a server. You may accomplish NFS failover quickly but then wait minutes for NIS clients to time-out and rebind to the secondary (or a different) server. Separate the servers and spare yourself the headache. Naming services can be run on small, easily replicated servers, while NFS belongs on a disk-heavy, NIC-loaded box.

3. *Cross-mounting is evil.* Cross-mounting, or having NFS servers mount each other's disks, is a recipe for a deadly embrace where NFS servers crash and hang each other. In Chapter 8, we outlined a graphing strategy to prove your network is free from dependencies in core services. Add NFS to that service graph and ensure you are still service cycle-free.

4. *Journaled file systems speed recovery.* Once the secondary machine starts its takeover procedure, one of its first steps is to verify the consistency of the filesystems it is inheriting. The Unix filesystem check (`fsck`) utility can take an extremely long time to check large volumes—up to a minute per gigabyte of filesystem under duress. Since you failed over in midstream, without quiescing clients or attempting any cleanup on the primary server, you're under duress, and long fsck times are not out of the

question. Journaled, or logging filesystems, solve the problem by eliminating the `fsck` step. With a journaled filesystem, recent modifications to the filesystem are written into a log, as with a database. When the filesystem needs to be checked for consistency, the update log is replayed to flush out all of the filesystem redundancy and self-check data. Instead of crunching block-by-block through every file, logging filesystems cruise through an update history and complete in a matter of seconds per gigabyte. Some journaled filesystems do not perform as well on writes and modifications as their naked cousins; however, it's worth sacrificing the write performance, if any, to gain the better recovery time.

5. *Treat WebNFS like vanilla NFS.* WebNFS, the http competitor that allows you to use an nfs://host URL notation to walk filesystems via your browser, is really just NFS on the server side. You'll probably want to be more careful about security and auditing the content you make available via WebNFS, but the redundancy and availability rules are the same.

File Locking

File locking and NFS were never meant to mix gracefully. The problem stems from differing design constraints of stateful and stateless systems. Stateful systems "remember" information about previous requests, such as the holder of a lock or the byte range requested. Stateless systems retain no information between requests. It's easy to recover stateless systems, since they don't need to go back and rebuild their internal "remembered state" based on what clients tell them about previous requests. On the other hand, stateless systems can't handle every situation. File locking is stateful, and requires coordination between the applications that use it. NFS was meant to be stateless so that it would recover from server crashes quickly. NFS servers therefore require an adjunct protocol to handle the locking functions. As a result, file locking makes NFS server recovery more complex. Fortunately, few applications use NFS-compatible file locking, making this less of an issue in practice.

NFS-compatible is stressed for a reason. You can only do advisory, or gentleman's locking, over a network. Mandatory, or blocking locks, are not supported across machine boundaries because the crash of a client holding a mandatory lock would render a file inaccessible by other clients. Advisory locking provides a primitive access-allocation scheme that is essentially interoperable with PC filesystem locking. It's good enough for most of its uses.

What happens when the primary crashes and the secondary takes over? It's not a whole lot different from the case when the primary recovers by itself. Before going into the gory details of recovery, you need to understand how NFS monitors file lock holders. When a client-side process requests a file lock, the request is passed outside of the NFS RPC service to the network lock manager

(NLM) RPC service on the server. The lock is acquired, the client is notified, and the server and client then begin monitoring each other. Clients with NFS locks verify that they still want what they previously requested, and servers verify that the requesting clients are still around and functioning as they were when the lock request was made.

The status monitor (`rpc.statd`) makes sure that locks are freed or restored in the event of a system crash on either side. If the client crashes, the server removes its locks when the client stops responding to monitor probes. A server crash causes each lock-holding client to be polled. Clients are given a short grace period in which to reestablish their locks.

When performing an NFS failover, you need to make sure the directory used by the status monitor to note lock holders is included on a shared disk set that migrates to the secondary server. This may require passing a command line option to the status monitor so it can find the state directory in its nondefault location. In addition, locks can only be acquired from the public, or virtual, host name of the NFS server, since that's the name that moves and will be contacted for lock restoration by the clients.

Some operating systems support an option for mounting a filesystem without network locking, using `-llock` or a similar flag in the mount syntax. If your applications want to coordinate locking intramachine, without any regard for other applications on the network, this is sufficient. Unless there's a specific requirement that processes on different clients coordinate locking with each other, local locking or no network locking is ideal. You want to ensure that all of your applications agree on locking mechanisms, possibly including a long time-out waiting for a lock that is in transit between servers. If some of your clients don't renegotiate locks after a server failure, avoid using locking at all—think about databases instead.

USE BIG GUNS

In the first *Indiana Jones* movie, Harrison Ford is confronted by a saber-wielding maniac who threatens him with moves normally reserved for circus performers. Ford resolves the situation with a single shot from his gun. (The oft-told and probably apocryphal story is that the script originally called for a much more elaborate fight scene, but Ford was ill that day, and decided to avoid the fight.) Such is life when you depend on gentlemen's agreements about access—if you rely on applications to coordinate their own access to files and obey advisory rules, at some point you'll have to support an application that's packing the equivalent of a large gun. When you have applications that don't play nicely in the locking sandbox, ensuring serialization of access and consistency requires an even larger gun in the form of a database.

—Hal

We'll cover database recovery and consistency later in this chapter. For now, realize that we're not fans of file locking for a reason: It has a bad return on complexity and it's not foolproof. Gaining availability means getting rid of those fool-susceptible things like applications that don't cooperate or users that remove files others have in use, creating stale file handle problems. Now that we've blasted file locking, it's time to deal with stale file handles.

Stale File Handles

Probably the most common complaint we hear about NFS failovers is that they aren't transparent to clients suffering from stale file handle problems. The short, snappy answer is that stale file handles are a bug, not a feature of failovers, and well-conditioned NFS failover systems don't produce buckets of errors. Before we rail on stale file handles, you'll need a bit of background.

NFS clients identify every file and directory with a file handle. Locally, you'd use an inode number and filesystem number to locate something on a disk; however, over the network you need to know the server's identity and also the modification history of the file. An NFS file handle is an opaque, or server-specific, structure that contains the server's IP address, the filesystem ID number on the server, the inode number on the server, and the inode generation number. The last item is used to make sure inodes that are reused don't get picked up by file handles that referred to their previous lives in older, deleted files. Let's say two clients are working on the same file, and one of them deletes the file and creates a new, unrelated file on the same server. Because of the way inodes are allocated it's highly likely that the new file reused the inode most recently freed, so the second client's view of the file is now invalid.

A popular cause of stale file handles is multiple clients accessing the same files or directories. One client removes a file while another is working on it, and the second client gets a stale file handle error. These situations are typical of software development or web authoring environments, where files are shared by multiple users and may be modified by several people during the course of a day. Stale file handles that arise from user access collisions can't be fixed with failovers or HA pairs; you'll need to use a source code control system to serialize access to the files that are being manipulated from multiple clients.

Much more common in the failover scenario is the situation where the filesystem ID numbers are not kept consistent between primary and secondary. In most operating systems, the filesystem ID number is assigned in the order in which the server mounts filesystems. Change the order, and the filesystem ID numbers change. This means that seemingly innocent changes to your `/etc/vfstab` or your FMS's mounting configuration file can paralyze all of your NFS clients when the server reboots or fails over; make sure that your system administrators add new filesystems to the *end* of the filesystem table to make the upgrades and reboots as transparent as possible. If the secondary fails to preserve the filesystem ID numbering of the primary, all NFS clients will see stale file handles after the failover, because one component of the file handle no longer matches their pre-failover view. The only way around the stale file handle morass is to reboot the client (or fail back to a happy primary).

EVERYTHING YOU KNOW IS WRONG

One night in the early days of a startup, we decided to add some disk space to our primary development server. While we had the guts of the machine arrayed on the floor, it seemed like a good time to juggle some directories and make better use of the space. We did full dumps of the filesystems and restored them in their new, larger homes. As soon as we rebooted the upgraded server and exported the enlarged filesystems, the network essentially came crashing to a halt. The server's CPU was pegged, and the blinking lights on our network hubs were twinkling at high speed. Looking at the client closest to the machine room door, we saw a stream of stale file handle error messages. The network was full of NFS requests and immediate replies of "stale file handle," resulting in retries by the clients that firmly believed they had valid file descriptors. In our predawn haze we realized that we had invalidated every file handle held by every client system when we shuffled the disks. The restore was successful, but it also made everything the clients knew about filesystem IDs and inode numbers ancient history. We went on a rebooting spree, and things settled back to normal—or as close to normal as you get in a startup.

—Hal

We've spent the early part of this chapter lamenting the lack of strict transactional control for client access to shared data in files. When you want transactions, you want a database, and with it comes a new set of challenges for optimizing recovery times.

Database Servers

Databases provide transactional, recoverable access to persistent storage. You can argue about the merits of object-relational or relational or next-generation databases, but the basic mechanisms are the same. Database systems obey the ACID properties:

- **A***tomic.* Transactions are demarcated and either complete or do not complete. There are no partial insertions or updates.

- *Consistent.* All parts of the transaction complete, and all modifications that comprise a transaction complete within its scope.

- *Independent.* Transactions do not affect each other, so that one failure is isolated from other successful completions.

- *Durable.* Even after a failure, committed data is accessible and correct, while uncommitted or inflight transactions can be backed out, restarted, or discarded.

Atomic and independent transactions are the domain of database management systems. Making sure that the database is available, that it can be recovered quickly, and that it provides a consistent view to clients falls under the availability umbrella, so we'll focus mainly on the "C" and "D" parts of the property sheet.

Managing Recovery Time

As with NFS servers, it's helpful to know what happens when a database server fails and goes through a takeover cycle, and how clients are likely to react to that chain of events. We'll look at the usual failover and recovery cases, and then go into the more sinister setting where the failure also causes the database to be corrupted.

Database Probes

The first order of business is to be sure you truly have a database failure and not merely a break in the action. Some database transactions can be intense and long-running, making the server appear to be unresponsive when it's crunching through millions of records. Unlike NFS clients, who resend requests that appear to have vaporized, database clients have to respect state, transaction boundaries, and sequencing that are enforced by the ACID properties. It would occasionally be nice to have the ever-popular interest rate calculation example (where an application applies interest to some accounts, crashes, and then starts over again recrediting interest to the first few accounts updated before the crash) performed a few dozen times on your bank account, but database application designers are smarter than that. In the cases where the IT people fail, the bean counters pick up the error; there's always another level of management. You want your failover management system to check several test points in the database.

Listener processes or backend reader/writer processes may fail, leaving the data incommunicado with the server; or the database engine may seize up or the SQL interpreter fail, allowing the database to receive requests but not do anything useful with them. It's a good idea to check the operation of the database, using a short piece of SQL that looks up values in a small table reserved for the purpose of a health check. Think of this as the *nullproc* equivalent for databases; you may want to use the internal statistics tables of the database since you know you'll be testing something that resides deep inside the database engine.

If you're using raw disks for the database, there's not much benefit on your insistence that the test actually tickle the disk. Without a layer of filesystem and other kernel code between the database and the disk, you can rely on the disk management subsystem to recognize and repair disk failures. Checking the database health using an in-memory table is sufficient in most cases. Of course, if you're using a database on top of a filesystem, you may want to go through the whole database-to-disk path to be sure the filesystem internals aren't causing problems.

Database Restarts

Preserving the ACID properties of a transactional system requires more work on recovery. It's also not completely invisible to clients connected to the system, as we'll see shortly. When the primary database server fails, the secondary does a cold start of the database, either as a second instance in a symmetric configuration or as a new database instance in a master/slave setup. The first order of business is to get the disk sets from the primary to the secondary, just as in an NFS server takeover. If you're using raw disks for the database, the disk consistency check will happen at the database level, so the failover system just has to move ownership of the disk sets. When the database gets layered on a filesystem, however, you have the same recovery time headache inherent in an NFS server, namely, checking the filesystems for consistency. The database will still have to confirm that its data structures and transactions are clean, so this data storage consistency check only gets you partway there.

RAW OR COOKED?

Should you run your database on raw disks or cooked filesystems? This is the "tastes great" versus "less filling" debate of the digerati. (Although some database products have a definite preference for one or the other, most database applications run adequately in either environment.) This was the one issue in this book that caused the most debate and discussion between your two authors.

Hal, taking the "less filling" argument, prefers raw disks for their ease and surety of recovery, and their enhanced performance. Evan takes the "tastes great"

position, and prefers filesystem-based databases for their ease in backups, the ease in restoring a single filesystem from tape, and for all of the features that modern filesystems can deliver.

In some ways, the debate boils down to a safe-or-fast debate. Raw disks have one less layer of operating system overhead between the spindle and the SQL, and therefore reduce complexity (generally a good feature for critical systems). Filesystems can add the issue of recovery: If you're recovering a 300GB database on a filesystem and you have to `fsck` the whole disk farm, you'll learn that the "mean" in mean time between failures has other, more personal interpretations besides the mathematical one. Attempt to turn on journaling for the filesystem and you end up logging every disk update twice—once in the database and once in the filesystem. This is going to impact your update and insert rates. What if an application core dump fills up the data space filesystem you were counting on for the next hour's worth of inserts? You lose automatic recovery when a system administrator has to figure out why there's no more disk space left for the database tables and logs.

On the other hand, more advanced filesystems add the ability to checkpoint and rollback filesystems, which can eliminate concerns over database corruption; and they also add the ability to perform block-level incremental database backups, which can reduce backup times by 90 percent or better over fulls.

Filesystems that cache pages produce a super-caching effect for read-only or read-mostly systems: Much of the server's memory is used to cache database blocks, eliminating disk I/O and improving response time. Supercaching can boost performance tremendously, especially for very large databases on large memory machines where the elimination of disk I/O improves whole-table scan times by orders of magnitude.

Again, Hal's preference for reliability lies with the raw disk design, in the most general case. It's simpler to manage and it eliminates nasty interactions between filesystem effects and your database. Your mileage will vary depending upon the filesystem, operating system, and database system you've chosen, and the benefits of supercaching may thoroughly outweigh the recovery aspects. (If you're doing a read-only database, you're probably not going to worry about checking filesystems because they're not modified at all.) As Hal points out, "Sometimes cooking can be hazardous to your health."

Evan can't help but wonder if Hal has ever eaten bad sushi. This is not intended to sound like a commercial—but VERITAS Software has a product called Quick I/O that sits on top of their journaling filesystem. It has the advantage of making the database space part of a filesystem. However, Quick I/O removes the usual filesystem overhead of logging, journaling, caching, and buffering to deliver raw disk performance. For more details, pick up the white paper describing Quick I/O use and implementation with Oracle from either company's web site.

When the database engine starts up, it goes through its redo or undo log files to locate transactions that were in-flight when the failure occurred. These logs were brought over to the secondary from the primary, along with the data spaces, and are the critical component for rolling back any incomplete transactions. Typically, the database system completes any transaction that was in progress that can be completed, and that was acknowledged as complete to the client system. Transactions that weren't acknowledged, weren't completed, and can't be rolled forward are backed out. So much for your duplicate interest payments; you either snuck in under the wire or the client system recognizes the failure and knows it's safe to resubmit the whole transaction. Replaying the log files is the largest component of database recovery times, and shortly we'll look at how you balance performance and transaction shapes against recovery.

Once the database has completed its cold start, you are left with a system that is internally consistent, obeys the ACID properties, and is ready for action again. In NFS server recovery, there's nothing else to do because the clients were tapping their network fingers, retransmitting, and waiting for the server to recover. Database systems, however, are not stateless with respect to the clients. They see their database server connections get dropped, and may see transactions abort or return error codes, requiring some client-side cleanup.

Client Reconnection

Ideally, a well-written database client application recognizes a broken server connection and rebuilds it, without notifying the user of any problems. Transactions that were aborted or backed out can be resubmitted, possibly with user authorization. If there's a possibility that another transaction occurred while the system was recovering, the client-side application may want to ask permission before blindly sending a backed-out transaction again. Consider the case of a stock trading system, where a trader's desk is locked out for two minutes during a failover. When the client is connected to a live system again, the market may have moved away from its previous price point, making the previously submitted trade less profitable. In this case, the client application should notify the user of the failure, and let the user make the choice to resubmit or discard. In most cases, early notification results in the user solving the problem through another channel when time is critical.

Less-than-perfect database applications abound. They cause user headaches in a variety of creative ways:

- Instead of reconnecting, they crash or sit disconnected from the real world.

- They force the user to log in again, or to provide other startup information. The surest way to annoy a time-stressed user during a failover is to require more user intervention.

- They remain strangely silent as soon as a disconnect or transaction abort is detected. When you're driven by transactions, it's best to let users know exactly where those transactions stand. If there's a sign of trouble, tell the user so that corrective action can be taken in other ways.

We'll come back to the issue of well-written database applications and failure detection on the client side in Chapter 11. Now, however, to round out our examination of recovery time, we need to look at the nightmare case where the failure causes the database to become unrecoverable.

Surviving Corruption

Some database shops insist on checking the consistency of a failed database before bringing up the redundant server, thereby eliminating the possibility of running with bad data. While database corruption is a rare event, once it happens you'll be spooked by the thought for a long, long time. Databases are supposed to enforce the ACID properties; however, durability is remarkably hard when the database is corrupted.

What causes database corruption? In addition to the usual issues of bugs in the system, you need to look out for external impacts on the database's storage. Random processes that write to the disk, or database processes that write bad data, can blow out log files or data spaces. If you're using a filesystem for database storage, you run the risk of user-level processes with root permission writing or corrupting named files and wiping out your database. If this sounds fatal, it is. We were tempted to title this section "Death of a Database (Salesman)," but respect for Arthur Miller and our high school English teachers won out.

There is no silver bullet that enables you to fix database corruption. You need to recover from a redundant copy of the database, or restore from tapes, or roll back to some well-known, precorruption state. Corruption introduced as a result of database bugs may make this process difficult, which is why the database vendors tend to fix these issues rather quickly. We'll look at replication techniques and cost trade-offs in the next chapter.

Unsafe at Any (High) Speed

"Do it quickly or do it safely" sounds like something the metal shop teacher drills into your head before you turn on your first power tool. The quick-or-safe trade-off also exists for database systems. The more you focus on high performance, the more you risk increasing the recovery time. Database insert and update performance comes from increasing the depth of the replay logs, and from caching more structures in memory. The deeper the logs, the longer they take to replay. The intent is to allow the system to catch up and flush out the logs once a peak in inserts or updates has passed, but if you happen to crash at the apex of the performance peak, you'll have an extra-long recovery window.

Transaction Size and Checkpointing

You can attempt to strike a balance between transaction size and recovery time. Consider the difference between a transaction that updates every customer record in a single SQL statement and one that walks through the index sequentially, updating each record as a separate transaction. Clearly, the second approach takes longer, as it eliminates any benefits of caching and bulk data retrieval that the database might perform for you. Large transactions are the norm, but they aren't always the easiest to recover.

Database crashes between separate transactions mean the client program can pick up where it left off, possibly repeating the one transaction that was in-flight at failure time. This requires that client-side application know how to walk through the table, and also how to determine what the pick-up point is; a client-side crash will require the application to query the database to find its last update. Involving the client in the reliability design makes recovery easier but makes the client more complex; it also requires you have the political clout to get the application designers to sit down and consider recovery issues when doing their design. If you're successful, you'll have an easier time in the data center and might consider using your newly found spare time to run for public office.

Another independent approach is to trim the logs more frequently. This process, called *checkpointing*, forces the database to verify that any transaction represented in the logs is written out to disk, and then to discard the related log file entries. There's another balance between performance and recovery in setting the checkpoint interval: A longer checkpoint interval means that you can survive higher peaks of logging activity, while a shorter interval means that you clamp the recovery window based on the depth of the log file. If you build in sufficient disk I/O capacity, and the database storage can handle the activity using whatever CPU and memory resources are required, more frequent checkpointing will be a win in the longer run.

You'll probably want to try smaller transactions and more frequent checkpointing. Both introduce minimal complexity and don't require major server-side changes. The next step is to use a parallel database to improve recovery time, but this, too, comes with a performance consideration.

Parallel Databases

Parallel databases like Oracle Parallel Server (OPS) use multiple database engines on a single, shared disk set or on multiple, independent (shared nothing) disk units. The goal is to provide a single view of a large database with more than one host, operating system, and database engine underneath it for performance and reliability. Note that a parallel database in this context is not just a database that parallelizes activity using the operating system's threads model; that form of parallelization is expected and provides a solid performance improvement. We're going to look at the case where you have multiple servers and multiple database engines, and have to coordinate availability and performance between them.

Scaling up with multiple engines sounds nice in theory, but the drawback to parallel databases is coordinating inserts, updates, and cache information between the instances. The problem is about as complex as trying to get a group of your friends to decide where to go for lunch. Who's driving? What restaurant? Who should reserve the table if you arrive there out of order? The coordinator among your cohorts is probably the largest or loudest person; in the parallel database world this function is performed by a *Distributed Lock Manager* or DLM.

The benefit of a parallel database is that the recovery window is reduced to the time required to back out in-flight transactions on the failed node. Consider a two-node HA pair running a database; when the primary fails, the secondary has to restart the whole database engine and roll the transaction log. In the parallel database, the second database node rolls the relevant portion of the log for the failed node, and continues with its existing work. There's no cold start, only a warm recovery, making the typical time for database restart much shorter.

And there's the rub. Reread the previous section where we pointed out that replaying the transaction log is the greatest contributor to database recovery time. In insert-intensive or update-heavy environments, the transaction log is going to take a relatively long time to recover, whether it be on a parallel database or an HA pair. For read-mostly or read-only applications, parallel databases offer both performance and recovery advantages because there's little work involved in failing one node over to a sister node in the parallel cluster. In general, parallel databases can be slower for heavy insert and update work than their single-instance relatives, given the overhead of the distributed lock manager and multiple cache instances to be maintained.

This holds true for shared nothing and shared disk parallel databases. In the shared nothing case, a transaction has to be routed to the instance that "owns" the most data for the work required; if portions of the database owned by other nodes are needed you start routing traffic on the server interconnect, resulting in higher overhead than a shared-disk DLM. Shared nothing databases are good for decision support or warehousing work in which you apply transactions to all rows of the database, and parallelization at the node level is trivial. Of course, these types of marketing applications tend not to be highly available, so you can make the performance-versus-recovery trade-off without negative consequences.

There are cases where shared nothing, parallel solutions are ideal, typically where ACID properties and state persistence are recreational rather than managerial considerations. Web servers fit this bill nicely, because there's no state between the browser and web server other than a TCP connection that is easily rebuilt, and the http protocol doesn't care what server is behind the host name associated with a URL. We'll conclude our look at data service reliability with a departure from the sanctity of HA pairs and a foray into replicated, shared nothing servers.

Web Servers

It's something of a misnomer to title this section "Web Servers" because we're really concentrating on serving up files through http, and only http. You can use some of the designs here for other web services like ftp servers or even anachronisms like gopher sites. Today the emphasis is on http and on making other services appear through HTML pages, both for the visual niceties and wide support in the browser community. Since http is file based, it's similar to NFS in availability options. However, http doesn't use file handles or other server-specific identifiers to locate files, so it's easy to have several servers provide http service to a group of clients without confusing them. Our goal is to provide a roadmap to these availability options for web servers.

Availability Constraints

Your choice for server availability is probably going to be driven by scale, and by what clients see during the failover period. If the switchover time is short, and clients either don't request new pages or have previously cached pages available, they may never detect the outage. It's more likely, however, that a browser will sit spinning its logo until the request times-out or the user clicks the "Stop" button. As soon as the user hits "Reload" or goes to another page on the same server, a new request is issued that can go to a different server. It's likely that commercial failover management systems would have been developed for web servers had not NFS driven the requirement. However, the massive scale required of web server farms, coupled with the simple nature of http, has driven alternative availability designs.

Overall, there are few design constraints for making web servers available:

- The web server should be the only application on the server. As repeated before, this is good practice for avoiding complexity.

- CGI scripts must be well-conditioned to restart after a failure (a topic that we'll cover in Chapter 11 as a client-side issue). CGI scripts that talk to databases or other services are in fact clients, further confounding the stereotypical "two-tier" design notion.

- You need at least one server to represent the host name and IP address of the web server, possibly as a virtual IP address. This server (or group of servers) should know the "right" address and answer requests directed to it.

- All of the servers need to present the same view of the http name space (filesystem) to the world. This doesn't require shared disks, merely replication of the HTML files so that all files appear on all servers in the right paths.

We'll look at the classic redundant host design, multiple hosts with DNS round-robin naming, and dynamic IP redirection.

Web Server Farms

Thoroughness dictates that we discuss HA pairs for web service, even though this is the least attractive and efficient design. We'll also look at the name service configuration tricks that provide a poor-man's replication, and also dig into the mechanics of IP redirection.

High-Availability Pairs

Redundant host configurations for web services are similar to those for NFS servers. After a failure, the secondary host needs to import the disk sets, run fsck or otherwise check for consistency, and add the files to those it serves via the httpd daemon. Sharing a disk set between servers is a guarantee that you'll have the right files and pathnames on the secondary machine, although it's possible to run the HA pair with redundant, replicated disk sets and simply use the HA framework to handle allocation of host names and IP addresses.

HA pairs and the corresponding failure management framework offer some other advantages. Because you're monitoring the hosts, you can detect open-loop or out-of-control CGI processes, and do failover between multiple network interfaces. If you're using large web servers, you may find that a symmetric HA pair suffices for the expected load, with a slight hit to performance when the secondary machine handles all incoming traffic solo.

The downside to using an HA pair is that it's limited in scale. Even in an N-1 configuration, you can't scale N arbitrarily large due to I/O and network connectivity limits. You also have a challenge with input distribution; if you are running four web servers in an attempt to scatter the load over all of them, you need some way to ensure the load is fairly evenly disbursed. There's nothing inherent in an

HA configuration that does load balancing. Perhaps the most important draw-back to HA pairs is the failover time. If you suffer an outage of several minutes while failures are detected, disk sets get imported, and IP addresses moved, users of that web server will quickly find the stop button. Web time is real time, and it demands more immediate resolution of failures.

Building up servers with independent, non-shared disks is a form of shared-nothing replication, a departure from HA pairs that reply on replication and independence of client requests to go both fast and reliably.

Round-Robin DNS

Round-robin DNS is a form of shared-nothing clustering. Each web server has its own filesystem, its own IP address and hostname, and its own interface to the world. DNS does the heavy lifting by associating multiple IP addresses with the virtual hostname; for example, you may assign four IP addresses to www.blah.com so that incoming traffic will go (fairly evenly) to all four addresses over time. Some implementations of DNS do this automatically, cir-culating through all available IP addresses for a given host name. In other con-figurations, you're going to need to get a copy of the publicly available load balancing BIND daemon (lbbindd).

When a client gets an IP addresses via round-robin DNS, it will use it until the DNS lifetime has expired. Sites using round-robin DNS typically shrink the DNS lifetime to several minutes, forcing clients to rebind the hostname to an address more regularly and reducing the average window of an outage. Done well, round-robin DNS is a low-impact and low-budget solution with its own good and bad points:

Good. There aren't any real failovers to manage; clients just find alternative servers when they get new IP addresses for the virtual hostname.

Bad. Downtime windows can still be minutes, or as long as it takes to spit out the defunct DNS mapping and get a new one.

Good. Scaling up is as simple as adding hardware and IP addresses, then mixing until blended.

Bad. Reducing the DNS cache lifetime means more DNS traffic for you. You're trading availability for load. Best to beef up the DNS servers.

Good. With N servers, you're only taking down $1/N$th of the clients when a server fails and even then the outage is limited by the DNS cache lifetime.

Bad. You're assuming that all clients have nice DNS configurations, and that they'll play by the lifetime and time-out rules, and not make mappings per-sistent or copy IP addresses into local state files.

Bad. Implicit load balancing doesn't take into consideration the duration of a connection. If every fourth connection is for a rather large file, and all other http hits are for small graphics or HTML files, you'll find that a 4-way server farm has a real hotspot where all of the large file transfers cluster. This is an extreme case, but it points to the unpredictability of load balancing via round-robin techniques.

What started off as a balanced point-counterpoint on DNS round-robin techniques ended up with an extra negative point. This isn't meant to dismiss round-robin DNS out of hand; in some cases it will be the best, quick solution you can implement. However, the Internet market seizes opportunity, and when web server farms became de rigeur, new and established players in IP switching filled the gap in IP traffic distribution.

IP Redirection

IP redirection is essentially DNS round-robin service in a box. The IP redirector assumes a well-known, "public" hostname and IP address, and then translates it into multiple backend, private IP addresses. When combined with routing functions, the IP redirector can talk to backends on multiple networks. Figure 9.1 shows a typical IP redirector configuration, using a redundant IP switch to avoid a single point of failure at the public/network interface.

Normally, you'll set up the redirector behind a firewall or external router, replacing what would be a single web server's network interface with the redirector complex. Because it uses only one public IP address, an IP director does

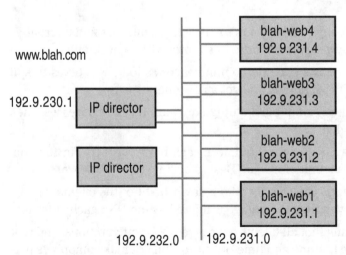

Figure 9.1   IP redirection.

not need DNS round-robin support. Clients resolve the public name through DNS, and are connected to the appropriate backend server based on load, time, equal distribution, network radix or distance, or other metrics particular to the manufacturer of the IP traffic router. By eliminating DNS as a point of control, and by consolidating all load balancing decisions into a redundant configuration, IP redirection provides the best solution for horizontal scaling (by adding more servers) and reliable scaling (by minimizing downtime). Clients will still notice that a web page isn't loading, but the next hit on that site will be directed to a different, and hopefully more functional, server in the farm.

Deep or Wide?

What's the best way to get high performance and high availability for a network service? Is it a stack of low-end boxes, or a pair of high-end, symmetric multiprocessing servers using a commercial failover product? There is no single right answer for all configurations, because the deep-or-wide controversy depends on the code paths taken by applications through the operating systems, the amount of state generated and accessed, and the eventual scale required of the service.

But dismissing this question with "it depends" is the easy way out. If you've made it this far into the chapter, you deserve a Big Rule, and you'll get one: The Big Rule of Code Path Ratios. The *code path ratio* reflects how much time is spent in user-level work versus system-level work. Routing packets and running NFS are system-level work. Doing I/O for a database and locking pages are system-level work; running the database optimizer and interpreting SQL statements are user-level work. Web servers shuttle files from the disk to the network, typically mapping the data from one controller to another and rarely coming up to the light of user level. Pure web servers have code path ratios of close to zero (mostly system work); databases can range from 80 percent user work to 10 percent or less user work, and NFS is nearly 100 percent system work, with a resulting code path ratio of close to zero as well.

If you can estimate your code path ratio within about 25 percent, you're ready to go through the decision tree for the rule:

1. *Is state involved?* If the user applications create state, then the state needs to have persistent, single-source storage. State can be records in a database or changes to a password file or even history files that are referenced in the future. Applications with state need to be run on deep Symmetric Multi-Processor (SMP) servers, since the state is very difficult to replicate across many small machines.

2. *Are clients server-agnostic?* If the clients don't care about the identity of the server providing them with data, they are suitable for a wide strategy.

If clients need to know the identity of a server (NFS file handles, for example), then you need to go deep with HA pairs. Databases can go either way—a read-only database of stock quotes or a data mart has no persistent state, so clients can send their SQL to any available machine. Inserting records into a general ledger, on the other hand, creates state that is better handled by a single, large multiprocessor server in an HA pair.

3. *Is the code path ratio close to zero?* The closer you are to zero, the more the model fits the stack of boxes approach. With a small code path ratio, the operating system can become a rate-limiting factor in performance. Adding copies of the operating system through multiple servers is your best path to high performance and rapid failure recovery. This rule comes third because the server and state limiting requirements can make the code path ratio meaningless. NFS has a nearly "ideal" code path ratio (almost zero), but NFS relies on server-client relationships and the state represented by files to which those clients are writing.

Of course, there are times when you can't build a bigger box, and simply need more servers to meet performance demands. There are also recovery time windows smaller than the relatively uncontrolled database failover, and disaster recovery scenarios where entire machine room environments need to be recreated. In these cases, you want to use replication, the next powerful tool in your reliability utility belt.

▶Key Points

- In addition to building a highly reliable hardware platform of servers and disks, you need to take additional steps to be sure that your data management service will recover quickly.

- NFS servers need to recover all of the supporting services like lock managers in addition to moving disks between servers; you need to be sure that you end up with identical configurations after a failover.

- Database systems can be optimized for performance or reliability, but it's hard to aim for both.

- Web servers fit the "stack of boxes" scalability model, provided you take care of IP address distribution.

CHAPTER 10

Replication Techniques

Most of this book concentrates on reducing the Maximum Time To Repair (MTTR) in a variety of network and data service configurations. There are cases when merely reducing the time to the range of a few minutes just isn't sufficient to satisfy operational requirements. Trading floors and other financial applications, as well as highly trafficked web sites that support real-time purchasing and e-commerce applications all demand near-real-time failover and close to continuous uptime of applications. Growth in Internet usage has given weight to the "web time is real time" camp, and sometimes that growing sense of user impatience demands that we all be a bit more creative in designing failover systems. As mentioned in the previous section, various kinds of data corruption also require replication so that a copy of the data in a well-known, reliable state can be brought on line quickly.

This chapter addresses replication and all of its impacts on availability, starting with simple filesystem replication for handing files to a web server, and working up to transactional replication of a high-insert volume database used in a real-time trading application. We'll also dig into process replication and the differences between replication for failover speed and replication for ease of disaster recovery.

What Is Replication?

Replication techniques move data from one set of disks to another completely redundant set of disks. Replication is not the same as disk mirroring, because mirroring treats the disks as a single, logical volume with enhanced availability, while replication treats the disk sets as two completely independent items. When replication is done properly, the same ACID properties used to assert correctness in database systems will be present in the replicated databases. You end up with two consistent and equally viable data sets, ideally in distinct physical locations, connected to distinct physical hosts. Replication further increases your disk space requirements above mirroring or RAID-5, because each replicated disk set is usually a RAID-1 or RAID-5 volume. What you gain in return for the investment in disk spindles is the ability to recover from a large variety of performance and operational outages quickly and with deterministic downtime.

Replication Applications

Why bother with replication when mirroring, RAID-5, and failover management systems bring the time to repair a failure down into the range of a few minutes? As previously discussed, some applications require failover times on the order of a few seconds, and some operational guidelines demand that data corruption or database inconsistency be resolved with the last known, good copy within minutes, not the hours required to restore a clean copy from backup tapes. We hinted at the need for replication in Chapter 9, with the code path ratio rule indicating where you should deploy racks of small servers with the same content.

Here are five recipes calling for replication as a primary ingredient:

1. *Load balancing with replicated servers.* Replicated web servers are expected to have exactly the same content with the same URL and filesystem structures accessible from any host. Creating a scalable server farm using replicated servers requires at least some level of filesystem replication. You may use large NFS servers for several front-end web server clients, but in exceptionally large farms even those NFS servers will be replicas of each other. In software development environments, commonly used filesystems such as developer tools, libraries, and documentation are good candidates for replication, ensuring that every developer's seat has high performance access to the environment.

2. *Resolving the WAN bottleneck.* NFS and other file access mechanisms are designed for local area network usage. Run over wide area networks

(WANs), file access protocols are tolerable for browsing or quick reference use, but they suffer from latency and bandwidth limitations when used for on-demand, real-time access to files. If you need access to the same data in more than one location, and the average network bandwidth is small or the typical round-trip latency is high, you'll need to use replication of the filesystem or database to remove the WAN bottleneck. One rule of thumb is to look for cases in which the average access time is doubled; if you are receiving 2KB rows on each database lookup over a 56KB WAN, you're adding about half a second to the average response time of a query. That's only for the first user; if you have 10 users running these queries over a WAN, you may find that requests pile up at the WAN interface on the database side for several seconds. Local access to a replicated database is the answer.

3. *Deterministic, short failover times.* When time is money and the absolute value of the money involved is large, the time left for repairing system failures is very short. A telecommunications application that does call routing or provisioning may be expected to be operational within seconds; an order routing and matching server on a trading floor may have to survive with less than 5 or 10 seconds of downtime in one single failure. Replication of the application and all of its processes is the only solution that ensures there's some running system capable of completing the transactions within the desired time window. This is normally the domain of mainframe systems, and you should tread carefully here in Unix and NT environments.

4. *Corruption fallback and recovery positions.* What do you do if your database declares itself inconsistent and wants a full recovery along with a multiple-hour trip to the tape drive health spa? If you're an on-line service, you start answering the customer service line using executives who are "pitching in" during the crisis. In the time- and mission-critical environments that demand replication, database or filesystem corruption are additional reasons to invest in multiple copies of the data on multiple physical servers. You can also use checkpoints of the database, built using redo logs, or a product such as VERITAS's Database Edition to roll back to a particular state if you're sure you can isolate when the corruption occurred. If you want to solve for disasters in multiple flavors, you'll need full replication.

5. *General disaster recovery.* Blowing out a database is a logical disaster. What about physical intrusions into your data center's health and welfare, like fire, flood, locusts, or other natural disasters? With a fully replicated site up and ready to go, you can be online again quickly without starting a tape backup or full system reconfiguration and restore

process. You'll find that recovery from data corruption or disaster is about the same, and requires careful coordination with application developers to ensure that all corner cases are covered with at least some plan of action. We separate the issues of system-level disasters, for which replication is ideal, and physical or environmental disasters requiring replication of data and environments. You can use the techniques described in this chapter for all of the scenarios covered in the disaster recovery discussion of Chapter 14.

Any time you move entire databases or filesystems around on a network, you're going to have to balance network bandwidth and latency against the time necessary to bring the replicated copies into synchronization with the master. You'll also have to weigh complexity of the replication system, including manual checks and system administrator intervention, against the benefits it provides. If your only motivation for making remote copies is to make it easier to perform disaster recovery in a short time window, you may be better off relying on backup tapes and well-written procedure manuals. To help you walk through these cost/benefit trade-offs, we'll briefly cover the different types of replication and then discuss applications of each to the various data management services.

Overview of Replication Techniques

Replication can refer to something as simple as doing a complete backup of a disk and reloading it onto another system, or as complicated as replicating the in-memory state of a process to one or more replicas across the network that provide backup service in case of excessive load or failure. There are five major categories of replication techniques, listed from the simplest to the most complicated:

1. *Filesystem-level copies done at user level.* As implied, this is the quickest and easiest way to make remote copies, and it's also the one most fraught with failures, incomplete copies, and other problems. Filesystem copy tricks include using `ftp`, `tar`, `dump`, `rdist`, or proprietary backup utilities (see Chapter 12) to send files from a master server to one or more slaves.

2. *Device-driver-level write propagation.* This is the lowest level form of automated write replication. Disk write operations going through the replicating driver are copied to other systems, with the entire write operation blocking until the remote copies are done.

3. *Disk unit replication.* Similar to the host-side replicating driver, this technique uses a hardware disk array controller to send the modified data to another disk array. Like the previous technique, disk unit replication

copies a disk block at a time, which may have serious impact on your network under high write, update, or insert volumes.

4. *Transactional replication.* In this scenario, transactions coming into a database are distributed to two or more database systems. Some database applications can do this within the bounds of a single transaction, using two-phase commit to ensure that the transaction is applied to both systems. Other implementations of transactional replication include *Transaction Processing Monitors* (TPMs), such as IBM's CICS, BEA's Tuxedo, and Microsoft's MTS; and *asynchronous queuing systems* like IBM's MQ Series or BEA's Tuxedo/Q, that sit logically in front of the database and send the transactions to multiple systems at the same time.

5. *Process-level state replication.* The first four techniques ensure that persistent storage is copied to multiple locations. In high-update, high-volume environments, it's frequently necessary to keep in-memory structures updated on multiple servers. Process-level state replication ensures that updates are sent to all interested applications. This technique also encompasses *checkpointing*, where an application copies its vital internal state to disk so that it can be restarted later, possibly after a crash or during off-peak processing hours.

We'll fill in this cursory explanation of replication with examples specific to each kind of data service: filesystem, web server, and database server, as well as some process checkpointing techniques commonly used in high-performance computing and long-running scientific codes.

Filesystem Replication

Filesystem replication is the most common application of the techniques just described. You'll want to replicate filesystems when you have enough developers to demand the capacity of multiple servers' worth of tools, library files, and manual pages. Multiple servers provide a first level of redundancy against the failure of any one server, and can remove performance bottlenecks by distributing the client load over several copies of the data. Replicated read-only file servers are also frequently dropped in behind web servers, providing load balancing across multiple sources for the same content with the same measure of availability and performance.

Read-write replication of filesystems is primarily used for disaster recovery, providing a "hot spare" remote site that is as close to a perfect copy of the primary site as possible. Using the remote copy is faster than restoring from a backup, an ideal situation when you have hundreds of gigabytes of data that may be divorced from your users by a fire or water penetration problem. Read-write replication can also be used to update multiple filesystem copies continuously, with one master server feeding the updates to the slaves in a steady stream instead of in discrete chunks.

Filesystem replication is not a panacea. It's not a substitute for backups, because replication only captures current state. If you want to restore your director's e-mail spool from last Thursday, not even Siegfried and Roy could make it appear from a remote copy. You need a multiple-level backup strategy (as we'll discuss in Chapter 12). Replication also is not a snapshot mechanism, or a "point-in-time" backup system. Snapshots give you a copy-on-write filesystem; you can go backward in time and look at the filesystem before any particular change was made to it. Snapshots are useful for recovering damaged or missing files, because they track changes to files. However, those changes are only tracked on one filesystem, making it just as susceptible to single-site failures as a normal, nonsnapshot-based system. If you want to be able to recover quickly from complete site failures, you'll need read-write replication.

Archive Distribution

Most filesystem replication techniques rely on checkpointing of the master volume. A copy is created, or all of the files that have changed since the last copy are rolled into a package, and the set of changes is applied to the remote side. The simplest approach is to use the built-in backup utility to create an image of the entire filesystem, and apply it to an empty filesystem of at least the same size on each replicated, or slave, server. If you're going to be doing dumps several times a day, you'll want to have multiple landing spots on the slave servers in case your copy process happens to crash in midstream, leaving you with at least one good, albeit slightly out-of-date copy.

A decidedly nonautomated but completely safe way to work around the midpoint crash risk is to use physical tapes for the replicas, restoring the tapes at the remote site. For exceptionally large replication tasks, on the order of terabytes or hundreds of gigabytes that change every day, consider using tapes to alleviate network congestion and improve your remote restore bandwidth. Never underestimate the aggregate bandwidth of a Federal Express truck carrying a load of DLT tape cartridges to your disaster recovery site; with enough tape drives you'll be able to recreate the primary location at better than DS3 WAN speeds.

You can use multilevel dump approaches to only grab the entire filesystem at the beginning of key parts of the day, relying on incremental dumps every 30 minutes, for example. Realize that with this approach you run the risk of having files in the replicas that were deleted from the master, and won't be "removed" until the next full dump creates a baseline without the deleted files, unless your backup utility is smart enough to keep track of deleted files, and not restore them. For more on backups, again, see Chapter 12. If you choose to go dump trucking, make sure your media management software does not confuse or interfere with the tape-based backups you'll need as part of normal operations. It is best to send duplicates of your on-site backups off-site; sending the originals off-site without making copies is a surefire route to trouble and delay when you need to restore from them.

Next in efficiency are the archive-based transports `cpio` and `tar` in Unix and the variations on `zip` utilities in Windows. Creating a Zip- or tar-ball isn't much different from a full backup, although some backup utilities are smart enough to do multiple passes on filesystems that are changing while the dump is being taken. If you are modifying the filesystem while also making your tar archive, you run the risk of sending a corrupted or inconsistent replica to the slave servers. The `cpio` utility, long overshadowed by its cousin `tar`, is useful for checkpointing because it allows you to include files from a list passed on standard input. Whether you're using tar or `cpio`, construct file lists using a timestamp file and the `find -newer` construction to locate files changed since the timestamp file was created. Once your file list is generated, touch the timestamp file again to seed the next replication wave. If you want to have consistent home-brew utilities for your Windows and Unix systems, consider a Unix-like shell package for Windows that will let you use `find` and other Unix staples. Of course, hearken back to the key design principle about homegrown software; you may find commercial tools that are multiplatform and more stable over time.

Last on the efficiency and safety scale are remote access and copy scripts. In their simplest form, they amount to remote mounts of a filesystem, followed by a script that copies selected files onto the local disk. Remote access has the single advantage of working across different operating systems, so that you can access an MVS system and copy files from a Unix server to it, or use an NT filesystem share to copy files from an NT fileserver onto a VMS server for safekeeping.

The risks of an archive-based replication approach include failure during the copy or remote restore steps; distribution of a corrupted, inconsistent, or incomplete archive; leaving orphaned files on the remote sites; and running out of space to receive the updates on slave servers. Note that in the timestamp case previously mentioned, there's a small window for a race condition in which a critical file can be created in between the time the find utility starts walking the filesystem tree looking at modification dates until the timestamp file is updated. Files created in that space of a few minutes will not be included in the next incremental file archive. You also need to worry about hardware failure in the midst of a copy operation; how long does it take to recover the primary or replica systems and then restart or back out the copy and begin a new, clean take? You're creating manual intervention after a system failure. For a first pass at replication, and for many high-update environments, archive-level distribution works well because it's low-impact and easily tended to by the system administration staff.

Distribution Utilities

Next in complexity are distribution utilities like `rdist` and its secure cousin `sdist` that uses the `ssh` secure shell to create a data confidentiality wrapper around the file transport. `rdist` is almost always built into Unix systems, and a version is publicly available for consistency in options and configuration across multiple-vendor Unixes. Comparing the local and remote timestamps, `rdist` will only send files that require updating on the remote site, conserving network bandwidth and time. It also has limited error checking and a powerful configuration metalanguage, allowing you specific replication at the filesystem, file tree, or subtree levels, down to the granularity of individual files you need to keep synchronized.

In exchange for this flexibility, `rdist` is more complicated and can break in more colorful ways than a simple dump-and-restore process. You need to be wary of network outages (even temporary ones) that could cause `rdist` failure. File and directory permissions can also create problems for `rdist`, so it's best to carefully test configurations and replication end-to-end before putting an `rdist`-based system into production.

Designing to work on local area networks, `rdist` doesn't incorporate many security features to prevent unauthorized or unintentional exposure of data. Furthermore, it may not be the best tool to push files outside of your internal firewall to an external or DMZ-located web server. You can use `sdist` to wrap up the whole transfer in an `ssh` session, such that outsiders can't see the file content being moved by `rdist`, or you can use an ftp script to push files from inside the firewall to the outside. If you need to move complex packages of files, consider bundling up the `ftp` script with `expect` to script the command line interactions with firewalls, choke points, and remote authentication systems.

There are other products that replicate filesystems at the disk block level, using either modified disk drivers or disk array controllers. With these products, you're assured of a clean remote site; however, you may experience slowdowns in write performance as the remote write operations add to the latency of the single, local write operations. The issue of orphaned files—those deleted on the primary but not on the secondary—is addressed with remote block level copies, because the process of removing the file updates the directory entry and inode blocks in the filesystem, which are then replicated to remote sites. Because it sits at the physical disk level, block level copying commonly interferes with filesystem logging, so you'll have to run a full filesystem check in the event of a server crash and recovery. Again, the trade-off is window of consistency and time to update the remote versus time to recover from any or all failures.

File Replication with Finesse

What we've described are bulk-loading techniques that allow you to move all or part of a filesystem from one server to another one with a high degree of confidence that what you'll get on the other side is functional and essentially complete. There are minor tricks that should round out your arsenal of big filesystem slingshots:

- Web servers are really file servers with http instead of NFS as the primary protocol. Replicate to them as you would to a fileserver; however, realize that changing HTML pages in-place may seriously confuse web-surfing clients who see parts of parallel realities while the new pages are being installed. It's best to replicate to a staging area, verify that the new packages have been correctly copied over, and then move the root area of the web server to the new root of the copied filesystem. Consider this a form of "double buffering" for maintaining a consistent client view of the web server.

- Read-only doesn't imply "never changes." Filesystems that are mounted read-only may change on the server-side, and the client eventually has to realize that the data changed and reload its copies (which may have been cached for a long period of time). This means that NFS clients mounting read-only filesystems should not set arbitrarily long attribute cache time-outs, or they'll fail to notice the server-side change for files with long-duration cache survival skills.

- Versioning helps make sure you know what is where. When you're replicating web server content to 40 servers in 8 countries, once an hour, there will be failures. At some point, you're going to have to intervene and decide what updates get propagated around the world to catch up with failed distributions. Having timestamp or timestamp and version number files included with distributions makes your life much easier.

- Checksum-generating tools like `tripwire` help even further by verifying the integrity of what you've copied over. Get in the habit of putting a checksum in your distributions so that you can use it for timestamps, content integrity checking, and debugging purposes.

- Sparse files wreak havoc with utilities that read files block by block. A sparse file is one with a "hole" in it, where there are blocks allocated at random points in the file with no intervening data blocks. These files read back as zero-filled in the "holes" between valid data blocks, and can cause a file-oriented copy to explode in size. Database applications, even NIS or NIS+ systems that use DBM files, tend to create these sparse files. If you're using `perl` scripts that create and maintain DBM database files, or other tools that create index files based on block numbers, you probably have sparse files around and should be sensitive about copying them.

- Large files are becoming commonplace, and all utilities should know how to handle a 6-GB log file or a transaction log that's over the default signed, 32-bit file size limit of 2GB. Make sure all file transport products handle files larger than 2GB, or you'll find that you corrupt files and/or truncate them during the replication process.

Be sensitive to the timeframe for propagating file changes. web content that's created hourly as a summarization of news items should be pushed at least hourly; if your web server is an NT share client and caches files for two hours, it's going to miss one of those updates. Change management becomes more of an issue when you're dealing with software packages and supporting tools.

Software Distribution

We're going through this exhaustive discussion of filesystem replication and software distribution because it produces a client-side reliability issue: clients that have the wrong versions of something, or that try to mix-and-match old and new versions, are invariably going to cause intermittent and vexing failures. Software distribution is a special case of filesystem replication because of the number of ways in which it can go wrong. At the basic level, there's nothing special you'd do for a software package or a set of developer libraries as opposed to taking an intraday checkpoint of a mail spool or a home directory. Here are some other rules to live by:

- Versioning of the entire package, including libraries, tools, header files, and intermediate object files, is critical. Once you've spent half a day convinced you have a bug in your code or in your compiler, only to find that you were mixing an old header with a newer library, you'll make sure you use versioning on every file that gets replicated. This requires that you maintain "parts lists" of the files that need to be kept together, at the appropriate revision numbers. List mastering is worth the effort if you're going to be copying all or part of that tree around your network.

- Applications with local configuration requirements, such as printer lists or user authentication tables, need to be separated into the fully replicated parts and the locally managed pieces. If the package you're working with doesn't allow for easy separation of the custom and common components, consider using a shortcut or symbolic link to a nonreplicated area for custom files. Every distribution will have the same link, pointing to a per-machine area with local information in it. Devout Unix automounter users will find ways to build hierarchical mounts or multiple mount points that layer local information on top of the common base package.

- Don't change binary images in-place. Make sure you do the distribution to a new directory, and then move the entire directory into place. Clients that were using the old binary will continue to do so until another reference opens the newly deposited file. If you replace files on the fly, clients that are demand paging text (instructions) from them may become confused or crash when the text pages change underneath them.

An example of software replication helps to illustrate these rules. Consider how you build up a directory in which local tools, libraries, manual pages, and other locally-important files reside. The standard approach is to have one tools directory on a large file server that all clients share; changes are made to the file server, and all of the clients see them within a short window. Note that the quick-and-dirty method introduces a SPOF at the file server, and isn't scalable for performance. If your client load is going to increase over time, you'll need to be able to crank up the horsepower of the tools directory server at the same time, and that means multiple copies of it, close to where its users are on the network.

The single tools directory also leaves you open to process weakness in change management. What if your latest software installation has a broken install script, and trashes the tools directory? With replication and change management you have built processes to recover from internal corruption. Testing a new tool can be accomplished by building a new area within the shared directory, verifying operation using the master, and then pushing the replication to the slave servers.

When dealing with files and filesystems, you generally have the advantage of being on a lazy time schedule. You can generate replicas on an hourly schedule, or do updates when sufficient content has been added to the master copy. If your primary data service is a database, however, you'll need a stronger replication technique and a more timely propagation mechanism.

Database Replication

Database replication buys you protection against several disasters: corruption of your primary database; failure of an operational system when the MTTR is measured in seconds not minutes; and protection from a full-fledged physical disaster. Database replication can rely on variations of file distribution tricks, using log replay, built-in database features such as distributed transaction management, or third-party transaction processing and queuing systems that guarantee delivery of transactions to multiple database instances on multiple servers.

Log Replay

Database log replay is the simplest approach to database replication, taking a page from the filesystem replication playbook. Every database logs all changes to permanent structures, typically in an "undo" or "redo" log that is used for rolling the transaction forward in the event of a system failure. Log replay involves copying these log files to another machine, and then reapplying the transactions from the logs to the replica databases using the recovery manager, creating a near-mirror copy of the primary with some slight time delay.

It's possible for some transactions to fall into the "gutter" between the primary and secondary database machines, if the primary crashes and takes its log files with it before the final transactions are copied from the log. If you replay the log file, then accept five new transactions in the primary database, then suffer a crash, those five transactions won't make it to the secondary server.

Database log replay is a relatively big win because it requires no application changes for the replication. The database administrators can configure the log copy and recovery steps, setting the time interval between copies and the verification of updates on the replicated machines. Some applications are better suited to this technique than others. Here's a checklist of features that make an application fit the log replay model:

- *Low volumes of inserts and updates, so that the log files do not grow rapidly.* Applications with high rates of change generate large log files, and can induce a backlog on the replica database servers as they struggle to keep up.

- *Applications that can tolerate a small time skew between the live and redundant sites.* If the primary site goes down, and the application has to reconnect to the redundant site, it may have to wait for several transactions to be played through the recovery manager before it can reconnect to the database.

- *Applications that can easily detect missing transactions when connecting to a database for the first time, and know how to find the right "starting point."* This is a critical consideration for stating that "no changes" are necessary to the application—if the application can look for transactions that fell into the gutter, then it will tolerate log replication well.

In some cases, asking the user for verification of a missing transaction (resulting in a user query of the secondary database) is warranted or desired; this puts recovery with precision back into the hands of the end user. In some cases, if a few minutes have gone by between the time of the original transaction and the time the redundant database is available, the user may no longer wish to start the old transaction. A clear-cut example is that of a trading floor, in which a user may choose to hold a trade that was not accepted by the primary database if the market has moved adversely during the recovery window. It's better to let the user make this call than to blindly apply the transaction under a different set of environmental conditions.

LOG-ROLLING COMPROMISE

At one banking customer, tensions arose between operations people running a trading system and business people looking to real-time reporting of activity to help identify trades that went outside of acceptable risk levels. The operations crew felt that adding a risk management step would slow down trade reporting, possibly introducing some regulatory issues. How to get through the impasse? Log replication to the rescue! Logs from the trading system were copied to the risk management system, where they were used to insert transactions into the risk management database as if it was directly connected to the trading system. The trades were entered into risk management in real time, plus the log transfer interval of a few minutes, making everyone happy and eliminating a possible bottleneck on the trading system.

—Hal

Database Replication Managers

One step above database administrator-directed log transfers are commercial database replication management products. Some, such as Sybase Replication Server, are offered as part of the database management system, and others are third-party products. To replicate databases, a database replication manager application walks through the log files and copies the transactions to one or more replica databases. Instead of relying on the recovery manager to roll the logs, the replication manager mimics an application performing the workload represented by the log files. The process that picks apart the log files and reconstructs the transaction is commonly called a *transfer manager*, and it can write to one or more target machines that have a local replay manager acting as a database application.

Replication is typically done asynchronously; that is, the log files are walked by the manager after the transaction has already been applied to the primary system, and without any locking or checkpointing to ensure that the transfer manager and the primary application coordinate updates to all databases. As a result, it's possible for the transfer manager to be several transactions "behind" the primary application database, slowed by the time required to walk the logs and apply transactions to the secondary machines.

As with log replay, there are design considerations for database replication managers:

- Understand the relationship between insert rate, update rate, and the log transfer manager's ability to extract transactions. Under high insert and update conditions, does the transfer manager run into contention for access to the log files?

- Estimate or benchmark the longest delay you'll see under these extreme conditions, watching the number of transactions that go into the log transfer manage queue. If you can only replicate 10 transactions a second but have insert peaks of 50 transactions a second, you'll push 40 transactions a second into the transfer manager. You may end up with a delay of a few minutes, while waiting for the replicated databases to absorb these load peaks.

- What happens when the primary database fails? Does the transfer manager fail as well, requiring applications to do the "ask then restart" recovery outlined above? If the transfer manager continues to apply updates, how can a client application determine when it's acceptable to connect to another copy of the database?

- When the primary returns to service, what happens to the log transfer manager? The secondary database (now acting as the primary) has probably reinserted all of the transactions that were enqueued in the transfer manager at the time of the primary failure; should the transfer manager flush its queue? Should it remain quiescent until restarted by the database administrator?

As with all commercial tools, you should get slightly better results using the commercial tool rather than building your own log transfer mechanism. Be sure to look for third-party tools that handle log transfers before you delve into log copying.

To Block Copy or Not?

Why not use block-level copying (at the disk unit level) for replicating a database? While this approach works with about the same degree of certainty as log replay, there are some less-than-obvious drawbacks to block replication with live databases:

- You get the on-disk data but not the in-memory database state. Block level copying is great for disaster recovery, but it doesn't save you time when dealing with a failover situation. You'll need to fire up a copy of your database on the replica site, and have it do a cold start to be able to handle the incoming transaction request stream. Do log transfers and you're talking to a live database that has enough in-core state to go live after you check for missing transactions.

- Failures in the middle of a large number of updates may leave the remote side in an inconsistent state. One of the advantages of doing replication at the transaction level is that you're fairly certain the replicated systems also obey the ACID properties.

Some transactions may be described simply but require many disk write operations; it's easier to replicate these at the application or transaction level, as described in this section, than by sending large volumes of disk writes over a WAN. One way to replicate the contents of a database (or a filesystem) is with VERITAS Software's Storage Replicator for Volume Manager (SRVM). It replicates block updates, basically using the same logic as the VERITAS Volume Manager, extended to run over a wide area. It maintains write ordering, and replicates any type of data in a volume manager volume across any TCP/IP network.

If your primary goal is to provide a measure of disaster recovery, without regard for the maximum time to repair a failure, you can use log replay or block copying, although the advantage of the latter is reduced when you can simply stack up log files for replay on the recovery site. When optimizing for recovery speed, you want to use log file transfers with support from your applications to find those transactions that fall in the gutter. If you want stronger guarantees that updates are applied to all replicated databases, you may want to engage a transaction processing monitor in front of the databases.

Transaction Processing Monitors

Transaction Processing Monitors (TPMs), now sometimes referred to as "transactional middleware," are your best bet for hard, reliable database replication. They're also the slowest and hardest to implement, a trade-off you'd expect for a solid guarantee. You can use some distributed transaction features of some databases to accomplish the same results described in this section, with the same upsides and drawbacks.

Two-phase commit (see Figure 10.1) ensures that two databases are updated in a transactionally consistent manner. The resource manager, or transaction processing manager, makes sure that both systems can proceed with the transaction, then it applies the transaction to each, verifies completion, and completes the higher-level transaction it is managing for the application. If either side fails to complete the transaction, the TPM can rollback the other side, aborting the entire sequence of events. There's no requirement that the transactions be the same; TPMs are commonly used to ensure that updates to multiple, different databases occur as a single transactional unit.

The problem with two-phase commit is that it's slow. The TPM has to coordinate with each database, and every intermediate transaction has to complete before the application is notified of a successful transaction. You can use a TPM

1. You ready?
3. I'm ready
5. Commit
7. Done

2. You ready?
4. I'm ready
6. Commit
8. Done

Figure 10.1 Two-phase commit.

for database replication simply by writing transactional code that applies the same transaction to the primary and any number of secondary databases, letting the TPM update them all in lock step. Advantage? Recovery is no different than reconnecting to a single database. After all, the TPM was managing all updates in lock-step, so if the application sees the last transaction rolled back, it's been rolled back in all copies of the databases. You'll need to make sure your application follows the right transaction interfaces supported by the TPM and databases, possibly requiring some application coding changes. You'll also need to make sure you can find the redundant copies of the database and reconnect the client application quickly.

So how does having a redundant, live copy of the database allow for predictable failover times? The trick is moving the point of control from the system administration domain, where systems monitor each other for failure or signs of failure, to the application domain, where the application itself or the transaction processing monitor drives recovery via a time-out or *deadman timer.* Let's say you want less than 10 seconds of downtime for any transaction. After submitting the transaction, set a timer for 8 seconds; if the timer expires, then you can forcibly abort the transaction, apply it to the secondary system only, and pro-actively declare the primary system "dead." Of course, you may want your application to begin queuing updates for the primary, or to note that the primary fell behind at a certain time so that it can be recovered later. Many TPM systems allow deadman timers to be set by the resource manager coordinating the transactions, proactively alerting applications if the entire set of updates cannot be performed within the desired time window.

What do you do if you can't trade off insert and update performance for fast failover times? Look for an intermediate solution that guarantees transactional integrity but allows for asynchronous updates to the replica systems. So-called *asynchronous,* or *reliable* queuing, mixes the best of the TPM and log replication models.

Queuing Systems

Most transaction processing monitors operate in a bulletin board, or memory-based mode. Transactions that are in-flight are posted to the bulletin board until they are committed to all systems. Recovering a bulletin board system is similar to recovering a database; the log of applied transactions results in roll forwards or rollbacks to bring the transaction monitor into a state of consistency with the databases it is front-ending. A reliable queue, or transactional queue, uses disk-based transaction "waiting areas" to ensure that no transaction accepted by the queue is ever lost. Reliable queues that allow transactions to be inserted and processed later are known as store-and-forward queues or asynchronous queues.

Examples of reliable queuing systems include the IBM/Transarc Encina RQS, IBM's MQ Series, Microsoft's MSMQ, and BEA's Tuxedo/Q and MessageQ products. There are other commercial products that perform some of the store-and-forward distribution of messages but lack strong recovery or replication features. Use the design rules and requirements in this chapter to help guide you through product selection; you may not need all of the transactional recovery if you handle corner cases in your application.

Applications can send their transactions into the queue and then continue with other tasks, safe in the knowledge that the queue manager will forward the transactions on to their next destination. Generally, it's a bit faster to insert a transaction into a queue than into the whole database, because there's no data manipulation work involved in the queue. The transaction is copied to disk, logged, and the writing application is free to continue. The queue manager then forwards the transaction on, possibly replicating it to other queues on multiple machines, or doing the replication in-place by replaying the transaction across several machines before removing it. Queues allow transactions to be routed, merged, and distributed without impacting the application, provided the application can handle asynchronous notification of transaction completion or failure, and that the application is "pipelined" enough to benefit from asynchronous operation.

WEDDED ASYNCHRONY

When talking about asynchronous queuing systems, I often point out that they work best in optimistic designs; that is, in cases where you try to cover the average case instead of the oddball but serious failure mode. I was once asked point-blank by a customer, "What do you mean by asynchronous but optimistic transactional systems?" It's a model that was popularized inside of Sun by Alfred Chuang, who went on to become the "A" in BEA Systems, but the examples seemed particular to Sun and computer sales operations. Here's the example I used to explain asynchronous operation:

Consider how you and your spouse manage your checkbook. In a synchronous world, you would write checks together, go to the ATM together, and even balance the checkbook register together in a true fit of happiness. This model is impractical because it assumes you're physically together and in total agreement for every single financial transaction. In real life, you operate asynchronously;

you each visit the ATM separately and write your own checks, confident that
the other person won't suddenly withdraw 99 percent of your available funds
and head for Las Vegas. The ability to handle your own slice of the financials
is the asynchronous part; the assurance that most transactions don't produce
exceptions is the optimistic part; the monthly discussion over who gets to sort
through receipts and checks to balance the checkbook and produce the truth is
the transactional part. Eventually, all assumptions are cleared and exceptions
processed, and you're back on your own tracks.

—Hal

Applications that can operate optimistically while recovering an asynchronous queue are ideal. It's possible to "execute ahead," with the optimistic
assumption that transactions in the queue won't interfere with or invalidate
transactions being currently processed. As the queue of transactions is applied,
those assumptions are tested and any exception conditions are handled, allowing the system to continue functioning even while it performs recovery. This is
vaguely similar to a disk mirroring system that does disk rebuild after hot spare
replacement on the fly. The system makes the optimistic assumption that you
won't suffer another failure while it is copying data onto the new disk, and it
allows the mirror repair to proceed asynchronously with respect to the other
disk activity that is generating independent I/O operations.

Be careful not to leave single points of failure when designing with queues. If
you leave the receiving queue on the same machine as your primary database,
but have the queue write to two intermediate queues on other machines, you're
exposed if one of the intermediate machines crashes and leaves the queue inactive during the downtime. See Figure 10.2 for an example of two databases that

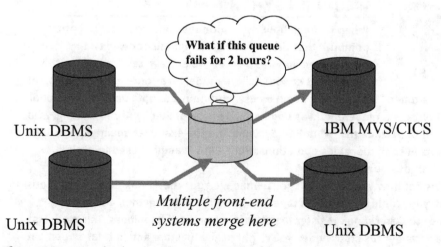

Figure 10.2   Two databases with an intermediate queue.

populate an intermediate queue which is used to replicate the transaction stream into two disparate databases. If the intermediate node fails, without any redundancy, transactions in the queue are left in limbo until the node is repaired. When using asynchronous queues, keep the queues close to the databases that they're responsible for updating, so that they fail and recover consistently with the database servers.

We've shown you how to make filesystems and databases appear in multiple places, with the same content and attributes, and offered advice on reducing failover times to short, well-defined windows. In some cases, even these steps aren't sufficient, and full replication of server-side processes is required to ensure that there is a minimal break in service in the event of a failure.

Process Replication

Process-level replication ensures that you have another copy of a server at the ready, with all of the intermediate, in-memory state and supporting data it needs to take over for a primary or peer process. Replication at this level buys you the shortest time to repair, because you can redirect client connections or route transactions to a replicated process in near real-time. To be complete in our discussion of replication, we'll also look at checkpoint and restart techniques typically used to restore a system to a well-known state after it has been running for a long period of time. Checkpoint and restart and process replication are similar in their efforts to reduce time to repair a server fault; however, process replication can take you from minutes to seconds, while checkpointing is most commonly used to go from hours down to minutes. We'll look at each technique and provide thoughts on its ideal applications.

Redundant Service Processes

Redundant service processes are used to provide more CPU cycles for an application. The simplest example is the implementation of NFS in the Unix operating system, where the nfsd server-side process spins up multiple copies using multiple threads of execution. Each `nfsd` thread can handle a different incoming request, and adding threads adds parallelism and headroom to the NFS server. The best-case scenarios for redundant service processes are applications that have little state retained between requests, and where the requests can be multiplexed over a single incoming connection.

The usual startup sequence is something like this: A master, or controller process, creates sockets for incoming connections and requests, and then creates (forks) subprocesses that do the actual work. The more subprocesses, the more capacity (subject, of course, to the physical limits of the server). Since all of the subprocesses inherit the open file descriptors from the master process, they all are connected to the stream of requests, and have control, configuration, or other utility files open when they are started. How does this provide redundancy? All processes can read from the same socket, allowing for a demultiplexing of requests on the back end. If a process dies, others can continue reading from the same input stream. The master or controlling process may choose to spin up another subprocess, or run with fewer worker processes.

Think of the overused bank teller example as a model for multiple service processes. Once the bank opens the front door (the common input socket), and sets up the ropes to define the teller queue, all of the tellers are essentially identical. If one teller leaves for a bathroom break, the line's progress slows. Astute branch managers notice lines heading for the door, and add tellers or step in themselves to help absorb the volume. Any state information, such as your balance, credit and identification, is stored in a back-end database where it can be equally accessed by all tellers. The advantage of the multiple teller model, like that of the multiple process model, is that a failure or grand pause with one server does not impact the others; you get a very rapid failover at the application level or continuity of service through the multiple back ends.

Redundancy at the process level has limitations. Each process must ensure that it remains independent of others, not moving file pointers or modifying shared file information. Output must be coordinated and serialized so that there is no contention from the writing processes. If there is intermediate state managed by the worker processes, that state needs to be broadcast to the all processes since a future request looking for that state information might end up on another process. Ideally, you want as little state as possible managed on the server-side within the application process; state belongs in a database or filesystem where it can be made recoverable, persistent, and easily accessed from any process. Note that with multiple processes trying to coordinate read and write access to files, and passing information through the filesystem, you may get better results and fewer development headaches by using a small database table to accomplish the same thing.

Multiple server processes can run on multiple servers. Classic example: httpd daemons running on a web server farm. They contain no state that lives beyond the scope of an http connection; they are identical from the point of view of a client, and they are easily replicated. If you choose the multiple server approach for scale or host redundancy reasons, make sure you use an IP redirector or other traffic distribution model as described in Chapter 9. Running multiple server-side processses buys you protection against application-level or logic faults; running them across multiple servers gains the additional protection against hardware, operating system, and peripheral failures as well. Designing an application to fit the multiple server model is complex, because not all applications can be stripped of their state. When you want the benefits of application-level process replication, but have to deal with state information, you need process state multicast support.

Process State Multicast

State multicast, or reliable multicast techniques, are used to distribute updates from one process to all of its peer processes on the same server or on the same network. Implementations range from serial unicast, in which the updating process sends updates to each receiver in turn to actual usage of Internet multicast class addresses with verification and logging to ensure that all recipients see all intended data. Most of the products in this space come from the middleware vendors such as Vitria, Active Software, TIBco, Talarian, and BEA Systems.

State updates are useful when an application has to maintain some in-memory information about transactions to process incoming requests. This might be an open order table, or an in-flight transaction history, or a list of available slots in a scheduling system. This data is also recorded in a persistent disk store somewhere, but the time required to query the disk system through a database or filesystem often makes it impractical for real-time request processing. The in-memory state offers a compromise, representing a cache of the persistent copy of the data. As such, the problem of state replication resembles that of processor cache snooping, ensuring that all CPUs in a multiprocessor system see all updates to shared, cached data addresses.

When you're designing hardware, though, you can set the hard and fast rules. In software, and over a network, you need to deal with a variety of failures and with a longer time scale. Be sure you understand the constraints and guarantees you're getting from any kind of replicating middleware:

- *What are the delivery semantics?* Do you get delivery of messages at least once, at most once, or exactly once? At least once means you may get duplicate messages if the middleware believes a message was lost on the network. At most once means you have no duplicates, but lose messages that are eaten by the network or by overloaded servers. Exactly once is the transactional, ACID-property friendly behavior that's ideal, but often the slowest and hardest to guarantee.

- *Deal with duplicate messages.* If you may get duplicates, make sure you know how to suppress them or filter them out. In some cases, duplicates are immaterial, and can be ignored. If you get the same quote on a stock once or five times, only the last reported quote really matters. Similarly, if you run the risk of falling behind in processing state updates, determine if you can compress the updates and take the last one or the net-net change of all of them. Being flexible with the update stream allows processes to pick up and remove slack from the distribution system.

- *What's the latency under load?* As with queuing systems, you want to be sure the distribution middleware holds up with increasing request volumes.

As you compare various state replication techniques and application issues to handle duplicates, lost messages, and updates, the process replication problem bears an uncanny resemblance to a transaction replication problem. The same concepts are involved, and the same constraints and concerns should guide your selection of technologies and designs. With some good groundwork and developer guidance, you can build a system that tolerates failures at any level, from the hardware to the application coding.

Checkpointing

Not all processes handle short-lived requests. Reliability engineering also has a place in the scientific and modeling worlds, where codes may run for several hours, days, or weeks. Taking a hit due to insufficient memory or a network error in the middle of a week-long simulation run incurs about 50 hours of recovery time to get the simulation back to the point of failure. Given that most simulations are run to reduce time to market, wasted simulation cycles and dead time are not easily forgiven. You need to add reliability at the process level to ensure rapid recovery of long-running jobs.

Checkpointing can be done at the application level, with extra code to handle writing out critical state information; it can be done using a job scheduler or tool such as the Load Share Facility (LSF), or it can rely on operating system support for preserving an entire process and its in-memory state at any point in time. Checkpoint-restart facilities are not common, so we'll stop at this brief mention of them. All of the techniques and issues described in the following text apply to OS-level support as well, but we're going to focus on more application-controlled techniques to allow restart and recovery.

What kind of failures scare the scientific coder the most? Obviously, resource shortages such as memory, swap space, and filesystem space represent threats to the completion of a long-running code. There are also issues of poorly conditioned inputs, application bugs, and floating-point exceptions that can cause a finely-tuned, sensitive piece of code to crash if given slightly erroneous inputs midway through the simulation. With checkpoints made along the way, the application can back up to a well-known point in time and restart, perhaps with finer input checking or resolution of system resource constraints.

The most obvious approach: At well-defined intervals, copy out state information such as in-memory matrices, file I/O position indicators, locking information, counters, and intermediate results. After ensuring that the disk I/O has completed, and that the state variables dumped are consistent with each other, the application can continue. When the application is restarted, it should check for the existence of a clean checkpoint file or have a flag passed on the command line indicating it should resume a checkpointed operation. You'll need to manage the time required to create the checkpoint and write out the state information as an overhead factor; if it takes you 6 minutes to write out state for a 200GB memory segment, you don't want to do this every 10 minutes. Once an hour reduces your duty cycle to 90 percent, with 10 percent of the time spent writing out checkpoints.

Balance the checkpoint interval against the difficulty in backing out changes made since the last known good point. If you're walking through a file, updating records, make sure the checkpoint contains a copy of the file as it was at the time of the checkpoint, because you may update another 3000 records before crashing—how do you back out those changes when the checkpoint file reflects the total system state 3000 records ago? Coordinate file I/O, lock files, counters, and other indications of progress with the data recorded in the recovery area, and you'll be able to move backward in time to recover from a variety of faults.

Operating system or job control level features such as LSF and OS checkpoint merely make the checkpointing process easier for in-core state. You'll still have to worry about file I/O and interactions with other data services such as databases. Make sure you understand all of the dependencies of an application, and you can engineer a recovery technique that provides rapid recovery as required. Your job, as you've probably deduced from other sections of this book, is to make the choices in trading off complexity, time, cost, and resiliency.

▶Key Points

- File system replication is useful for improving performance, but it requires careful selection of tools and methods.

- Database replication can protect you from a variety of corruption problems while providing bounded, low response, and failover times. It comes at the cost of complexity.

- Asynchronous systems scale better than those that operate in lock-step, but require that you design for optimistic cases rather than the failure modes.

- State replication of multiple processes gives you even finer control over request execution.

- Checkpointing is useful for preserving the state of long-running applications for later restart or recovery.

CHAPTER 11

Application Recovery

Architects and interior designers revile and battle each other.
—*Stewart Brand, in* How Buildings Learn

Stewart Brand's book is a wonderful resource for all architects, whether you're working with silicon, steel, or sofas. The above quote captures the tension between those who design structures, like availability platforms, and those who make things happen within them, namely applications that run on those platforms. We've been describing availability building blocks in layers, starting with a foundation of hardware and data management, working up through failover management systems and network redundancy, and concluding with design rules for data services such as database and web servers. Together, these components comprise an application *platform;* that is, they are the pieces you use to support an application that actually does something interesting. Unless you run benchmarks for a living, you probably don't just run "a database," you run an application that talks to the database. Keeping the database online, available, consistent, and performing with snappy response time has been our focus up to this point.

At the apex of the availability pyramid is the application. There are two aspects to application recovery: First, how does the application react when a data service fails; and second, what else might go wrong within the application code that would cause a failure? Sometimes it's the application to blame, dumping core or behaving erratically when the network and all of its services are just fine. In this chapter, we'll top off our analysis of design rules and building blocks with an investigation of application-level recovery, starting with a list of failure modes and application reactions, then a brief look at internal application failures, and concluding with an overview of good developer habits that improve overall system reliability.

Application Recovery Overview

Service availability, as discussed in previous chapters, only ensures that there is a data management service at the ready on the network. Your clients may not be able to access it because they are not configured to deal with redundancy and get confused after a server failover. Applications may not deal with failures in a gentle manner, resulting in application crashes or endless streams of errors while they try to recover or reconnect to the wrong server. Application-level reliability is a trap for finger-pointing: the front-end team blames the back-end team for making their part of the application crash; the web designers insist they didn't do anything on the edge that would make a browser seize up; the database team blames the middleware selection for failing to route transactions after a failover, while the middleware team insists it's a database recovery problem. Developing good detection and prevention techniques will help you sort through these situations.

Application Failure Modes

From a network client's perspective, a server failover is indistinguishable from a fast reboot. The client needs to reconnect, restart any in-flight operations, and continue from where it left off. If the application happens to be running on the machine that crashes, obviously it will be restarted when the machine comes back up. These are the two extreme cases, where there's a clear failure and recovery at the system level. But what about nonfatal system or software logic faults? These can impair or crash an application, even while the system is still running. Commercial failover management systems often let you try to restart a crashed application at least once before taking down the entire server, so you'll need to make sure your applications tolerate these "soft crashes" well.

The following are the application failure modes we'll dissect in detail in this chapter:

Improper handling of a server restart. Networked client applications must be able to detect the corner cases when data management services restart or failover, such as a long break in service or an aborted transaction. Many of these conditions are the same for server reboot and failover, so ensuring proper restart behavior is a good idea even without high availability or other server management software in place.

Nonfatal system or external failures. How does your client application react if it can't find a remote server? What if a disk quota is exceeded and a write operation fails? None of these conditions is strong enough to cause a failover immediately, but they may have adverse affects on applications. When a disk fills up, failover isn't going to help, as the overflowing disk is going to be imported on the other side of the HA pair. Persistent failures, such as a network segment that fails and requires redundant routing, or a disk that presents media failures, may be handled automatically, but you want to be sure your application will tolerate the intermediate failures well. There's little point in having automated recovery if the client application has already failed.

Internal memory and state management. In the vernacular, this category is filed under "bugs." We'll restrict our discussion to memory-corruption problems and their detection. Memory-related problems are probably one of the most common sources of application-level failures, and developer difficulty with memory management was one of the key drivers behind the memory access constraints in Sun's Java environment.

Logical faults. Examples of these include looping or hung code, deadlock conditions, improper handling of unexpected input, or merely wrong answers. We'll include some boundary condition handling in this category (these are also known as "bugs").

Many of the topics in this chapter may seem like common-sense items, but even obvious application safety mechanisms fall by the wayside when customer deadlines, urgency of bug fixes, or upcoming trade shows in Las Vegas demand swift development. "Damn the torpedoes, full speed ahead" works in the movies, but not in the real world, when you've got a beeper attached to your waist. It pays to invest time with the developers up front to be sure the applications under development fit your models for cost, complexity, and time to recover, and that the development and operational camps are aligned in terms of priorities. This often means crossing political boundaries and offering some value in return for a series of meetings. Set your sights on the level of continuous application uptime that you need to achieve, and you can generally coax all of the teams into the same goals. Our goal in this chapter is to show you where the torpedoes are and what you can do to avoid them.

Application Recovery Techniques

Investing in application recovery is akin to the message sent out by health management organizations: If you do a good job of early detection and prevention, you won't get too sick. Given that software failures account for a large portion of system failures, your applications need to be sensitive to the different types of faults they'll hit. Job one is to decide how you'll react to each type of failure.

These are cost-time-benefit evaluations, balancing the time required to implement a recovery technique against the cost of having or not having that recovery, with the possible benefit of the automated recovery considered. There's no sense in adding checkpoint features to a database application if it can be easily restarted and the database handles transactional integrity. On the other hand, if an application crash runs the risk of corrupting data or propagating wrong answers, you'll want to invest in taking the necessary steps to keep your data flows clean.

We've broken down recovery techniques into five major categories. We'll provide an overview of these categories here, and then dive into detail on how the most appropriate ones apply to each type of data management service crash, nonfatal system error, and internal logic problem.

- *Detect and retry.* Images of "Abort, Retry, Fail?" haunt DOS-literate users. This is the simplest approach, and while it seems obvious, you need to be sure your application "tries enough" to achieve reconnection to a data service or recovery. In the event of memory exhaustion or network disconnects, for example, it's possible for an application to punt and simply crash, or for it to sleep for a few seconds, try to wait out a short-term memory deficit or network glitch, and then retry the failed call again. Patience is sometimes rewarded.

- *Gentle shutdown.* Faced with a case of memory exhaustion that doesn't resolve itself quickly (perhaps another application has a memory leak and has consumed the entire machine), or a floating point exception that can't be fixed, it's necessary to save state and make sure files are left as consistent as possible. Client applications should try to fail gently, leaving clear messages for users about what happened and what to do next.

- *Crash, burn, and restart.* A variation on the gentle shutdown, when either the application exits abnormally due to a signal, exception, or other internal failure, or when the failover management system decides to kill it because it's not responding. In most cases, the failover management software will try to restart the application at least once before declaring the entire system unusable and instigating a failover to a secondary server. On the client side, recovery isn't always possible, but in the case of violent death users usually know what to do when they see their application window vanish or end up looking at a Blue Screen of Death for a few minutes.

- *Restart from checkpoint.* This assumes, of course, that you have a valid checkpoint file somewhere. If your failure was caused by an internal application error, like a memory exception, restarting from a checkpoint may result in you taking the same exception later on. Applications that handle streams of requests may be able to recover from a checkpoint, since the new request stream may go through different code paths in a different order. Memory exceptions and other internal errors are often exposed randomly, so mixing up the input may allow you to continue past the fault. Further, if the problem was caused by poorly conditioned input that slipped past the default boundary checking, then executing "past" that request may eliminate the problem as well. As discussed in the previous chapter, checkpoints are useful if you have a long startup or recovery period for an application, typically one with significant internal state or computation required to regenerate that state.

■ *Escalate to a higher management authority.* Otherwise known as "pager pandemonium," this technique is used for nonfatal system faults that can and should be resolved with human interaction. Disks that fill up, networks that appear partitioned or unreliable, or memory exhaustion may not be fixed with a failover. The time to repair these failures is dependent upon the time to locate someone who is available, awake, and accessible to fix the problem. Escalation paths, as we'll discuss in Chapter 13, are critical for continuous operations.

It's always a good idea to have an application clean up as much as possible if it fails, or if it knows that it's going to fail. For some fatal exceptions, this isn't possible, but even problems like floating-point exceptions often give the application a chance to be notified and deliver some last-gasp information useful for tracking or preventing the problem in the future.

Kinder, Gentler Failures

When an application is terminated by the operating system, there isn't much it can do. Its open files are closed, locks released, and other resources returned to the system pools. In some cases, the operating system may deliver a signal to the process, allowing it to perform some last-minute cleanup or diagnostic message printing. In other cases, where applications recognize failures for which they have no recovery path, it's up to the application to exit gracefully under pressure. One example is a database client application that tries to reconnect after a failover, finds it can't reach the server, retries a few more times, and finally gives up. The application should at least give some warning to the user about the state of the last known transaction, and the reason for the failure. When users are expected to call the help desk to report application outages, the application can help its own cause by reporting problems automatically to the help desk facility and interactively to the confused or angry user.

What else goes in the kinder, gentler application failure bucket? Ensuring that all files, counters, and indexes are kept consistent helps. The operating system will close files automatically, flushing out whatever data was queued for the disks. If there is additional information the application needs to ease recovery, or if an indication of the last action of the application is helpful, then this data can be written as well, provided the internal application failure doesn't prevent it from doing so. When developers add last-gasp features to applications, these should be self-contained, simple, and use a minimum of system calls. A memory access failure, leading to an exception, may be "caught" with a signal handler that prints out some diagnostic information. However, if the diagnostic routine tries to allocate memory to format a print string, the diagnostic routine is likely to fail as well.

Providing as much information as possible about memory-related problems such as access protection faults may be helpful to developers looking to fix the problem. It won't help bring the application back quickly; you'll need to restart the application or do a failover to recover. Note that Unix operating system failures, or panics, are sometimes due to memory access problems within the kernel. Other application-specific failures, such as floating-point exceptions, should also deliver a signal to the offending process. If possible, the process can take corrective action—sometimes these failures are due to code that attempts to be more precise than input or data items allow, resulting in an underflow or divide-by-zero problem. In other cases, a floating-point exception is entirely unexpected, and dumping out whatever state information is relevant will help in diagnosing the problem further.

None of these graceful exit techniques improve recovery or reliability; they merely make life easier the next time by helping your development teams locate and eliminate problems or by gently steering users to corrective action. However, the best failure is one that doesn't happen, so we're going to turn our focus to preventing application level failures, starting with adding resiliency and recovery in the face of data management service faults.

Tolerating Data Service Failures

Client applications have a hard time detecting the difference between a successful server failover and a fast reboot. Most database applications will recognize that a server connection has been broken, and will try to reconnect to the server and restart in-flight transactions. Other types of clients may not be so optimistic, or may require system administration changes to make them tolerant of short breaks in service that are handled by failover systems. File server clients are probably the biggest culprit in this class.

File Server Client Recovery

Setting up a high availability pair for an NFS file server is only half of the battle. You'll need to be sure that your NFS clients are tolerant of breaks in service and continue to retry requests and recover gracefully from server outages. Again, the clients don't really see the difference between a single server reboot and a failover; your goal is to use failover to make the time to client recovery as short as possible. You also want to be sure there are clients at the ready.

NFS Soft Mounts

The default mode for mounting NFS filesystems is with the "hard" option, indicating that the client should continue to retry operations until it receives an acknowledgement from the server. The alternative to hard mounts is "soft" ones, in which a request is retransmitted a few times and then the client gives up. Five retries is the default, although this parameter can be set as a mount option.

NFS soft mounts and reliability do not mix. Data integrity has to have the highest precedence. NFS soft mounts do not ensure data integrity on the server or application correctness on the NFS client.

If your goal is to make sure that servers recover quickly and clients continue from where they were waiting, you cannot use soft mount operations to give the clients a chance to abort operations in progress. Some system administrators prefer soft mounts to hard ones because they allow clients to "break" operations that are stuck on NFS servers that have crashed. Note that this is precisely the behavior you're seeking to fix by investing in availability techniques in the first place. You want clients to be as insensitive to the server's state, and even the server's identity, whenever possible. Mixing hard mounts and the "intr" mount option to allow NFS operations to be interrupted may give you control of the NFS clients more quickly than a server failover, but it kills the application process that was hung on the nonresponding server. Again, your goal should be to improve server reliability to the point where client-side behavior isn't your concern. You can focus your attention on a room of NFS servers, but it's nearly impossible to scale up your system administration staff to handle floors of NFS clients in various states of hanging and abnormally terminated applications.

What happens if you use soft mounts, and a client request times out? The process making the system call to the filesystem that was converted into an NFS call will eventually run into trouble. On a call to get the inode information from a file, possibly as the result of an ls command or part of the file opening sequence, a null structure will be returned to the calling process. A well-written process will detect an empty structure and complain (see "Boundary Condition Checks" later in this chapter). Most applications, however, will dump core when they attempt to use the zero-filled values in that file information structure. Similarly, an attempt to read a page from a file that fails returns a zero-filled page; a failed write operation leaves a hole in the file on the server. Both of these failed operations cause data corruption. Writes that fail on soft mounts are particularly tricky to identify because the error may be returned to the calling process long after the error occurs (again, see the following text for more details on why this happens).

Big rule with NFS servers: If you make them highly available, make the clients highly patient and persistent in sending requests until they are serviced. Soft mounts are a poor man's way of regaining client control; they were introduced in the early days of NFS when server uptime was measured in days, not months. With improvements in operating system reliability, network engineering and hardware improvements such as switches, and the introduction of server-side redundancy, soft mounts no longer really have a place in NFS environments. You'll get better predictability from server-side controls, and you'll only get control over data integrity with hard mounts.

Automounter Tricks

Another common approach to improving NFS client resistance to failures is to use the automounter (or the publicly available amd) to load balance across multiple, replicated servers. You'll recall that we discussed the merits of replicating file servers in Chapter 10 (it's done primarily to improve performance and improve reliability when many geographically dispersed clients are involved). The automounter on the client side is not an availability technique for the long haul. Replicated filesystems give you load balancing and some measure of protection against servers that have gone down for long periods of time, but they don't give you the rapid recovery of an HA pair.

When the automounter is given a list of fileservers for the same mount point, it tries to find the one "closest" to the client by matching network numbers. Once network distance is determined, the automounter then pings each server by calling its null procedure (as described in Chapter 5) and measuring the response time; the fastest local network server is chosen. Mounts are only completed on the first reference to a filesystem; once the server's volume has been mounted on the client, the automounter is no longer involved in references to that filesystem. If a server is down while the automounter is searching for a potential server, you'll safely skirt it. But if that fileserver later crashes after a client has mounted it, the client is blocked waiting on the server. Replicated filesystems don't help at this point because the client has file handles, mount information, and other state tying it to the particular server that serviced the mount on the first reference through the automounter.

Many system administrators find the amd alternative attractive because it has a "set-aside" feature. When a fileserver in a replicated list stops responding, amd "moves" the mount point aside, and the next reference to that volume causes a fresh mount from a different server to be completed. This has the nice feature of preventing the next process from stumbling into a crashed server, but it doesn't help the processes that already have operations in progress on open files on the now-defunct server. Those processes are blocked, waiting for the server to recover. The set-aside feature and soft mounts may be used to essentially fast-crash applications that get caught waiting on a crashed, replicated server; soft mounts mean that the process will eventually recover from its wait and can be killed and restarted; when it is restarted it will use the new and improved mount point for the same filesystem. This is a bit heavy-handed, since it requires restarting a client application and is far from transparent; it's going to require at least a user adept at sending interrupt signals to a process or system administration help.

Sun's Solaris operating system includes a client-side NFS failover feature that works for replicated, read-only volumes. When multiple servers are listed for the same filesystem and one of the servers crashes, a client will recognize the failure when NFS requests begin timing out repeatedly. At that point, the client unmounts the volume, chooses another server from the list, remounts the filesystem, and renegotiates all of the open file handles in use, using mount path information and permissions stored on the client side. Client-side failover is useful for replicated volumes that are subject to random outages, such as those in a development environment that is not well-controlled, but it is less deterministic than recovering the server quickly. In general, replicated volumes should be used for performance and ease of administration; each replicated server may be part of an HA pair to ensure shorter maximum time to recover from failures.

In the Windows NT arena, file sharing resembles NFS soft mounts. When a server fails, the mount eventually times out; if the server recovers quickly enough, then the client resumes the mount. Clients run a process known as a *redirector* that intercepts file references and sends them to related processes on the server; the redirector binds to a specific remote server instead of one in a list of replicated servers. NT does offer network-based file locking, although it is not implemented by default. In general, if you're providing an NT file server to NT clients from a Unix host, you'll want to go down the high availability path.

Database Application Recovery

Database clients are much easier to recover than NFS clients. When the database server fails, client applications determine that they have lost their server connections and can abort in-progress transactions. Some transactions may have rolled forward when the server recovered, so clients need to reconnect and check on the status of in-flight transactions before restarting them. In general, database client libraries handle reconnection, transaction restart, and recovery gracefully. When using an HA pair, the IP address and host name used for the data service migrate to the secondary server, so clients reconnect to the "right" machine. The generic case is the easy case.

It's possible for stored procedures or triggers to fail on an otherwise normally functioning database. These failures may be due to internal database problems, errors in the logic, external problems such as a full log device or lack of data table space, or a lack of available memory on the server. Client applications must check the return values of stored procedures, looking for all possible failure modes and exception conditions. Also watch out for long-running transactions. Clients that set time-outs (or "deadman timers") for some transactions may inadvertently abort transactions that are blocked by a large SELECT or other transaction that consumes most of the database engine's cycles. Application developers may be tempted to break up the single large transaction into several smaller ones, performing part of the work in each transaction. This attempt to break the logjam works well if you are certain that the other transactions are lookup or read oriented, and won't change data that impacts parts of the broken-up transaction that occur later in the overall timeline. Part of the advantage of a single, large transaction is that you're guaranteed to have the database state remain consistent during the course of the entire work unit. You need to manage your recovery time exposure against the smallest logical unit of work done by the application. You want the right answer with the least application work, provided it gives you the right recovery window.

Replicated database systems also pose problems for client applications. If a client is going to failover to a replicated system that uses a different IP address and host name, it must know how to connect to that server. Some application frameworks and client libraries support lists of IP address and host name pairs that represent a "search path" for applications, giving them some of the benefits of the NFS client using replicated NFS servers with the automounter. Many publish and subscribe state management systems use this technique to ensure that clients can find a valid, functioning server on the network even after a primary server has failed, without requiring IP address and hostname information to migrate (which might confuse the configuration of the state multicasting engine).

Finally, most database applications require a client login to authenticate the user to the database server. Even if the client application reconnects after a server failure and restarts in-flight transactions, the additional step of logging in with a password makes the failover visible to the user. If you can automate the authentication step, by using a tool like `expect` or by caching the user password in memory (encrypted, of course), then you can make database-client reconnection completely transparent to the user. Even without a failover management system, this is a good developer practice, as it reduces the impact of server failures on the user community.

Web Client Recovery

Web clients have the easiest recovery path of all application types discussed. When a web surfer notices that a page isn't loading, the conditioned reflex is to hit the "Stop" button, followed by one or more tries on the "Reload" button. With replicated web servers, the first reload should start a new connection,

routed to a different server, which completes the HTTP operation successfully. If the failure occurred at the level of a cache or proxy server, there will
be a small performance hit as the cache reloads, but aside from the user-
driven click-and-start operation, the failover to alternate servers happens
automatically.

Pages that are forms-driven or are used to create shopping baskets on the
server side introduce a bit more complexity. Most browsers ask if the user
wishes to repost form data; this is resent to (hopefully) the new server when the
page is reloaded. Any transactional back end called through a CGI script should
be hardened the same way other transactional data management services are
handled. If the shopping cart or other back-end state is maintained in dynamic
web pages, these will likely be lost when the primary server crashes unless they
are written to a file server or other single data source on the back-end. Ideally,
systems that capture user profile and choice information should isolate the
dynamic state in a database or file server if the web server front end is a stack
of boxes that handle availability through replication.

Clients that are viewing secure pages using Secure Socket Layer (SSL) connections will have to reconnect to the server. There are two parts to client
recovery from within an SSL session. First, SSL is typically used to secure transactional information such as credit cards, user name, and passwords, so the
user may need to reauthenticate; there's no problem in presenting the same
page used when the user's session times out or when you want to reverify user
credential information. Second, the client needs to rebuild the SSL connection
to the new server, which may incur a few seconds of overhead. A simple user-
intelligible message about restarting a transaction or verifying work done to the
point serves to make the user verify everything has recovered properly, and that
you're proceeding from a known point.

Client applications are fairly easy to condition to handle server-side failures
and recovery; if you focus on separation of state and replication, and make sure
that client configurations are consistent with server failover mechanisms,
clients should see little if any disruption when your HA system kicks into gear.
However, applications on both client and server can still fail due to other errors
caused by system failures or internal problems. We'll now go on from data service dependencies to application structural analysis.

Application Recovery from System Failures

External events such as a disk filling up can cause application failures. In
this section, we'll look at system-level failures that create headaches for applications, and some common workarounds or early detection steps. We'll
also cover network programming interactions and dependencies, since some
network-based applications don't restart well after they have failed and been

restarted. We'll cover the easy ones (memory exhaustion and I/O errors) first, then look at how network failures impact application flow.

Virtual Memory Exhaustion

Even with large physical memories, systems can exhaust their virtual memory. In some operating systems, this happens when swap space (or paging files) is full; in others, it's when the sum of physical memory and swap space is allocated completely. In either case, virtual memory exhaustion is an external, system-level failure that can crash, confuse, or otherwise impair the reliability of an application. The two most common causes of virtual memory depletion are memory leaks, in which one or more processes grow in size until they occupy all of memory, and endless forking (spawning) of new processes due to a bug in a script. Even forking a large application can cause a temporary shortfall as the system cleans up the copy of the large application to make a process container for a new job.

When you run out of memory, normal processes start to act like denizens of the twilight zone. Checking all return values from `malloc()` is the first step in reducing memory-related failures, but that only tells an application if there's enough virtual memory left to satisfy a request of the stated size. An application may try to dynamically allocate a full megabyte of space, and fail, but the system has 512 Kbytes free. On the other hand, the system may be down to only a few tens of Kbytes of available memory, and out-of-memory errors start to pop up in many places:

- Attempts to create new processes fail, because there is not enough memory left to copy the parent process's state.

- Attempts to dynamically allocate memory, even in small cell sizes, also fail because there is not enough virtual memory left.

- Network clients attempting to create sockets to the machine cannot complete their socket connections, because there is not enough memory left for TCP data buffers and socket control block structures. Similarly, attempts to create new sockets on the memory-starved machine also fail because the necessary kernel data structures cannot be allocated.

- System calls fail, often producing the `EAGAIN` error on Unix systems, indicating that the error is temporary and may be recoverable, but at the time of the call there were not sufficient resources to complete it. Generally this indicates a lack of space for I/O buffers.

How do you resolve a memory shortfall? If the problem is due to a memory leak, killing the offending process should restore order to the system. If it's an overall load issue, or a process that has gone out of control forking copies of itself, then system administrator help is often required to reboot the machine or kill the root process in an attempt to clean up all of the rampant children processes. Remote help isn't always a possibility, as a machine in a memory contention fight may not have the resources to open up a new `telnet` or `rlogin` session. This is a corner case that may best be handled with automated failover management systems, adding memory exhaustion to the list of monitored conditions that make a machine go out of service.

I/O Errors

For the most part, I/O errors are caught and suppressed by the data integrity techniques discussed in Chapter 4, such as disk mirroring and RAID-5 redundancy. If you start building in redundancy at the data storage level, disk errors due to media failures, I/O failures, or systemic failures in the disk storage unit should never be seen by the application. In the rare event that a disk failure manages to bubble up to the application level, you'll want to be sure that the application handles it cleanly.

Read errors are usually obvious; instead of a buffer full of data you get back zero bytes and some indication of an error. Make sure that the error isn't that the input pipe is empty; there's no point in going through corrective action only to find out that the "problem" was a zero-length input item. The gray area between what volume management systems provide and what applications demand is filled with failures in write operations on filesystems. On raw disk partitions, write operates synchronously, and there is no intervening data structure to add to the complexity of the problem. Working through the filesystem, the `write()` system call is asynchronous in Unix operating systems, meaning that the actual data block is written to a disk after the system call has returned. In the event of an uncorrectable disk system failure, errors are returned to the calling process in a later `write()` call or when `close()` is called on the file (see "Return Value Checks" later in this chapter).

Two filesystem-related problems comprise this gray area between predictable disk systems and well-defined system call behavior. First, what happens when the filesystem fills up? The lack of space is detected immediately, causing the `write()` operation to return an error with some indication that the disk is full. No data is queued; no asynchronous reporting is needed; the application just realizes that it's staring at a full closet while holding an armful of dry cleaning. In some cases, this problem resolves itself when a large temporary file is removed, but usually it requires help from the SA staff to enforce good disk usage habits. What should an application do? Generally, retry a few times if the shortfall in disk space is expected to be resolved quickly; otherwise do as gentle a shutdown as possible, given that there's little or no room in which to write out a checkpoint image.

The second problem: user quotas. Quotas are like payphones installed in your home to control garrulous teenagers. Seems like a good idea until you need to make the critical call to your client and you're without change or a calling card. To be fair, quotas allow large time-sharing systems to ensure that individual users don't inadvertently seize control of a filesystem with downloaded files from the Internet and PostScript output from graphics-laden presentations. If a write operation fails because a quota would be exceeded, it's up to the application to notify the user (and possibly the SA authorities) via other channels, and then again either wait it out or gently fail. With an NFS-mounted filesystem, the quota may be exceeded on the server side, and there is no immediate notification since the quota check is done once the call reaches the server, not at the local client side. A good rule of thumb is to manage disk space carefully and aggressively on servers, and avoid the use of quotas except in interactive, many-user environments.

Network Connectivity

A well-functioning application that needs to use network services is at risk of network connectivity impacting its predictable behavior. To continue functioning normally, the networked application relies on routing, remote host availability, and name service configuration. The most common error is that a host or network is unreachable, meaning that either the network is partitioned due to a routing failure or some intermediate routing information is no longer valid, so that clients on one end of the network can't find the servers on the other end. Assuming that you've done a bare minimum of redundant network design with multiple routers and rapid detection of outages, connectivity failures reflecting network outages should be short-lived. On the other hand, without network redundancy, you need an alternative plan—either another server for the same service, or some way to stall the requesting application. If you are merely waiting for the routers to reestablish end-to-end connectivity, a short wait-and-retry loop should make your application tolerant of these network hiccups.

A second network connectivity problem is when your application and a host undergoing failover or reboot engage in a network footrace to see if the server can start listening on a port before the client's request arrives there. If the server wins, there's no visible impact; but if the client wins it may see a "port unreachable" message indicating that the remote host was there but nobody was home on the desired port number. Again, if you assume that the remote service is on its way back to full health, then a short time-out and retry should establish a connection on the next attempt.

Another set of network problems has to do with connections reset by peers. This is the networking equivalent of "I don't like you anymore." Usually a network connection reset occurs when one end of the connection reboots, telling the other end to drop as soon as it's able to do so. Resets can also be sent on connections that do not respond to any traffic for a long time, typically at the expiration of a "keep alive" timer that sends periodic probes to the other end to be sure someone is still listening even if there's no traffic on the socket. When a database server reboots, all of its clients see their TCP connections reset by peers, and they have to reconnect. This should be handled transparently by applications; there aren't many worse ways to annoy a user than indicating that an application has to be restarted because the socket connection code is buried somewhere in the startup sequence.

Finally, network applications have to be sensitive to connection-request time-outs. If the TCP connection can't be built up when there's a valid route, one or more of the following problems is at work: The remote host has crashed; the remote side's connection queue is too small; there's a network latency problem or some piece of network hardware is dropping packets; or a bona fide denial-of-service attack is under way and absorbing all of the server's capacity. Your best approach, from an application perspective, is to try several times before declaring the remote server inaccessible. Consider the typical user reaction to "404" type errors from browsers. Users want applications that produce meaningful diagnostics when they have trouble reaching remote servers. Your tolerance for pain in this case is at the threshold where a user goes to click on the equivalent of the browser "Stop" button.

Restarting Network Services

Recovering services by restarting applications on an otherwise functional host requires that you tune network traffic parameters to allow the same TCP/IP ports to be reused. Anyone who has restarted a database on a machine without rebooting has probably seen "Address already in use" error messages, caused when the database listener processes attempted to bind to a well-known port for incoming requests. If the server can't bind to the port, clients won't be able to find it at the agreed-upon location, and to the clients, the server is still down even though the host is running and the application has restarted. Guaranteeing that well-known addresses can be reused is critical for restarting applications without a complete cold start via server reboot.

Only two knobs need to be turned to ensure that server processes can reuse their previous network registrations. First, make sure that you are specific that a socket address can be reused, by handing the SO_REUSEADDR option to a setsockopt() call (using Berkeley socket semantics). This system call indicates that even after the socket owner crashes, the socket's port number can be reused later on by another process. The second knob is a TCP/IP configuration control that sets the TCP keepalive interval and the close wait interval, both of which are used to determine when a socket that has one end closed is really, totally, most sincerely dead. The defaults for these values are generally in the range of several hours—not exactly the time-out you want before you restart an application in an attempt to recover a service without a reboot.

Here's where your challenge as a high availability system architect arises: Set the time-out too small, and heavy network congestion coupled with lossy networks (such as clients connecting over the Internet) may result in discarding sockets that are functional, but moving little data. Set the time-out too high, and you might as well reboot or failover to another server because you'll have to wait for the entire time-out period before restarting the application that wants to reuse its previous port registration. Using a lower bound of three minutes is fair—meaning that you can restart applications after three minutes of a crash. Any network connection that remains data-free for three minutes is suffering from other problems, and abnormally terminating a socket connection is the least of them.

That completes the list of external failures that may impact application reliability. To be thorough in our discussion of application operations, though, we need to take a brief look at ways in which applications fail through nobody's fault but their own.

Internal Application Failures

Probably the most common cause of application-level failures is improper memory accesses. The usual suspects include array indices that go past the end of the structure, use of a null pointer, using an uninitialized piece of memory as a pointer, yielding a random data address, and overflowing a buffer with unterminated or unexpectedly long input.

Memory Access Faults

Accessing the wrong piece of memory or attempting to access an invalid piece of memory produces either a segmentation violation or a bus error if you're on a Unix system, or a general protection fault on a Windows system. In any language, the cause is the same—a piece of code used a memory address that wasn't valid and ran into memory that didn't belong to it, or memory that shouldn't be accessed because it was in a "red zone" between valid segments of a process. Dereferencing a null pointer, or using it as a base for an offset into a data structure, produces this "red zone" fault where the resulting data address points into the invalid first page or so of an application's address space. There is little help for these kinds of faults after they occur; mostly your work is preventive medicine in terms of testing and using memory checking tools that look for invalid pointer arithmetic.

Memory leaks are another class of fault that can cripple an application. When a data item is dynamically allocated, it can only be found if there's at least one pointer to it in the process's address space. Reassign a new value to the last pointer, and the data item is "orphaned," left in the address space without any way of being reclaimed or returned to the pool of available memory cells. If this orphaning process happens regularly, the process has a memory leak and will grow to consume all available resources on the machine.

Memory access faults don't always cause application termination. If the problem results in a pointer being moved to another valid location in a valid page, then you'll corrupt data and possibly get the wrong answer, but you won't suffer an application crash! More common are wild pointer references that cause the text segment of a process to be damaged, or that damage the dynamic linking information so that a future library call goes into hyperspace. Applications that crash with illegal instruction errors or data alignment errors generally suffer from wild (uninitialized) pointer problems. In nearly every case, there's some element of data corruption, making it a chore to determine what's valid and where to pick up from a well-known state.

Memory Corruption and Recovery

How do you know that you're suffering from memory corruption? First of all, attempts to solve problems involving wrong answers or invalid calculations usually involve adding output statements to the code. If these make the symptoms disappear, you have a memory-stomping problem that was rendered less fatal by the introduction of new code and data structures. Similarly, moving or adding data items may hide the problem, or changing from dynamic to static linking rearranges the code segments so that the damage is hidden for a longer period. None of these "answers" is sufficient, because they only defer the point at which the application will use an invalid piece of data and crash.

Some application developers attempt to recover from an invalid memory reference by catching the signal delivered by the operating system. In Unix, when you get hit with a SIGSEGV on an invalid memory access, you're probably in irreversible trouble. Flush out some state, if possible, and pick a point at which to restart the process from a known good state, using a checkpoint if one exists. In highly sensitive and time-critical operations, it may be beneficial to add intermediate checkpoint and consistency checks on vital data items. Like the checkpointing process described in Chapter 10, there is a cost to performing these checks, and they can't be done on every item after every reference, or you'll slow your whole application down to the speed of a simulation. On the other hand, running a checksum on some key, in-memory data items and comparing it to a known, good value from time to time may help detect when any of those items is damaged by a bad, but not invalid, memory reference.

Hanging Processes

Our final flavor of internal failure is the good, old-fashioned infinite loop. Generally, loops are caused by unexpected input that sends the input parsing routing into a cycle or a deadlock on threads or other scheduling facilities that results in a deadly embrace followed by a break followed by another deadly thread embrace. Even network events, such as having a client disappear when a server is sending a UDP packet to it, can cause a loop, because there's no way of knowing that the system responsible for the next event in the processing chain has disappeared. There are a few ways to deal with habitually locked-up processes:

- Use an application-level heartbeat to learn whether the application has returned to its "main loop" or listening state. It if gets caught processing a request, the heartbeat stops and the equivalent of a failover management system can step in and kill it with the intent of restarting it, or can try to send it "secret input" to grab control of the application.

- Make sure you understand the deadlock detection and back-out procedures for whatever scheduling facilities you use. If you need to back out or reschedule a task, don't just blindly go down the same path; execute with a delay or out-of-order to prevent future deadlocks.

- Don't mix and and match locking mechanisms. If two applications are locking the same pieces of data in different orders, or using different granularities of locks, eventually they're going to deadlock and get stuck in a deadly embrace, where each one waits for the other.

Most of these issues won't affect system administrator- or architect-level work; we include them to be sure that you know the warning signs of a variety of failures and common courses of corrective action.

Developer Hygiene

In a USENIX keynote address a few years ago, John Perry Barlow remarked that the early American West was inhabited by adventuresome, aggressive men with poor hygiene—a situation that resembled the frontier of the Internet at the time. We're not going to make disparaging remarks about anyone's personal grooming. We want to concentrate instead on the adventuresome and aggressive parts, and how to balance the "need for speed" in Internet time with the good grooming required to ensure that your network applications run reliably.

No matter how much diligence the system administration staff and operations design architects apply to a problem, you still run the risk of a poorly written application reducing availability. This section is not meant as an exhaustive list of "how to" techniques for application development, code quality standards, and secure applications. Instead, use this as a checklist of minimum functionality required to eliminate the most common mistakes at the application level.

Return Value Checks

Programmers tend to pick system calls out of manuals and programming examples to accomplish a specific function without concern for how that function might fail or otherwise impact the application. The best example is the behavior of the Unix `write()` system call. Delivering acceptable write performance to a filesystem requires that the write operations be done asynchronously; that is, the `write()` system call returns as soon as the operating system has copied the data into a memory buffer and scheduled the disk write, possibly for some future time. Asynchronous writes are one of the things that makes filesystem checking so laborious, because information about the file (like its last update time and size) are modified at the time of the `write()` system call, but the data blocks aren't updated until the write operation percolates to the top of the I/O queue.

What happens if there's a problem finishing a write operation? Let's say a disk has a media error. There's no way to tell the application about the exact write operation, because the system call that schedules it has come and gone. Instead, the operating system returns an error with the next `write()` call, even if that succeeds. As a result, the application cannot tell precisely which write operation failed, and if the application developer doesn't arduously check the return value from `write()`, the failure may be missed entirely. When a file is closed with outstanding write operations, the `close()` system call waits for the writes to complete and reports any errors back to the application. Errors from any outstanding write are compressed into the single return value, even if multiple, different errors occurred. Here's an example involving a network client and a remote `write()` operation: If an NFS client writes to a filesystem and exceeds a hard or soft quota, the write on the remote end may be aborted. The client won't know about the quota problem until the write hits the server; the server can only report the issue in a subsequent `write()` call. Applications that continue to stream data to the server even after a reported failure essentially dump that data down the bit bucket, since enforcing quotas on the server suppresses new writes to a user's home directory. Net result: a hole in a file, or at least some incomplete filesystem data.

What are the issues? First, always check the error return value on a system call, even a "trivial" one like `close()` that can "never fail." (Yes, closing a file can return an error if there was an I/O problem not reported back to the application previously.) Next, I/O errors reported back through the `write()` system call do not necessarily correspond to the operation scheduled by that call. Whenever there's an error on an asynchronous call, whether it's `write()` to the filesystem or an explicit asynchronous I/O thread, you need to back up in the output file and determine exactly where the error occurred. Finally, failure to heed error return values can lead to data corruption or application failure. When a `write()` operation fails, it can leave a "hole" in a file, since successive completed writes will move the file pointer ahead and fill in data beyond where the failed operation should have done its work. When the file is read at a later time, the hole is returned as a block of zeros, which is likely to cause problems for the reading application expecting something else, or for an application that was attempting to use the block as part of its text segment.

System calls have a well-defined interface to an application, and therefore have a nice way of handing errors back to the calling process. Life is a bit more complicated for problems that arise in the normal flow of control of an application. In addition to aggressive checking of error values from system calls, developers need to perform regular checking of bounds and input values.

Boundary Condition Checks

Remember the Internet worm incident of 1988? The Morris worm used a buffer overflow problem to inject its code into a running process; many of the Unix security holes discovered since have also utilized a buffer overflow or improper input checking as a vector. Boundary condition checks, where you test the assumptions of a developer against the randomness of the real world, are an important reliability feature because they prevent spurious crashes, wrong answers, or security holes. Checking input values against constraints is another cost/benefit trade-off; if you run every value through a sieve of checks you'll burn a nontrivial amount of CPU and user time. If you worry about the index into an array exceeding the dimensions of the data structure, you can have the developers trace back the code to where the index is calculated, and determine what inputs affect the index value, or you can insist on periodic bounds checking.

In general, you want to question odd results or outcomes that are dependent on seemingly unrelated events such as link order or inserting of debugging statements. Here are some guidelines for making your life easier in terms of instituting and testing boundary condition checks:

- Utilize testing and development tools that look for boundary condition exceptions, memory leaks, and other internal structure problems. Most vendors' in-house compiler suites include this functionality today, and it's available from third parties like Rational/Pure Atria.

- When there's an input, make sure you span the entire dynamic range expected, and then cover all of the unexpected values. A FORTRAN application expecting a positive integer value may try to digest a negative number that shows up in the input file; the developers will be quick to point out that no rational person would use a negative number for something as obvious as, say, the number of iterations of a simulation. But connect applications together in a script, mix in some 32- and 64-bit type casts that may sign-extend values, and fairly soon you're passing the wrong input value to a long-running application. Test the unexpected.

- Watch out for testing results that vary each time you relink or rebuild the application. In particular, if an application works well when statically linked but fails when dynamic linking is used, you're looking at a buffer overflow or boundary problem. The different linking techniques rearrange data structures such that in one case, the error damages something critical, and in the other, it merely steps on memory in a nonfatal way. Both applications will fail, at some point.

- Use a programming language, such as Java, that hides memory allocation and size matching problems from the developers. Java applications don't suffer from random results due to buffer overflow or index values out of bounds because these structures are handled dynamically.

EXPECT THE UNEXPECTED

Opening slide from a USENIX talk: `/* not reached */` **is the surest way to be sure that piece of code will be executed. If there's a code path that can only be reached through the right combination of bizarre inputs, corner cases, and ill-advised user actions, it will happen. Test this combination, and see how the application behaves; at the least make sure it complains nicely and produces diagnostics.**

—Hal

Boundary checking from a technical perspective requires that you understand how an application will handle or mishandle the entire range of inputs and index values. There is also a business aspect to boundary checking—is the application doing something that makes sense? The second aspect of boundary condition checking is to add these business-rule-driven checks, sometimes called *value-based security checks*.

Value-Based Security

Assume you have an inventory application that lets you move from 1 to 1000 widgets at a time between warehouses. The lower bound is simple logic; the upper bound is set by the size of a truck or the number of widgets in a packing crate. What if a user requests a transfer of 547 widgets, but only 13 remain in the source warehouse? The request is perfectly well-formed, but it doesn't make sense in the business context. As an application developer, you have no insight into these business rules; as someone charged with improving reliability and predictability, you need to capture these rules and cast them as simple boundary condition checks that can be added to the application.

THE $300,000 LETTER

Several years ago, a Wall Street trading firm received some negative press for processing a perfectly valid trade for the wrong security. A trader had written a ticket for several thousand shares of NYNEX, ticker symbol NYN, but, probably due to sloppy handwriting, it was read as symbol NVN during trade entry. NVN was another valid symbol, only instead of a high-volume, well-known utility stock, it was a small bond fund that traded only a few hundred shares a day. The resulting sell order for NVN sent the stock into a downward spiral, until someone noticed that the order size and average volume simply didn't make sense. The firm found the error, corrected it by buying back the NVN and properly selling the NYN, but not until a number of holders of NVN had the color drain from their faces. How do you fix something like this? Checking the size on a ticket versus the average volume is a start—and is now standard practice for trading floors. Wall Street adopts the exceptions and corner cases as standard practice quickly to prevent the same mistake from being made twice.

—Hal

Typical business rules that need to be included in application logic include checks for quantity desired versus quantity on hand, or average size versus requested size; time and sequence problems; and dollar amount or value of a transaction versus the permitted or valid amount for that user. Some of the more complex uses of value-based security entail adding authentication checks for certain transaction types, such that first-level employees cannot move millions of dollars, or employees below VP level cannot adjust salaries more than 15 percent without additional authorization. Typically, value-based security can be enforced by a database, using stored procedures or triggers to run additional checks on the records about to be inserted or modified, but it can also be done at the application logic level.

Logging Support

If you assume that you're going to have problems with applications at some point, you'll be well-served by insisting that applications log messages when practical. As with nearly all other topics in this chapter, it's a balance between logging everything and computing nothing; logging is overhead and consumes disk space. If you chose to write out a 500-byte log message for every transaction, you'll be logging 50 Kbytes/second at 100 transactions a second. Let that application run for a few days and you've filled up a filesystem. In general, log all fatal or near-fatal but recoverable problems; log anything that might help with performance modeling or prediction; generate period logs of response time and load metrics; and log anything unusual, such as input that comes close to a boundary condition.

How do you add logging support? Writing to a log file is the most obvious approach, although some applications use a centralized logging facility like syslog in the Unix operating system. Here are some practical concerns for logging activities and log entry formats:

- Logs are almost always read by people, so make them easy to parse by carbon-, not silicon-based, readers. Not everyone reading the log will know that "mkttfxcp" is the "make trade ticket FIX-compatible" step, so take the time to spell out exactly what happened, where, and why.

- Sequences of events help determine why a failure occurred; timestamps that are coordinated across all log entries help tremendously. Make sure that you're using a common time base (see the discussion of ntp in Chapter 13) and include a timestamp in every log entry. It's going to be hard to diagnose problems at the millisecond level via logs, so you can stick to minutes and seconds in the timestamps.

- Nobody can digest megabytes of logs, even with significant doses of caffeine. Keep the logs short, using circular log buffers or trimming the logs frequently. The exception is logs that may be used for tracking security incidents; if you're going to go back through the logs looking for patterns, you'll want to keep them accessible and complete.

- Logs should be located where the operations staff can find them, but not in a public place so that nonprivileged users can glean information from them. The /var/log directory is an ideal place on a Unix system, because it is persistent across reboots and expected to contain files that grow over time. Don't use temporary directories, because your logs may vanish after the mysterious reboot you're trying to explore. Don't use filesystems limited in space, or those that are already under high load, because logging will fill up the disk and add to its write load.

- Think of logging as primitive engineering journalism: who, what, why, when, how did something fail, or why was the log entry made? If there's a reference point back in the code such as a routine name, or a trail (routine XYZ called by routine ABC), leave those clues for the folks who will read the log entries later on.

Assume Nothing, Manage Everything

Sounds like being a parent of a toddler.

No matter how well-designed something is, and despite all of the effort put into testing, verification, and logging, something is going to break. You may get hit with something subtle, like a filesystem filling up such that your database can no longer log transactions, or you start dropping incoming mail. Perhaps most vexing is the universe of user inputs, which range from the bizarre and unexpected to the truly random, usually when a user's mouse wanders and changes window input focus on your application. If you weren't expecting a 22-character string of the letter "d" as input, and your application crashes, or worse yet takes down a server-side application, you'll learn to expand your input testing to cover the completely irrational but possible cases. When you take no assumptions for granted; when everything is suspect; and when you itemize, prioritize, and then test your risk tolerances, you're ready for production. Or so you assume.

Beware of "quick hacks" meant as stopgap measures. They tend to live on and have other applications piled on top of them. Unless the quick hack really is an overnight or hour-long fix to buy time to get the real solution in place, you'll find enough application weight heaped on your quick fix to compress it into something resembling architectural rock. Once in place, the fixes don't come out. Remember that COBOL programmers thought of 2-digit years as a necessary hack to get around short-term memory constraints; few thought such techniques or assumptions would still be in place two or three decades later. Your quick and dirty fix is the next person's millennium bug.

Baking in the reliability aspects at design time isn't sufficient for smooth, predictable operations. You'll also need management, operations, and backup support to ensure that you handle all failures as predicted, repair outages within your expected time windows, and bring the world back to a state of serenity. The remaining chapters deal with the operational aspect: eating your own reliability cooking.

▶Key Points

- Applications need to be tolerant of data service failures. NFS and database servers crash and recover, and your applications should be ready and waiting for the service to resume.

- External system conditions and intermittent network outages affect application reliability. Understand them and deal with them.

- Developers share the responsibility for application correctness. They need to test return values, institute boundary condition checking and business-rule conditions, and accept the entire range of possible but unexpected input streams.

Backups and Restores

Never underestimate the bandwidth of a station wagon
full of tapes hurtling down the highway.
—Andrew Tannenbaum

In this chapter, we will look at backups, one of the greatest nuisance tasks in system administration. We will also address the flip side of the problem, restores, one of the most critical tasks to maintaining system availability. The two are intricately entwined, in that the more time and effort you assign to one, the less time and effort you need to assign to the other.

The Basic Rules for Backups

In many ways, backups are the heart of any design of critical systems. Handled properly, they represent the last line of defense against just about any catastrophe. Even if your building or your entire city is wiped out, your business can be restored on other computers from properly generated and stored backup tapes. But there are several "if" conditions you have to satisfy for everything to work out properly.

There are a number of backup guidelines. By keeping them in mind as you design your backup environment, you will make the best advantage of your backups, and they will serve you best when you need them:

Mirroring does not replace backups. This hard fact runs counter to a very old and unfortunate myth. Mirroring protects against the failure of storage hardware, but it does nothing at all to protect you from a deleted file. If a file is deleted (or corrupted) on one side of a mirror, it is gone from both sides, and therefore must be retrieved through some external means. The most common (but by no means the only) external means of recovery is the restore of a backup tape.

The most common use of restores isn't after a catastrophe. Yes, of course catastrophes do happen, but it is much more likely that a user will accidentally delete or dramage a single file, or even a directory, than it is for the contents of both sides of a mirror, or two disks in a RAID stripe, to fail at the same time. So, design your backups to shorten restore times for a single file.

Regularly test your ability to restore. Backups are wonderful, but if you cannot read their contents, you have wasted a lot of time and effort creating useless tapes. You shouldn't need to test every backup tape that you create, but certainly every tape drive should be tested regularly to ensure that the backups it makes are readable, and a random sampling of tapes should be tested to ensure that they can be read, and restored properly.

Keep those tape heads clean. Dirty tape heads may cause writes to appear to complete successfully when, in fact, they have only written garbage to the tape. Clean the tape heads as often as the manufacturer recommends, if not slightly more often. If your backup utility reports tape read and/or write errors, clean the heads immediately. If errors continue, see if they are present on other tapes, and if they are, then contact the vendor.

Beware of dirty tapes. No, not adult videos, but rather the tapes themselves. Sometimes a single bad spot—a crease, a fold, or a smudge of dirt—on a tape can prevent the entire tape from being read. Store the tapes in their cases in relatively clean rooms, and test them from time to time.

Pay attention to MTBF numbers for tapes. If the manufacturer suggests that a tape's useful life is 1000 backups, then use it 1000 times, and get rid of it. The time to find out that a tape has gone bad is NOT during a restore. Good backup management software will keep track of tape access counts for you, and tell you when it's time to dispose of a tape.

Tapes decompose over time. Do not assume that the tape you made five or six years ago is still be readable today. Tapes break down; they may get exposed to weak magnetic fields that affect their quality; or they may simply age badly. It is very difficult for manufacturers who are introducing new tape formats to accurately determine the shelf life of such a tape. If they were to perform definitive tests, introduction of such tapes could be delayed for several years. Test your tapes on a regular basis, and copy them to new media from time to time.

Make two copies of critical tapes. Tapes are much less expensive to purchase and maintain than is recreating the data that is on the tapes. To better ensure the longevity and safety of your tapes and data, it is often wise to store one copy of your tapes off-site.

DRUM ROLL, PLEASE

A museum in California was producing an exhibit showing the development of a particular chunk of land over a period of several decades. The exhibit curators asked NASA and three-letter government agency contacts for satellite photos of the area, and were thrilled when told they could have the actual data in its original form. What arrived, much to the museum's chagrin, was a set of data drums: decades-old rotating storage without a device to mount or read it. The bits of data representing bits of land might have been a stellar addition, but without the ability to make sense of it the data was effectively lost. Beware of the longevity of the media format as well as the media's magnetic properties.

—Hal

Backup Software

Many of the same guidelines that we discussed in the section on failover management software apply equally to the selection of backup software. The key design principles come into play as well.

Commercial or Homegrown?

The issues that lead many users to consider homegrown failover management software lead many to consider homegrown backup utilities, too, particularly in Unix shops. (Windows systems are bundled with fairly intelligent backup solutions, so homegrown solutions in that space are usually a nonissue.) Homegrown backup solutions are almost always wrappers around standard OS backup tools like `dump` or `tar`, and as such exhibit the shortcomings of those tools. For instance, many versions of the Unix `tar` utility cannot handle long filenames, or backups that span more than one tape, especially if they don't start at the beginning of a tape.

HOMEGROWN BACKUP SOFTWARE

A few years ago, I was called on to write a backup utility for a development group, to whom I was consulting as a system administrator. (In the end it turned out to be a roughly 500 line Perl program.) Maintaining the program, not to mention the backups themselves, wound up taking an inordinate amount of my time because the requirements for the backups were constantly changing. (The initial request was "write a backup program for the developers.") What's more, I never got around to adding the fairly complex code that would have enabled my program to handle backups that spanned more than one tape. Fortunately for me (though perhaps not for my customer), I left that consulting assignment shortly before the backups outgrew a single tape.

My program also made no allowances for backing up open files. This came back to bite us all very badly, as the development group used a development environment product that required precise consistency across hundreds of tiny files throughout the filesystem. When the filesystem needed to be completely restored from tape, the backups did not contain a consistent view of the filesystem, and so the development environment could not be restored. The developers were down for a week.

And there were other problems. Some nights the backup would complete in 3 or 4 hours, while other nights it would continue from 8:00 P.M. until 10 or 11 the next morning. When that happened, we had no choice but to abort the backups, as they put such a load on the server that performance became unacceptable. On those nights, backups simply failed. We never did find out why. Admittedly, I did not have that much experience with backups at the time I did this work, but most likely, the system administrator being asked to develop a homegrown backup system at your site hasn't very much more.

—Evan

Poor and inconsistent performance are just two issues that mature commercial backup solutions have run up against and solved over the years. A homegrown solution is unlikely to have solved very many at all, leaving its users to settle for a second-rate product. In the sections that follow, you will see more cases where a homegrown backup solution will not suffice.

Examples of Commercial Backup Software

The backup and restore arena is filled with commercial products. Some of the leaders, and some of the operating systems they will back up, are:

- *VERITAS NetBackup.* Solaris, Windows 95, 98, NT, HP/UX, AIX, SGI, Novell Netware, NDMP, OS/2, Compaq Tru64

- *Legato Networker.* Solaris, NT, HP/UX, AIX, SGI, Novell Netware, OS/2

- *Tivoli TSM (formerly IBM ADSM).* AIX, Solaris, NT, HP/UX, AS/400, OS/2, MVS, VM

- *Computer Associates ARCserve (formerly Cheyenne).* NT, Novell Netware, Windows 95, 98, some Unix

There are many other entrants in the field, including Budtool (now a Legato product), Backup Exec (now a VERITAS product), SyncSort, and others.

Commercial Backup Software Features

What follows is a list of some features that are valuable when evaluating a backup product. This is by no means a complete list, and different users will surely assign different values to some of these features. Your mileage may vary:

100 percent hardware utilization. We spend quite a bit of time in this chapter discussing the best way to lay out your hardware to achieve the backup performance that you need. All that is for naught if your backup software cannot drive your hardware at its maximum speeds. Tape drives are designed to spin as much as possible, and will last longer and deliver better performance when they do.

Hot backups. You should be able to back up filesystems and databases, as described above, without having to take them off-line, and without an obvious performance impact to your applications.

Open tape format. In an emergency, you should be able to read and restore tapes without needing specialized software or license keys. The delay in obtaining software and keys will increase your MTTR in a crisis.

Speed. Benchmark backup and restore performance in your environment. Even if backup performance isn't critical today, you can safely assume it will be tomorrow.

Centralized management. It should be easy to administer your entire backup environment from a single console, if that is the configuration you select. If you prefer a few administrative consoles, that should be available to you.

Reliability. There should be no single point of failure in your backup environment. If a tape server or a controlling server fails, its functions should be picked up by another server on the network.

Quick disaster recovery. Some backup products require the rebuilding of their tape databases or catalogs before a postdisaster recovery can begin. If rebuilding indices requires prereading every tape in the library, it could add days to your recovery times. Make sure you understand the entire process for initiating a recovery from a major outage on new systems.

Hardware support and flexibility. When implementing a new wide-scale backup project, it is unlikely that you will have the luxury of purchasing all new tape hardware. Any backup solution you choose to implement should support as much of your existing backup hardware as possible.

Multiple platform support. You should not need to buy one backup solution for your NT boxes, and another for your Solaris boxes, and a third for your Novell servers. One backup product should suffice across all your major platforms.

Mature products with reference sites. Just as we have discussed with the other commercial products, always select your products with an eye toward mature products, with a proven record of successful implementations, and reference sites.

Efficient use of hardware. Most likely, you have a lot of backup hardware. Tape drives, tape libraries, dedicated backup networks, and tapes themselves are only a few of the expensive assets required to take and maintain backups. Surely the people who sign your purchase orders would prefer that you make full use of the hardware you have before you invest additional money on hardware that you may not actually need. Good backup software will drive your hardware at its maximum capacity, and will scale well as new hardware is added.

Media management. Although media management seems like an obvious feature, many vendors do not include such capabilities with their software. Media management includes features like tape labeling, bar code management, a database of tape locations, management of off-site media as well as on-site, robotic controls, and sharing.

A REAL DISASTER

When the World Trade Center terrorist bomb went off in 1993, many system administrators who worked in the building found themselves with nothing more than a bag of backup tapes from which to rebuild their business. Some backup vendors took several days before they were able to provide their customers with license keys that would enable them to begin the restore process. There was nothing those SAs could do except to wait for the keys to be delivered.

—Evan

Backup Performance

In order to get the best possible performance out of your backup software, you need to get the best possible performance out of all of your backup hardware. As you consider the issues presented in this section, we offer a simple rule of thumb: "Backups are only as fast as the slowest link in the chain." To that end, let's take a look at the speed at which backup (or any kind of) data can traverse your networks to your media or tape servers (Table 12.1):

We also need to examine the speed with which data can make it from a system (whether it has come across a network or from local disks) to a locally attached tape drive. There are two components to this: the speed with which the tape drive can write (Table 12.2), and the speed at which data can be sent to the tape drive, across a SCSI or Fibrechannel connection (Table 12.3):

Properly tuned and configured backups are really just an exercise in moving data. The process is very much analogous to moving water through pipes. You have to move a certain amount of water, but you are limited by the capacity of the pipes. If you want to move more water faster, you need fatter pipes or more pipes, or you need to make better use of the pipes you already have (get the hair out of the drain!). You can put a 12MB/second AIT drive on a system, but if the backup data only arrives on a 10 Base-T network, then your drive will only be able to write data at about 750 kilobytes per second (or roughly 6 percent of the drive's capacity), because that's how fast the data arrives.

Improving Backup Performance: Find the Bottleneck

Let's say that you have to back up 60GB of data located on five systems, as shown in Figure 12.1. There is 40GB on one system, and 5GB each on the

Table 12.1 Realistic Network Throughputs

NETWORK MEDIUM	THEORETICAL MEGABITS/ SEC	THEORETICAL MEGABYTES/ SEC	THEORETICAL MEGABYTES/ HOUR	REALISTIC UTILIZA- TION	REALISTIC MEGABYTES/ SEC	REALISTIC GIGABYTES/ HOUR
10 Base-T Ethernet	10	1.25	4500	60%	0.75	2.7
Token Ring	16	2	7200	60%	1.2	4.32
100 Base-T Ethernet	100	12.5	45,000	60%	7.5	27
FDDI	100	12.5	45,000	70%	8.75	31.5
Gigabit Ethernet	1000	125	450,000	60%	75	270

Table 12.2 Capacity and Performance of Selected Tape Drives

TAPE DRIVE	TAPE CAPACITY IN GIGABYTES (COMPRESSED)	WRITE PERFORMANCE PER SECOND (COMPRESSED) IN MEGABYTES/ SECOND	WRITE PERFORMANCE PER HOUR (COMPRESSED) IN GIGABYTES
DLT 2000	10 (20)	1.25 (2.5)	4.5 (9)
DLT 4000	20 (40)	1.5 (3.0)	5.4 (10.8)
DLT 7000	35 (70)	5 (10)	18 (36)
4-mm tape	4	0.733	2.64
8-mm tape	14	1	3.6
StorageTek 9840	20 (80)	8 (20)	28.8 (72)
AIT	50 (100)	6 (12)	21.6 (43.2)

remaining four. The systems are networked to a dedicated backup server, with no data of its own via a 10 megabit per second (10 Base-T) Ethernet link. The backup server has a single SCSI DLT 7000 tape drive on it, which can write compressed data at 10 megabytes per second. (Some data cannot be compressed as well as others, and so the 10MB/second is an estimate. Some sites report bursts of up to 12 or 13MB/second, while others see no more than 7 or 8.) The trick here is to find the bottleneck. Regardless of how fast your tape drive can write, it will only be fed data at 750 kilobytes per second, and that assumes that your data is the only data flowing on the network cable; in real life, your throughput will probably be less. Sixty GB at 750kb/second will take roughly 80,000 seconds, which is over 22 hours. And that assumes maximum efficiency from every

Table 12.3 Performance of Selected Local Data Buses

CONNECTION TYPE	SPEED
Narrow SCSI	10MB/second (36 GB/hr)
Wide SCSI	20MB/second (72 GB/hr)
Ultra SCSI	40MB/second (144 GB/hr)
Fibrechannel	100MB/second (360 GB/hr)

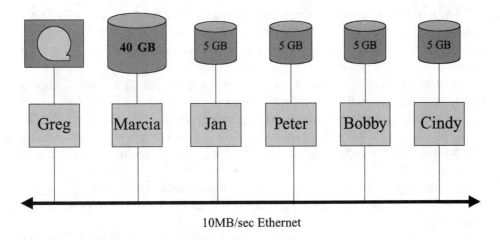

Figure 12.1 Basic networked backup configuration.

other element in the backup chain. In this example, the bottleneck is very much the network.

If we magically change the network to 100 Base-T (Figure 12.2), then backup times are cut by an order of magnitude to about 8000 seconds, or about 2 hours and 10 minutes. But since 100 Base-T can only send data at about 7.5MB/second and the tape drive can handle data at about 10MB/second, the network is still your bottleneck.

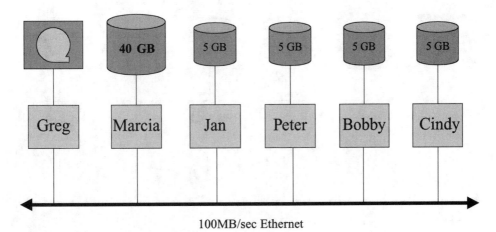

Figure 12.2 Backup with 100MB/second network.

What if we move our tape drive from the dedicated backup server ("Greg") and attach it directly to the 40GB server through a nice ultrawide SCSI interface that can pass data at 40 megabytes per second? We have eliminated Greg from the picture; Marcia is now our media server. (See Figure 12.3.)

Now the 40GB from server B will go to directly to the tape without hitting your network, and will do so at tape drive speed. Forty GB at 10MB/second will take 4000 seconds, or about an hour and 5 minutes. The remaining 20GB from the clients must still flow over the 100 Base-T network at 7.5MB/second, and so will take an additional 45 minutes, for a total of about an hour and 50 minutes.

The other advantage to putting the tape drive directly on the server is that the 40GB of backup data no longer goes across your LAN, leaving bandwidth for other applications.

To increase our network performance so that it approaches the performance of our tape drives, we can introduce a switched network (Figure 12.4). In a switched network, a private 100 megabit/second "tunnel" is opened between two of the network cards on the network. If we put four network cards in our main server, and connect them all to a 100 Base-T switched network hub, then each client can send data to the server at 7.5MB/second at the same time, for a theoretical total of 30MB/second reaching the server at the same time. Twenty GB at 30MB/second takes about 11 minutes. However, since our tape drive can only write at 10MB/second, our bottleneck has moved from the network to the tape drive. Assuming that we can throttle back our network usage, or limit the

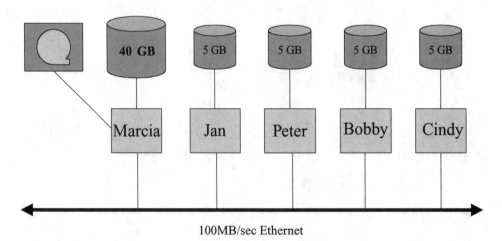

100MB/sec Ethernet

Figure 12.3   Backup with the tape drive on the main server.

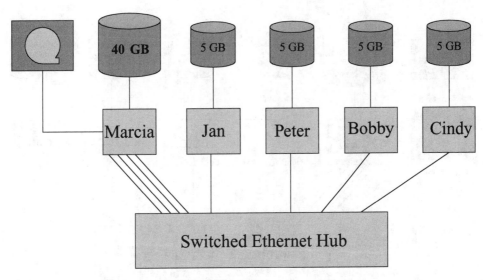

Figure 12.4 Backups over a switched Ethernet.

amount of data being sent over our networks to maximize the utilization of our single tape drive, we can write our 20GB of client data in 2000 seconds, or 33½ minutes.

We can cut still more time off of the backup by adding a second tape drive (Figure 12.5). Since the Ultra SCSI bus can handle 40MB/second (and Wide SCSI can write at 20MB/second), and our one tape drive only uses 10MB/second, we can add a second tape drive to the SCSI bus and effectively double our write performance. Used properly, our local backups are down to just 34 minutes. With our switched network still in place, the clients will back up their 20GB at 20MB/second, or 1000 seconds, which is a little less than 17 minutes. Adding the second tape drive cuts the total backup time to just 51 minutes. The bottleneck for our clients is still the tape drives, not the network.

Adding a third tape drive to the server, which would require a second Wide SCSI adapter card, but not another Ultra SCSI card (due to Ultra's additional capacity), reduces the time for the local backups to just 22 minutes. Our clients will send their data at the same 30MB/second that the tape drives can write, so backing up that additional 20GB will take another 11 minutes, giving us a total of 33 minutes for the entire backup.

In these examples we have shown that you could back up 60GB of data spread across five machines in times ranging from 22 hours down to a little over half an hour. It's all in the hardware. More tape drives, more SCSI buses,

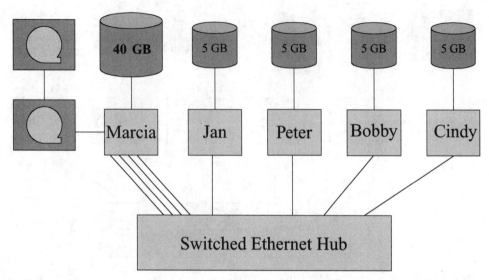

Figure 12.5 Backup over switched Ethernet with a second tape drive.

and faster and more efficient networks will yield faster and faster backup times.

Again, all of these idealized numbers are based on a fundamental assumption that all the other elements in the backup chain (networks, memory, CPU, disks, and tape drives) are used as efficiently as possible, and that your backup software uses the hardware that it's been given as efficiently as possible. Your mileage will surely vary.

The other assumption we are making is that you are backing up all of your data every time. For most environments, that is unrealistic. Backup times can be cut drastically further by reducing the amount of data that is backed up each time. (See "Backup Styles," later in this chapter.) The trick is to reduce the amount of backed-up data without compromising system reliability or lengthening beyond an acceptable level the amount of time it takes to recover lost data.

Solving for Performance

Most often, you will be given a set of systems with a particular amount of data on it, and a backup window, during which you must complete a full backup. Let's say you maintain a network, as in Figure 12.6, with one server, *elephant,*

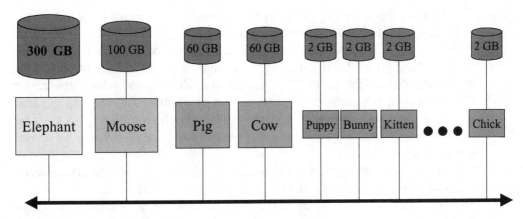

Figure 12.6 The backup problem.

that has 300GB on it; a second, *moose*, with 100GB; two more, *cow* and *pig*, with 60GB each, and 10 clients with 2GB each on them. And you've been given a window of just six hours to complete your backups.

Due to the wide acceptance of DLT-7000 tape drives, we are going to stick with them, and with 20MB/second SCSI buses. We will also assume that our network consists of switched 100 Base-T. The exercise would be similar if different hardware were employed. We will also assume that you get the full level of compression that the manufacturers claim. Your mileage will vary, based on the kind of data you are storing, your hardware, your backup software, and nearly everything else in the configuration.

The first thing we must do is to figure out how much data we're backing up:

$$300 + 100 + (2 \times 60) + (10 \times 2) = 540\text{GB}.$$

In order to back up 540GB in six hours, we must achieve a backup rate of 90GB/hour.

Our solution will include a deployment of local tape drives, as well as backups across the network. We will make no assumptions about network traffic outside of backups. Many users approach this style of solution through the use of dedicated backup networks, although many users do not have this luxury. If your backups will go across the same networks as your regular networked data, be sure to take that into account.

Another important timing issue to take into account is tape changing. We are not going to count tape changing times in our calculations. The most efficient way to change tapes is to use an automatic tape changer, usually a library or a stacker.

To limit network traffic, and to speed up backups as much as possible, we will put tape drives onto *elephant*. In order to back up 300GB of data in no more than six hours, we must install two local tape drives. At 10 megabytes/second, one tape drive would take 500 minutes, or about 8 hours and 20 minutes. Two drives would cut that in half, to 4 hours and 10 minutes, which meets our backup window requirement. Remember that *elephant*'s 300GB of data requires five tapes (four for the first 280GB, plus a fifth for the leftovers). We must be sure that whatever method we use to change tapes does not cause us to run past our backup window.

On *moose*, a single tape drive can back up the 100GB in a little less than three hours onto two tapes, easily meeting our backup window.

Solutions for *cow* and *pig* are not as clear-cut. If we choose to put a local tape drive on each of them, they can each complete their backups in an hour and 40 minutes. If we put a tape drive only on *cow*, and back up *pig*'s data across the network, then *cow*'s backup would still take 1 hour 40 minutes, but *pig* would take 2 hours and 20 minutes. Both backups would complete in an even four hours, and require two tapes.

There are other options for *cow* and *pig*. *Moose* still has three hours of unused backup window, and so we could network *pig*'s backup there, still leaving about 40 minutes within the backup window. Assuming that we want to make the best use of our hardware, that would be the most efficient solution. *Cow* would still need a local tape drive.

We still have our 10 2GB clients that need to be backed up. The 20GB of client data could be completed in 35 minutes. The clients could all be backed up to the tape drives on *elephant*, where we still have almost two hours of backup window still available.

So, the configuration requires four tape drives, two on *elephant*, one on *moose*, and one on *cow*. Of course, the tape drive on *cow* is very underused. You might choose to leave it underused, keeping it free for growth, or for restores that may be required during the backup window. Or you might choose to back up cow's data across the network to moose, and overrun your backup window by a small amount. The difference is the cost of that tape drive and SCSI bus. Or, you might choose to put the extra tape drive onto *elephant*, adding flexibility to *elephant*'s configuration, and leave it underused over there instead. Our preference is the last choice. Put the extra drive onto *elephant*, back up cow to elephant over the network, and give yourself a little extra capacity for growth. Remember, putting the third tape drive on *elephant* will require an additional SCSI card.

The completed configuration is shown in Figure 12.7. A summary of the configuration is in Table 12.4.

We were able to complete this design by using just four DLT-7000 drives, and we have capacity to spare. As we discussed, it could have been done with three

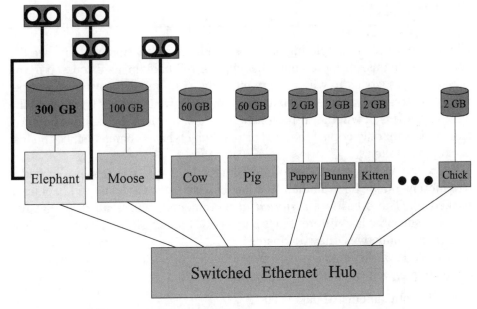

Figure 12.7   Solution to the backup problem.

DLT-7000s, but that would have left no room for growth and would have been an extremely tight fit. Since three drives would have a combined throughput of about 108MB/hour, all three drives would have to be operating for almost the entire backup window to complete the backups in the allotted time. Adding the fourth allows for additional growth and for tape changing, and makes it much easier to fit the backups in the window, especially if a tape drive failure or other problem interrupts the normal process.

Table 12.4   Summary of Backup Solution

HOST	AMOUNT OF DATA	SENT TO WHICH HOST AND DRIVE?	DURATION OF BACKUP
Elephant	300GB	2 local DLT-7000s	4 hrs, 10 mins
Moose	100GB	1 local DLT-7000	2 hours, 45 mins
Cow	60GB	3rd DLT-7000 on *elephant*	2 hours, 20 mins
Pig	60GB	DLT-7000 on *moose*	2 hours, 20 mins
Ten 2GB clients	20GB	DLT-7000s on *elephant*	50 minutes

Backup Styles

When we discussed completing backups within a narrow time window, we did not discuss the use of incremental backups. A full backup, as discussed in the last section, is a backup where every bit of data on the disks is copied to tape. Though extremely reliable, full backups can be slow since they back up all the data, regardless of whether it has changed since the last full backup. An incremental backup only copies the files or data which have changed since the last backup was taken.

There are, in fact, two kinds of incremental backups. The first is a *cumulative* incremental, where all data that has changed since the last full backup is backed up. The other is a *differential* incremental, where all data that has changed since the last differential is backed up. Since differentials back up less data than cumulatives, they run faster.

In Table 12.5, we compare three differing backup styles. For the purposes of our example, we made a few assumptions:

- The total amount of data is 60GB.
- Of the 60GB, 5GB changes each day.
- Each day the amount of data to be backed up by the cumulative incremental grows by a smaller and smaller amount (since, for example, some of the same data that changed on Tuesday also changed on Wednesday).
- For simplicity's sake, we are not going to change the quantity of data being backed up.
- We can back up the data at 20GB an hour.

Table 12.5   Durations of Different Backup Styles

	SUNDAY	MONDAY	TUESDAY	WEDNESDAY	THURSDAY
Weekly fulls and daily differential incrementals	Full backup (60GB; 3 hours)	Changes since Sunday's full (5GB; 15 minutes)	Changes since Monday's incremental (5GB; 15 minutes)	Changes since Tuesday's incremental (5GB; 15 minutes)	Changes since Wednesday's incremental (5GB; 15 minutes)
Weekly fulls and daily cumulative incrementals	Full backup (60GB; 3 hours)	Changes since Sunday's full (5GB; 15 minutes)	Changes since Sunday's full (9GB; 27 minutes)	Changes since Sunday's full (12GB; 36 minutes)	Changes since Sunday's full (14GB; 42 minutes)
Daily fulls	Full backup (60GB; 3 hours)	Full backup (60GB; 3 hours)	Full backup (60GB; 3 hours)	Full backup (60GB; 3 hours)	Full backup (60GB; 3 hours)

The conclusion one can draw from Table 12.5 is that differential backups are faster.

There are other varieties of the incremental backup. One of those is found in the standard Unix utility called `dump` or `ufsdump`. Dump permits up to 10 levels of backups to be taken; a level 5 backup backs up everything since the last lower level (say level 3) backup was taken. In shops where `dump` is employed, a common strategy calls for a level 0 (the whole disk) backup to be taken once every few months, level 1's once a month, level 3's every week, and level 5's every night.

The need for so much flexibility in backup strategies is apparent when we examine the requirements that are introduced when we need to restore the data. (For simplicity in this example, we will assume that each backup fits on a single tape, and is the only backup on that tape. In reality, neither of these assumptions will likely hold.)

Again, for the examples in Table 12.6 to work, we need to make some assumptions:

- Restores run at 15GB/hour. (Filesystem restores almost always run slower than backups, because the filesystem must place the data on the disk, and create a map to retrieve it again later.)

- It takes up to 2 minutes to unmount, remount, and position a new tape to begin restoring from it.

- The failure of our filesystem occurred on Friday, after Thursday's backups were completed.

Table 12.6   Durations of Restores

TYPE OF BACKUP	NUMBER OF TAPES TO READ FROM	OVERHEAD TO MOUNT AND UNMOUNT ALL THE TAPES	AMOUNT OF DATA TO RESTORE	TIME TO RESTORE THE DATA	TOTAL TIME REQUIRED
Weekly fulls and daily differential incrementals	5 (Sunday full, and incrementals from Monday through Thursday)	15 minutes	80GB	5 hours 20 minutes	5:35
Weekly fulls and daily cumulative incrementals	2 (Sunday full and Thursday incremental)	6 minutes	74GB	5 hours	5:06
Daily fulls	1 (Thursday's full)	3 minutes	60GB	4 hours	4:03

In a shop where full backups are taken every day, only one tape will need to be restored after a catastrophe. Restoring only one tape makes the process much simpler and much less labor intensive.

When fulls and cumulative incrementals are the rule, two tapes need to be restored—the full, and the most recent cumulative. This model is roughly twice as complex and labor intensive as the full backup method.

In the multilevel backup just described, three tapes are required to perform a complete restore—the level 1, the level 3, and the latest level 5.

To restore differential incremental backups, after the full backup tape is restored, all of the differential tapes must be mounted and restored, one-by-one.

TOO MANY TAPES

One user I know did a full backup on the 1st of the month, and differential incrementals every day after that. As Murphy's Law would have it, their disk crashed on the 30th of the month. To do the restore, they needed the 1 full and 29 incremental tapes. Since each incremental was on its own tape, in addition to taking time to actually read and restore the data, each tape had to be mounted individually (fortunately all the tapes were stored in a single tape library). It took roughly 3 minutes to unmount one tape, and mount and position the next. Multiply that by 30 tapes, and the restore already takes 90 minutes before a single byte has been restored. The users could have saved a lot of time by putting more than one differential on each tape. That admittedly can make the tape a single point of failure, so beware; but if MTTR is critical, time can be saved by minimizing the number of tapes that require mounting in a restore.

—Evan

When selecting the method that is best for you, you must strike a balance between the duration of your backups, which are probably a nightly event, and the duration and effort required during a complete restore. Complete restores may only be required once or twice a year. But the duration of the restore is your MTTR. As we have said so many times, you want to keep your MTTRs as low as possible, as some portion of your system is out of service until the effort is completed.

Incremental Backups of Databases

In general, incremental backups are limited to filesystems, although some backup vendors do have technology that will permit the incremental backing up of databases. Specifically, to do an incremental backup of a filesystem, the blocks that have changed must be backed up. Once they are backed up, pointers and indices must be maintained so that the blocks can be put back into the database upon restore.

Some solutions require a complete scan of the database for changed blocks. At least one solution (VERITAS NetBackup with the VERITAS File System; only available on Unix) keeps track of the blocks that have changed and does not need to do a full database scan in order to perform an incremental backup.

As with all incremental backups, in order to perform a full restore, the tapes from the full and all of the incrementals (or only the most recent cumulative incremental tape) are required.

Backup Windows

The bottom line on backup windows is that they are getting smaller and smaller, approaching zero. In many shops, they already are zero; backups cannot cause any service interruption at all. Fortunately, even tiny backup windows are no excuse to give backups short shrift.

In this section, we will look at some of the techniques for shortening the duration of the interruptions caused by taking backups. Some of these techniques reduce the amount of data being backed up; others require additional specialized hardware or software to get their job done. Some techniques are specific to one vendor or another, and others work only on databases, or only on filesystems.

Hot Backups

The ultimate in backup windows is one that causes no interruption whatsoever. This can be achieved on databases, and very nearly be achieved on filesystems.

The biggest problem in achieving hot backups is one of data consistency. Since it takes time for a backup to run and complete, files or data can change within the data store (filesystem or disks) being backed up. In order for a hot backup to be successful, there must be a mechanism inserted between the data store and the application that may be writing there.

Most good commercial backup utilities support online, or hot, backups of filesystems and databases. (Homegrown solutions generally do not.) To achieve reliable hot backups, the backup utility must interface, often at a very low level, with a utility specifically designed for the application or filesystem being backed up. For example, the Oracle database makes two different utilities available (depending on the version of Oracle you are running). The backup utility that writes data to tape (or other backup medium) must know how to speak with OEBU (Oracle Enterprise Backup Utility) or RMAN (Recovery Manager) and turn the data that those utilities provide into data that can be written to (and later read from) tape. MS-SQL, DB/2, Sybase, and Informix all have similar utilities to allow hot backups. In addition, some commercial backup products have their own agents that work with the published database APIs to enable hot backups without the need for utilities like RMAN or OEBU.

Normally, during a hot database backup, the database is put into a state where database writes are locked out of the actual database, and only written to a log. When the backup completes, the contents of the log are run as a batch job, and are added to the database. There are some performance implications with this method, because of the batched nature of the additions. There is also usually some overhead associated with logging the changes.

Hot database backups are very vendor-specific, and are an almost constantly changing technology. They are generally quite reliable, and so should definitely be considered when evaluating ways to shrink backup window requirements.

As for filesystem backups, there is a consistent problem across both Unix and NT filesystems. Filesystem backups are usually taken in two passes—a first pass which determines and backs up the file and directory layout, and a second pass which backs up the files and their contents. If a file changes between the two passes, inconsistent results can occur, but the most likely result is that the file will not be backed up properly. Another problem will occur if an application requires that two or more files are consistent. If they change during the backup, different versions may be backed up as the backup utility walks through the filesystem, resulting in inconsistent versions on the backup tape.

Filesystem backups vary by operating system. On NT, there is an issue with backing up open files. If an application has a file open, the file is locked. When locked, a file cannot be accessed by any other applications. Obviously, in order to back up a file, a backup utility must access the file. Most backup utilities attempt to lock the file during the period of the backup. If the utility cannot access (or lock) a particular file, it will time-out in its attempt to back up the file, and move on. When this occurs, the locked file will not get backed up at all.

There are at least two utilities for assisting in the backing up of open NT files: St. Bernard's Open File Manager, and Columbia Data Systems' Open Transaction Monitor. Some NT backup manufacturers integrate one of these products right into their software, while others deliver their own. These utilities operate in kernel mode, filtering I/O for calls to open or locked files. They keep a copy of the open file in cache memory, and present that copy to the backup software. In this way, this software guarantees that a consistent copy of the file gets backed up. The open file management software may also be able to cache the entire filesystem in memory (or on another disk) and present a consistent and unchanging copy of the filesystem to the backup utility.

On Unix, open files are not as much of an issue. A file that is written to disk can be backed up by reading it off the disk. If a file is open and being written to, then the disk copy of the file may not reflect its most recent contents, but your backup will get the most recent copy that is on the disk. Several products that do hot filesystem backup make multiple passes over the filesystem's inodes to be sure that file sizes and modification times have not changed during the course of the backup; if they have, the files that were being written to are dumped to tape again.

Of course, running backups while production is going on can have a discernable impact on overall system and network performance, so even if backups can be done online, we still want to keep them as brief as possible, which leads back to the earlier discussion of incremental versus full backups. There are other ways to shorten the duration of your backups, which are discussed next.

Have Less Data, Save More Time (and Space)

There are at least two ways to reduce the amount of data that gets backed up in a filesystem. Both involve removing older and less used data from the filesystem, and storing it someplace else.

Hierarchical Storage Management

A very interesting exercise for the system administrator in his or her spare time (ha ha) is to use OS utilities to generate an age report for all of the user files in the various home directories under his or her watch. Search for files that have not been accessed in each of two weeks, one month, three months, six months, and one year. Go back further if your systems have been around that long.

Consider this: Those files that haven't been touched in six months or more still take up valuable time, space, and bandwidth during your backups. Apart from simply deleting them, what can you do to recapture the resources that these files consume?

Welcome to the world of *Hierarchical Storage Management* (HSM). Hierarchical storage management is a grossly underused utility that provides a sort of automated archival system. An HSM process examines the most recent access date of the files in a filesystem, and based on rules set up and maintained by the system administrator, migrates the files to a less expensive, more permanent, and slower medium. This medium may be specially dedicated tapes, writeable CDs, magneto-optical disks, or some other not-quite-online storage medium. Left behind in the filesystem is a *stub file*, which is a special file that tells the HSM process to find the real file. Stub files are usually on the order of a couple of KB in size.

Once a file is migrated, a user need only access the old file in the usual manner, and the system will either locate and mount the appropriate tape, or place an operator request for a particular tape to be mounted. Once accessed, the file is returned to the local disk, and the clock on it starts again. While a file is migrated, it is no longer backed up; only its stub is. Obviously, the trade-off is that the first time a user needs to access a file, it may take several minutes, or longer, to retrieve the file from the off-line medium.

TUNING IN CHANNEL Z

There's a less-than-ideal way to test out the prospective benefits and user reactions to a hierarchical storage management system. Find large files that are more than six months old, and compress them in-place on the disk. You may reduce their size by anywhere from a factor of two to five times, and you haven't removed any data—only introduced a new access step for users who really need to get at the uncompressed original file. We tried this once without warning the user base, and results were good—few people noticed that their large, unloved files now had a ".Z" extension (due to the Unix `compress` utility's work), and the few engineers who found the files ran `uncompress` as needed. Of course, we had one employee who was complaining about all of "those stupid .Z files cluttering up [his] system," so of course he deleted all of them. Compression doesn't replace backups, but it sure can make them smaller and easier to handle.

—Hal

If properly implemented, apart from the delay in retrieving a file, HSM should be totally transparent to your users. A directory listing does not indicate that anything is unusual. The files appear to be present. Only when a user actually tries to access a file can any difference be detected.

If, like so many other systems, your user directories are littered with large files that have been untouched for months, and you need to shrink your backup windows and loads, HSM may be worth a look.

Archives

Archives are similar to, though somewhat less sophisticated than HSM. To archive a file, the file is written to tape (or some other off-line medium) and deleted from the filesystem completely. Some external mechanism must be employed to maintain the location of archived files. Otherwise, there is a very real risk that the file could get lost.

In some environments, users are allowed and even encouraged to maintain their own archive tapes. In others, the administrators maintain archives.

Use More Hardware

Vendors are developing new techniques and technologies, and exploiting old ones, to speed up backups through the use of additional hardware or clever software tricks. These techniques are of varying usefulness, depending on your environment. Some will surely work, while others could slow you down.

Off-Host Backups

The marketing hype for hostless backups (sometimes called *backdoor* or *direct* backups) says that they allow the backing up of data directly from disk to tape, without requiring an intervening CPU. In reality, the CPU doing the work is hidden, or is located off the host that actually holds the data. Today's technology does not yet support true hostless backups. In the future, enough intelligence will be placed inside the disk arrays to allow them to push their data directly out to a tape drive. However, the advantage that any hostless backup offers is that the backup can be performed without impacting the CPU or memory performance of the host holding the data.

If the backups are also performed over a dedicated backup network or a Storage Area Network (SAN), then little impact should be felt on production resources. Although EMC Symmetrix arrays have embedded PCs, they do offer off-host backups when combined with certain commercial backup utilities. More and more backup software vendors are adding this capability to their software.

Third-Mirror Breakoff

Some hardware and software vendors have implemented a backup model that involves keeping three disk mirrors of a filesystem or database. When it's time for a backup, the third mirror gets split off from the first two. New transactions continue to hit the first two mirrors, while the backup is started using the third mirror. At the end of the backup, the third mirror must be resynchronized with the other two copies, so that it's ready for the next backup.

The good news about third-mirror breakoffs is that the backup can be taken without taking the database or filesystem out of service for more than a few seconds (in order to ensure that the third-mirror copy is clean and consistent).

The downside to third-mirror breakoffs is the additional disk space required. Instead of the 100 percent disk space overhead that is required for regular mirrors, third-mirror breakoff requires a 200 percent disk space overhead. To mirror 20GB of disk space, you need 40GB of total storage space. To perform third-mirror breakoff, you need 60GB of disk. In addition, the act of resynchronization is very I/O intensive, and can be CPU intensive too. Depending on the implementation, there may be a very noticeable performance impact caused by the resynchronization process.

The other variation of third-mirror breakoff is to create the third mirror before the backup begins, instead of after it is completed. The I/O and CPU overhead is the same in this case. The potential is there to save disk overhead, as one set of disks could be reused as the third mirror for more than one filesystem.

EMC Symmetrix arrays use a utility called Timefinder that allow this resynchronization to be performed off-host, eliminating the impact to your server's CPU and I/O, and much faster than when the resynchronization is performed on a server.

Backing Up Directly to Disk

This is a myth. Writing streaming data to a tape is generally faster than writing it to a disk. SCSI disk write speeds top out from 5 to 8 Mbytes/second, regardless of the SCSI bus speed, because you're fighting the laws of physics governing a rotating disk platter. Reading and writing randomly placed data from a tape can be very slow. But backups are streaming by nature, and so are going to be faster to tape than to disk.

Backups to disk are more efficient when a single file needs to be restored, but when an entire disk must be restored, tape is going to be faster than disk.

DOING IT CAFETERIA-STYLE

File restore requests are fairly common in a university environment. Too late nights mixed with too few trips to Starbucks and you're looking at heavy-handed data corruption due to sleepy students. At Princeton, we did incremental dumps to disk to provide an online cafeteria-style restore system. It wasn't faster than dumping to tape, but it reduced restore times because you didn't have to look for the tape with the right files on it. Few things are more frustrating than slogging through four tapes to find a file, only to have a sleep-deprived, deadline-fearing undergraduate tell you it's the right file from the wrong date and he needs it three hours ago. Put the backup indices on-line, in such a way that each user can only read his or her own index files, and let the users self-select what they want backed up from the data available on-line. This will reduce your effective MTTR, but only if you do this in conjunction with a solid tape-based backup system. Disk-based backups are not a substitute for tapes (it's hard to get those disks off-site), and they're not ideal for large volumes of data, but they provide a nice middle ground between "snapshot" or point-in-time solutions and full, tape-based backups.

—Hal

From time to time, a disk vendor will release a new fast disk that is faster than current tape technology, for a while. But tape vendors soon leapfrog those advances. Note, too, that high-speed disks are going to cost a lot more money per megabyte than tapes, and a significant cost savings can be realized by taking advantage of the low cost of writing data to tapes instead of disks.

Sophisticated Software Features

Some commercial backup software offers features that can significantly reduce the overhead and the duration of backups, too.

Copy-on-Write Snapshots

A filesystem is nothing more than a collection of data blocks on a disk, with pointers to them so that data can be located and retrieved after it is written to disk. In a snapshot-style backup, the pointers are copied to a separate location, although they still point back to the original data. When a snapshot is enabled, and a transaction is about to overwrite a data block:

- The original block is read, and written to a new location, in a specially reserved snapshot region of the disk.
- The snapshot pointer is changed to point at the new location of the old block.
- The new data overwrites the original data in the filesystem.

The new set of pointers always points to a consistent copy of the data as it looked when snapshot was turned on. Of course, these steps are only necessary the first time a block is overwritten after snapshot is enabled; after that, we don't need to save the intermediate versions of the filesystem.

The end result is that we can take a clean backup of a filesystem even though it is continuing to receive new data. When the backup is completed, no resynchronization process is required. And the disk space overhead for a copy-on-write backup is greatly reduced. Instead of adding an additional 100 percent, only 10 to 15 percent is usually required, although that figure will vary depending on how much data actually changes during the backup.

Multiplexed Backups

Some commercial backup software is smart enough to take streams of data from more than one source, whether network connections or local disks, and stream the incoming data onto tape. This is especially useful in an environment where the tape drives can write much faster than any one client can send data to the tape server.

By keeping the tape drive spinning, data transfer rates will be much faster; each time the tape drive stops spinning, it must take time to reposition the tape against the head. This repositioning puts extra stress and strain on the tape transport mechanism, as well as on the tape itself, and will shorten the lives of the drives and the tapes.

Multiplexing can be slow to restore since the utility that reads the tape must read many more times the amount of data off the tape to get the same amount of useful information. Use of multiplexing may also counteract your backup software's ability to write in an open and generally readable format.

Fast and Flash Backup

The fast and flash methods of backups read the contents of a filesystem and write it directly to tape, as it sits on the disk, including portions of the disk that have no actual data on them. In a more traditional filesystem, backup files are backed up one at a time, which means that there is significant filesystem overhead associated with the retrieval of the file. Parts of files can be scattered all over the filesystem, and it is up to the filesystem to locate and retrieve the files. Fast and flash backup can read at raw speed, transferring data as fast as possible, without regard for file boundaries or locations. It also retrieves and stores the pointer (inode) map to the files, and stores that on the same tape.

To retrieve a file from a fast backup tape, the restore software must rebuild the map, and then rebuild the file from its potentially scattered parts on the tape. By putting the rebuild load on the restore end instead of the backup end of the process, backups are sped up dramatically.

Of course, in environments where filesystems are primarily empty, flash backup may not be the right answer, since all that empty space must be backed up too. These methods work best on filesystems where there are lots of small files, since small files introduce the most overhead during a backup.

Fast backup is available on Auspex hardware, while flash backup is available for Solaris and other Unix platforms from VERITAS NetBackup.

Handling Backup Tapes and Data

To put it bluntly, backup tapes are among the most valuable resources your company has. If they can rebuild your business after a major outage, then they also can enable a competitor to steal your business when no outage has occurred. They must be treated at all times like the crown jewels of your company, because that is just what they are.

The goal in handling backup tapes and data is achieving the proper balance between protecting them from inappropriate access and providing easy access for rapid recovery when the tapes are truly needed:

Restrict physical access to tapes. Access to a physical backup tape is about the same as root access to the disk on which the original filesystem or database resided. Give an unprotected tape to someone, and they can read it back anywhere else. Only personnel who have business seeing and touching tapes should have that access.

Magnetically erase tapes before they are reused. Many shops recycle tapes after they have expired. Since tapes can cost up to $100 each, that makes sense. But if you just toss an expired tape into a box, then whoever picks it up has access to all the data on the tape. If there is a recycled tape box, tapes must be erased before they enter the box. In especially secure environments, recycling should be carefully evaluated; destruction of the tapes may be the wiser approach.

Encrypt backup data. If this backup data can be picked up off the network, networked backups are also as dangerous as granting someone access to your raw disks. If you go to the trouble of securing user-level access to data, and database-level access by user, be sure that you secure access to backup data in transit over the network. It's the same data, perhaps with a trickier access mechanism, but you're still basically spewing the contents of a raw disk out in public unless you take the steps to encrypt it. Encryption may be as simple as doing network backups through an `ssh` tunnel or creating a disk-based backup image that is encrypted and then sent to a remote tape drive. Some backup utilities will encrypt the data before it flows over the network, if the option is enabled. Encryption will almost certainly impact the performance of the CPU of the machine doing the actual encryption. Regardless, make sure that you keep track of your encryption keys; otherwise those tapes may as well be blank.

Do not allow user-initiated restores without authorization. If you choose to allow users to run their own data restores, make sure they are restricted to data that they normally have access to. Make sure the right levels of passwords are required to restore data.

Protect tapes that leave your site. Once a tape is shipped off-site for long-term storage, what happens to it? Can you be certain that nobody ever has unauthorized access to these tapes? Would you bet your job on it? If you have the bandwidth, consider duplicating your tapes across the network (encrypted!), rather than physically transporting them.

Don't store originals off-site. You should only need to access off-site tapes in the event of a true emergency. Keep original tapes on-site. If they are stored remotely, then the MTTR is increased by the time it takes to find the tape off-site and then transport it back home.

Balance safety and rapid access. The ultimate in safe storage for your tapes might be in a waterproof, airtight, underground vault halfway around the world. However, since it might take 2 or 3 days to transport the tape back to you if you need it, that is probably unacceptable. The ultimate in rapid access for off-site tapes might be to store them next door. But a neighborhood-wide catastrophe might wipe the backup tapes out, too. Your solution should achieve a balance between these two extremes.

Label every tape. Unlabeled tapes may as well be blank. There's no easy way to determine what's on them, and they will get reused by some other operator.

Use bar codes. If you have a large library or silo, take full advantage of its ability to read bar codes, and use those codes to identify tapes. Bar codes are a simple, reliable, and uniform way to identify all your backup tapes.

General Backup Security

Backups are very valuable to an ongoing operation, but they can also represent a significant potential security hole. Everything you do to organize your backups, and make them easy to search through, and easy to restore from, also works against you. Those well-indexed backups are also easy for an "enemy" to rummage through, enabling him to examine and steal the very same data.

Can an intruder add an unauthorized client to your backup network? If he does, can he then spoof the identity of a valid client? Once he has spoofed a valid client, if the proper security is not enabled within your backup software, this intruder can restore from critical backups, or even erase backup tapes. Some backup software offers users the ability to initiate their own backups and restores. User-initiated restores can open a real security hole if intruders can gain access to your backup network. After all, good backup software makes the restores as easy as possible, finding the right tape, and either inserting it or requesting that an operator insert the tape, with little or no direct user involvement. If restores require security clearance and passwords, it becomes much more difficult for unauthorized restores of backed up data.

Most backup data travels across a network, whether a dedicated backup network, or just the regular internal LAN. If the data is not encrypted on the client side, this data can be read right off the network. If it can be read, it can be reassembled, and viewed by inappropriate persons.

Restores

There is a real trade-off between backup and restore speed. A lot of things you can do to speed up backups will slow your restores. Here we offer a few ways to speed up restores—but beware, some of them will increase your backup durations.

Do fewer incremental backups. Of course, fewer incrementals mean more fulls. More fulls mean that backups take longer. This can be a tricky balancing act. The best approach is probably to do cumulative incrementals once a week or so. Then you need only restore two tapes after a total failure. If you alternate between two or three cumulative incremental backup tapes, then the cost of losing one of those tapes will also be reduced. If you put all your incrementals on the same tape, then if that tape is lost or unreadable, you will lose all work performed since the weekly full.

Make the tapes accessible. Maximum time to repair grows while the operator looks for the right tape to mount. Don't let that happen. Keep the tapes near the drives, and keep the library neat and well organized.

Speed up disk writes. Build your systems with disk hardware that maximizes write speed. Some disk arrays use cache memory to capture large chunks of data before writing it to disk. If the writes are filesystem based, use a filesystem that optimizes performance.

Use the fastest path from tape to disk. Dedicated high-speed switched networks will move the data fastest across a LAN. Direct connections via 40MB/second Ultra Wide SCSI beats 100 Base-T (at 100 megabits per second) better than four to one. 100 megabyte/second FCAL beats them both. The downside here is expense. More hardware costs money.

Try not to have to do restores at all! The best way to speed up restores is not to have to do them at all. Since most restores are of a single file, rather than a complete restore of a catastrophic filesystem loss, by storing a snapshot or a checkpoint of a filesystem it may be possible to go back in time and restore a deleted file from an online copy rather than from a backup tape. The VERITAS File System is one product that supports this sort of filesystem snapshots. Note that this scenario does not eliminate the need to take backups at all; they are still needed as a last resort against a catastrophic loss of a filesystem.

Disk Space Requirements for Restores

Imagine the following scenario:

- On Sunday, we take a full backup of our accounting department filesystem, containing 8GB of data, out of a possible 10GB of space.

- On Monday, we learn that Joe, formerly in database design, is transferring to accounting, and he is bringing 4GB of critical files with him. Before Joe's 4GB can be added to our filesystem, which has just 2GB of free space, at least 2GB must be deleted. Word is given, and our friends in accounting delete 3GB of files containing pictures, music, and games downloaded from the Internet. An incremental backup of our newly reduced 5GB filesystem is taken.

- On Tuesday, Joe arrives, and his 4GB is added to our file system, bringing the total to 9GB. Another incremental backup is taken Tuesday night.

- On Wednesday, a disk crash occurs, so we must perform a full restore of the filesystem. (For the sake of this example, this filesystem is not mirrored.)

At the time of the crash, the filesystem contained 9GB. However, most backup software will try to restore all 12GB that existed during the course of the week. Since a 10GB filesystem is not large enough to hold 12GB, your restore will fail. If you know this is going to happen, you can sit at the keyboard and redelete those large music, picture, and game files as soon as they are restored, but that wastes your time and increases restore times. You also run the risk of missing one or two that got restored in error, and still overflow the filesystem. An overflowing file system will cause your restore to fail, and it will have to be restarted (On some Microsoft operating systems, an overflow may cause your system to crash entirely.) Chances are, if you are doing a full restore, you have other things on your mind besides sitting and deleting files that were restored in error.

The solution is to make sure that your backup software is smart enough to not only keep track of which files have changed from backup to backup, but also to keep track of which files have been deleted. Good backup software will simply skip over those unwanted music files. VERITAS NetBackup offers True Image Recovery, which prevents the restoration of deleted files.

Summary

Backups are tedious, dull, and a real pain in the neck, but they are your last line of defense against total loss of data in many types of disasters. Whether you suffer the crash of an unmirrored disk, the deletion of critical files, or the total loss of your data center, your backup tapes are the last thing between you and the irretrievable loss of this data. Sometimes, backups are necessary simply to reload a machine that has suffered hopeless data corruption and can't be brought back online with failovers because there's nothing left to failover. Last line of defense doesn't mean last priority; good, clean, regular backups must be a first priority.

The tapes containing the data must be treated as very real and very valuable company assets, and they must be given an appropriate amount of protection. The processes that perform the backups must be trusted and tested on a regular basis to make sure that they really work. If they don't, the time to find out is not when you need to restore from a tape that turns out to be invalid.

The software that does the backups must be fast enough to complete the backup cycle inside whatever window you have. It must manage the tapes properly so that they can be easily located. As with failover software, this is a job that should not be trusted to homegrown code. There are several examples of commercial backup software; compare them against each other for the speed and other features that you need; that comparing is a better use of your time than writing backup code with no support, no references, and inadequate testing.

If your backups work, but your restores don't, then you are wasting your time taking backups. Restores need to be quick, easy, and reliable. Make sure that whatever tool you use for backups create tapes that can be reliably restored.

▶Key Points

- Design backup systems to fit within your time window and tape space restrictions, while also optimizing the time to restore a single file from those backup tapes.

- Disks are not a substitute medium for tapes.

- Examine all of the facets of commercial backup software to be sure it handles your data service requirements, tape formats, and operating systems.

CHAPTER

13

System Operations

In this chapter, we take a look at some of the issues not usually thought of as part of high availability design. Often called the softer issues, they are less technical and more process and people oriented. This isn't intended to be an exhaustive look at system administration and network management, as there are many good books on those subjects. Instead, we cover the parts of the administrative realm that impact end-to-end reliability.

System Management and Modifications

Wouldn't it be nice if you could roll out a system and that would be the end of it? Imagine if you never had to revisit your systems for hardware, operating system, or application upgrades. As long as you're making wishes, how about a pony, too? Life just isn't that simple.

The first rule of system maintenance is that it will always be required. The trick is to perform the maintenance so that it has the least possible impact on overall system availability. The second part of that trick is to properly maintain your servers while still properly maintaining your personal life. Restricting all of your maintenance activities to Friday and Saturday nights after 8 P.M. doesn't leave a lot of time in life for much else. Of course, if your systems are used 24 hours a day, there may not be a noncritical time.

Maintenance Plans and Processes

The ideal way to perform ongoing system maintenance is to do so in a failover cluster, and to work on one server at a time. If *heckle* is running, perform maintenance on *jeckle*, and then failover to it when your work is completed to make sure that the changes worked. If they did, then you can follow up with *heckle* later. If not, you still have a perfectly good *heckle* to go back to, while you try again on *jeckle*.

Some other items will help to make your maintenance planning go a little better:

- If your systems are clustered or paired, additional complexities may be introduced by the very nature of the clustering. The best example of this is what happens when SCSI disks are shared between two servers. A SCSI chain cannot be broken while a system is accessing it. If the chain is broken (in other words, if the termination is removed), I/Os will fail, and users will be unable to work. (This is a SCSI-specific issue, and does not apply where other disk technologies, such as Fibrechannel, are used.)

- Be sure to consider the ramifications of your work on the partner server, clients, networks, and on your users in general.

- Always plan for the worst possible case. (It's easy to plan for the best case!) What happens if adding new disks somehow wipes out the contents or formatting of the existing disks? What if that static shock you got when you opened the case destroys the motherboard?

- Never begin any significant system work without a plan to back out the changes. That could (and probably should) mean taking a full set of backups before you begin. It could mean designating a system that you would cannibalize if you have no spare parts and some unexpected hardware damage occurs.

- The best way to develop plans, contingencies, and a list of possible external impacts is to work with a team. Run your ideas past your peers and/or superiors. Peer review is a wonderful way for all parties involved to learn to improve their plans. In the worst case, your plans are perfect; at very least others can learn from your wisdom.

System Modifications

The second law of thermodynamics states that disorder is going to increase. That means constant change for your systems. However, when change is uncontrolled and undocumented, systems become unmanageable. The worst kind of change is the quick temporary change that "I'll get back to and make permanent tomorrow . . ." Most of the time the temporary changes work fine, and there is no impetus to get back to them, nor to document the change. Hey, it's not permanent, right?

Some other things to aim for:

All changes must be documented. This means leaving comments in the files that get changed; comments should describe the nature of the change, the reason for the change, and include the name of the changer, and the date(s) the change was applied. If documenting the change in a file is inappropriate, then document the changes off-line in a notebook or other agreed-upon central location.

Try to limit the number of modifications applied at one time. If you apply five changes at once and something immediately goes wrong on the system, the debugging process becomes very complicated. Apply changes one at a time, until you can be sure that the change has fixed the problem and that it has not caused a new one.

Automate the distribution of files. Your operating system probably offers utilities to ease the distribution of files to several machines at once. If it doesn't there are public-domain utilities available on the Internet. Use them! They were developed by people in a similar situation to yours, and will probably handle your problems easily. Similarly, there are verification tools to make sure that files got to where they were headed. Use them to double-check your work. It is much faster to have a program check 20 machines for you than it is for you to manually log in to all 20 machines and poke around.

Use change management. There are public-domain and commercial utilities available for managing versions and changes in text files. These utilities allow you to roll back to previous versions of a file, if necessary, making it easy to back out the most recent changes. They can also generate a list of differences between one version and another. These utilities go by several names; SCCS and RCS are two of the most commonly used and mature of these change-management packages.

Watch for system file changes. Public-domain utilities such as `tripwire` can be used to keep an eye on certain key files, so that if they get changed accidentally or maliciously, the system administrators are notified in a timely manner. The time to discover that files have changed is not during a failover or a reboot. Something as simple as modifying the order of entries in the `/etc/vfstab` filesystem mounting table can result in a never-ending stream of NFS errors when the server with the modified filesystem table reboots. (This case is discussed in Chapter 9.)

Software Patches

System vendors such as Sun Microsystems are constantly issuing operating system and application patches. Some patches are revised and upgraded 50 or more times each as problems are fixed that depend on previous fixes. Usually, it's not 50 fixes for the same bug, but 50 (or many more) fixes that all change the same kernel modules, library routines, or other system software components. It is almost impossible to keep up with all of them. On the other hand, patches are the best way to get up-to-date fixes to bugs and other problems that inevitably occur between product releases. Microsoft's strategy is to release only the most critical patches, and to roll other fixes into service packs, which are released only occasionally. This method makes it easier to keep up on the fixes that the vendor has released; however, it can significantly delay receipt of a fix to an annoying or more serious problem.

Managing patch revision levels and patch interactions is a challenge when vendors distribute them individually. Consider all the permutations of patches that may be installed on a particular system. Let's say there are just 10 patches available for a particular operating system, and each patch has three versions. Ideally, you want to be on the latest version of whatever patches you have chosen to install, unless other considerations prevent you from upgrading (an application may break with a later revision of a patch, or regression testing or end-of-month configuration freezes may prevent system changes for a few weeks). Each patch has four states: It can either not be installed at all, or installed in one of the three versions. Think of the 10 patches as "digits" in a base-4 (for the four states) numeral. Enumerating every possible value of every patch in every state yields a total of 4^{10} (or over a million) possible combinations. It is unlikely that your vendor has tested every one of these to ensure interoperability.

If your vendor has more than 10 patches to choose from, we recommend a two-pronged approach to selecting which ones to install. First, regularly contact the vendor, possibly as often as once per month, to obtain the most current list of recommend patches. Be sure that all of those have been applied, and are right up to date. Second, maintain a separate list of patches that are specifically required in your environment, and only apply those that are required. Don't apply patches to systems where they are not needed.

Unless a brand-new patch specifically fixes a serious problem you are having, don't just drop new patches onto your production systems without putting them through some acceptance testing. Either test them on less critical systems, or wait a month or so before applying a new patch at all, so that others can test it and report problems. When a patch version number hasn't changed in a month or more, then it's probably acceptable to install it. If patch version numbers are changing all the time, keep away if you can.

When new service packs or jumbo patches are released, that is a good time to visit online bulletin boards or Internet newsgroups where such things are discussed. Get a feel from others who may have installed the updates for how they are working out. Try not to be the first one on your block to install patches or service packs.

Spare Parts Policies

If you choose to keep a spare parts inventory on hand, there are certain policies to follow that will help make your decision especially fruitful:

Inventory parts that fail the most. This will have the greatest impact on MTTR times, as you will not have to wait for overnight shipping. You can replace these items as soon as they fail. Disks and fans have moving parts, and as such generally fail the most. It doesn't hurt to have some spare power supplies and monitors on hand, either; there's no value in cannibalizing a good desktop system because you need a head for a critical system.

Inventory parts that are hard to get. If you find that a particular part is always back-ordered when you need it, it makes an excellent choice for inventorying. If you can wait for the part when it is not needed immediately, everyone will be happier.

Test your stock. When parts come in, make sure that they work. If they don't, there is no point to keeping them in inventory. Return defective parts before they are needed, rather than when systems are down and waiting for them.

Rotate your stock. Always put the oldest parts into systems, rather than the newest parts. If a part is too old to use, then exchange it for a newer version. Determining the minimum acceptable hardware revision level means having regular audits of the spare parts stock done by your hardware service provider.

Balance ease of access with proper security. Make sure that authorized personnel can access the parts at any time of the day or night. However, if unauthorized people can get to the spares, then they won't be there when you really need them.

Limit the number of system vendors and models. Limiting the number of distinct parts you need to inventory will keep your costs down, and will make it simpler to keep track of the parts you should have in inventory. Keep it simple!

Use multiple suppliers. If third-party vendors can provide high-quality parts, it is best to have more than one source for critical components. If one supplier is forced to cut off supply, or discontinues older models of equipment, you can still get parts another way. Think of the lone supplier as a single point of failure. The flip side to this approach is to be certain that the third-party-sourced parts will not void warranty or service agreements, and that you're certain they are interoperable with all of your system configurations.

Preventative Maintenance

It is definitely better to find trouble before it actually strikes. Like living organisms, hardware components get sick before they die. By monitoring system logs for recurring events like spurious memory errors, disk retries, and SCSI bus errors, you can predict the impending failure of system components.

If you know that a component is going to fail, you can replace it ahead of time, and at a less critical time of day. There is a software package called *Lookout!* from VERITAS Software that does exactly that; it monitors your system logs looking for component errors, and notifies you of these errors. The software claims better than 95 percent statistical accuracy in predicting component failures 24 to 48 hours in advance. It runs on Windows NT as well as Solaris and most other Unix platforms, and on some mainframes, too. Watch and learn the symptoms of failures, so that you can fine-tune your detection mechanisms and even extend the break-and-fix cycle to do root-cause analysis.

Environmental and Physical Issues

To drive home the importance of the physical layout of your systems, we offer an exercise that we call "The China Syndrome Test." Take one of those huge 64-ounce cups of soda pop available at many convenience stores in the United States. Fill it all the way up with real soda (no diet stuff, please; sugar works much better for this experiment). Set it on top of the cabinet containing your critical rack-mounted servers. Now knock it over. Watch as the sticky soda pop flows into all the ventilation holes and onto the systems and disks! Marvel as it runs out the bottom of one case and into the top of the next! Panic as you consider what happens as the goo runs down into your raised floor!

Are your systems arranged to minimize the effects of such a spill? Or are both of your failover servers arranged vertically in the same cabinet? Are both sets of your disk mirrors similarly vulnerable? What if the mess finds its way into your lone disk array? Would this spill take down critical servers? Chances are that they have become soggy, sticky toast.

Rules prohibiting food and drink in the data center are important, but they are often violated—especially late at night and on weekends. Don't assume that such a policy will keep all such contraband out of your data center. It won't. Of course, many data centers have no such prohibition, and moreover, you don't have to restrict your worries to soda, beer, and little ketchup packets. Glycol-based coolant from the air conditioner or water from a leaking overhead pipe can have the same effect.

Disclaimer: Please don't try this at home, kids! We accept no responsibility if a reader actually performs this exercise on his systems. The China Syndrome Test is best performed as a Thought Experiment. Offer void where taxed or prohibited by law, common sense, or management dictum.

Data Centers

Administered properly, data centers can be wonderful places from which to operate critical systems. But, just like anything else, if they are mismanaged, they can be bad news. Data centers are, in many ways, throwbacks to the days of large mainframe computing. Old mainframes required carefully controlled temperature and humidity, and they needed to be placed where certain people could get regular access to them. Since they had specific power requirements, these rooms represented a single place where 220-volt lines could be run and battery backup units could be installed. Raised floors made it easy to hide the spider webs of cables that often emanated from these machines to terminals, printers, and tape units. Fire protection could be centralized there; old Halon fire prevention systems could be deployed in a limited area.

Although most modern computers are not as picky about temperature and humidity, today's data centers have many of the same features. One reason, of course, is that many modern data centers still have mainframes happily chugging along. In fact, some high-end servers from vendors like Sun and Hewlett-Packard are looking more and more like mainframes. These data center features are still very valuable and practical with today's systems. Modern fire protection systems are safer and cleaner than Halon, but they can still be centralized into a relatively small space. Power requirements run the gamut, and 220-volt lines are still common requirements for larger systems.

Data centers offer significant advantages and disadvantages as compared to leaving critical systems in regular work areas. Advantages include:

Centralized resources. A data center is the perfect place to place all the specialized requirements of large machines: 220 volt power, fire protection, security, battery backups, raised floors, atmospheric control, etc. If systems were deployed at random throughout the facility, those resources would need to be available everywhere. By limiting their deployment to the data center, a tremendous cost saving can be achieved.

Physical security. Data centers work well to prevent inappropriate physical access to systems. (See the section on Security for a more detailed discussion of data center security issues.)

But there are disadvantages, too:

Limited possibilities for expansion. If your systems need to expand beyond the capacity of your rack, it may not be possible to get another rack adjacent to the first one. This can lead to complicated and messy layouts of systems, as they spread themselves in a seemingly random fashion all over the data center, analogous to the fragmentation of data across a disk. In that event, there may be issues with cable lengths, especially when SCSI is involved.

Putting all your eggs in one basket. Centralizing your systems can be a double-edged sword. Countering all the advantages we discussed above is the prospect that a single calamity could strike the data center and wipe out most or all of the company's computing resources at the same time. Of course, this can be addressed by maintaining multiple data centers at separate facilities, a topic we cover at length in the next chapter. Some people prefer to keep their failover systems at opposite ends of their data centers, to limit the impact of a localized external calamity such as a ceiling or floor collapse.

Too much physical security. Some security is critical, but too much security will do little more than impede the ability of system administrators to get their jobs done. In my experience, good security doesn't keep the bad guys out; if someone really wants in, they will usually find a way. All that overprotective physical security does is slow down the good guys, who have valid reasons for getting into the data center. The bad guys will often use a network back door anyway.

Perpetual construction. It is a rare data center that isn't undergoing some sort of construction. Often that means people unfamiliar with the nature of the equipment housed in the data center climbing ladders, pushing equipment through the room, moving ceiling tiles or floor tiles, or plugging large pieces of heavy machinery into the same circuits as delicate computer equipment. These same people are likely to prop open otherwise secure doors, allowing anyone in the room. Invariably, dust is stirred up and gets sucked into fans and filters, impeding system ventilation. Power interruptions (planned and otherwise) are common hazards of data center construction. Occasionally broken pipes (water, heat, fire protection, etc.) will interfere with the data center's operations.

TRAPPING YOURSELF A MAN

At one particularly security-conscious organization, I was taking a data center tour. In order to enter the data center, we had to pass through something called a "man-trap." One at a time, we went through the outside door, into a tiny room, basically big enough for one person. In that room, the man-trap, I was electronically sniffed for explosives and had to show ID authorizing me for entry into the data center. After each of us passed into the data center, we began the tour. As we neared the back wall, I noticed an open door that opened onto an unsecured corridor. On the back wall of that corridor was another open door, leading outside to the parking lot.

When I questioned the security of such an arrangement, I was told that there was construction going on, and that was the only door large enough to bring heavy equipment in and out. So much for the man-trap.

—Evan

Be sure that when you consider placing systems in a centralized data center, you consider all of these issues.

Data Center Racks

If you choose to locate your systems in a data center, then you will almost certainly mount them in data center racks. Just as with data centers, there are advantages and disadvantages to rack-mounting your systems.

Advantages include:

Neatness and organization. Racks place systems and their components near to each other, and allow for system grouping based on ownership in a large organization or based on system function.

Security. Most racks provide door locks to keep unauthorized personnel away from your systems. This makes it harder for cables and other components to simply vanish.

Centralized power. Racks are rated for power capacity, and provide ample, nearby power outlets for their components.

Cooling. Good racks have high-powered fans in them, and are designed for adequate ventilation.

Efficient use of space. Racks enable systems to be arranged vertically, so that additional equipment does not require additional floor space. In most data centers, floor space is at a premium.

LIFT AND SEPARATE

A system manager for a popular web site told me how he got "religion" about rack-mounted equipment. Two systems in an HA pair were sharing the same machine room footprint—one rested on top of the other. (Workgroup servers can be cajoled into this physical configuration by pulling their casters off.) When the machine on the bottom failed, and needed to be replaced, a system administrator lifted the top machine, yanking all of its network cables free, and taking the live half of the HA pair off-line.

—Hal

Of course, data center racks also have disadvantages, including:

Hard-to-relocate mounted components. Since components are usually mounted directly to the rails of the rack, moving a system around can require more than one person, including one to remove the screws and another to hold the system so it doesn't fall. The proximity of other racks may make it very inconvenient for more than one person to physically reach into the same rack at the same time.

Cabling issues. Commonly, cables in data center racks are tied together; moving a single cable from a bundle means disturbing all the cables in that bundle. Disturbing those cables adds risk, and could affect the services that those cables provide. Also, in a data center rack, there is a single best path between two components, say a system and a disk array. If the system and disk array are joined by two parallel cables for added availability, the physical arrangement of the equipment may make it difficult or impossible to run the cables along separate paths.

Danger of rack tipping or collapsing. Racks are extremely heavy, often weighing 500 to 700 pounds or more after they are fully loaded. If the weight is poorly distributed (i.e., the rack is top-heavy), someone leaning on it could cause it to topple over. Disregarding the effects on neighboring systems or on people standing nearby, especially those struck by the falling rack, the components inside the rack that falls are sure to be badly damaged. If components are not fastened down properly, systems could come loose from the rack, or the shelves inside the rack could come loose and crash down on the systems beneath them.

Clearances. This is generally a problem with or without racks: You need to make sure you have enough clearance to remove a board, drive, power supply, or other component from a racked system. If you place your racks in neat rows, the rows have to set back from walls and each other such that the largest clearance requirement is observed. This is a good argument for keeping like-sized equipment racked together, and for carefully studying how you'll service equipment once it's bolted in.

Too much security. If the doors on the cabinet are locked and the person with the keys is unavailable, you may have a problem if you have to access the system.

Effects of neighboring systems. Apart from the possibility of neighboring racks falling over and striking yours, nearby systems are probably administered by administrators who have nothing to do with your systems. They may not show the same respect to your systems that you would. If your racks aren't locked, they might "borrow" components or loose tools from yours.

China Syndrome Test. The China Syndrome Test is merely a single example of the kind of calamity that can strike systems when everything is lined up in a straight shot for the troublemaker. If it's not soda pop, then it could be water, or just a collapsing shelf that drops one component onto the one beneath it, and so on. Expect these sorts of problems, and plan for them.

Electricity

There is no better way to bring home our fundamental point—that achieving true high availability requires more than just installing failover management software—than to discuss electricity and electrical dependencies. A system that is functioning perfectly will, of course, stop instantly when its electrical supply is cut off. If two systems are connected together in a high availability pair, and their electricity is cut off, they will both stop working just as quickly. By providing electricity through separate paths, their power supply becomes more reliable. The further upstream the power source paths can be separated, the more reliable the power supply gets.

Plugging both systems in an HA pair into the same power strip is obviously silly, especially if the power strip has a single on/off switch on it. Running both systems through the same circuit breaker is almost as silly, but much more common, probably because it's a little harder to see which power outlets are on the same circuit.

POWERLESS

One customer I had was very concerned about power outages. He went to the extreme measure of running power to the building from two separate power companies. The problem was that they chose to run both lines into the building through the same power pole in the parking lot in front of the building. When a car hit that pole, power from both companies was interrupted until the pole could be re-erected and the lines rerun.

—Evan

Another way to defend your operations against power interruptions is through the use of a so-called *Uninterruptible Power Supply* (UPS). The "uninterruptible" part is pure marketing. UPSs are battery backups that will continue to provide power for a limited amount of time after electricity fails. But, like any other battery, they will cease to function after a certain amount of time has passed. The duration of the backup power is determined by the size of the battery unit and the amount of power being drawn. More size and less power means longer life. More size also means more money; UPSs can be very expensive. When you increase your power usage in the area that the UPS protects (e.g., new disks or tape drives), be sure that you get more and stronger UPSs.

One of the American tire companies recently released a tire that it says can be driven 50 miles after it has gone flat. The marketing says that this will enable you to get to your destination or to a repair shop without stranding you in the middle of nowhere. Sounds great, right? It might get you to your destination, but the only way the extra 50 miles can get you to a repair shop is if you *know* that the 50-mile countdown has begun. If you don't know, then you are just stranded 50 miles farther down the road. (To be fair, the fine print on the commercial makes reference to a monitoring device.)

The very same rule applies to UPSs. A UPS may get you to your destination (the restoration of regular power), but if it doesn't, then when the battery runs out your systems will go down just as hard as they would have before the UPS kicked in. Make sure that your UPS is smart enough to tell your systems or your administrators when it is running out of juice, so that they can be brought down in an orderly fashion. Be sure you leave enough time and juice for the graceful shutdown of your databases, filesystems, and network services to occur.

The other way to protect your systems against power failures is through the use of backup generators. We know of jet-engine-powered generators in at least two New York financial houses, and have seen elaborate diesel-powered generators in telecommunications hubs. Backup generators are no less likely to fail when they run out of fuel than UPSs are. The difference is that large backup generators can produce a lot more power.

MORE POWERLESS

One of my customers had a very expensive jet-engine-powered generator on the roof. One day the regular power went out, so it was up to the roof to start the engines. (He did have a UPS in place to bridge the gap between the time the power went out and when the generator could be started up.) Our guy ran up the stairs to the roof (remember, the power was out: no elevators), and, panting, tried to start the engines. Unfortunately, nobody had ever bought any jet fuel to power the generator, so it wouldn't start. When the UPS drained, they were out of power. Never assume; test everything!

—Evan

Cooling and Environmental Issues

Although today's computer systems are less sensitive to overheating than systems from 10 and 20 years ago, it is still important to maintain reasonable temperature and humidity levels in your computing environments. Failure of an air-conditioning unit can result in the total failure of the data center. The effects of extended exposure to extreme heat or humidity can be subtle, or in some cases can be quite noticeable.

The clearances between disk heads and their associated disk platters have become remarkably small. Heat can cause expansion in disk head arms, causing the disk head to make contact with the platter, destroying your disk and its data. The glue that holds the disk heads in place can soften or melt, causing it to move out of line.

In extreme cases, solders could melt or the fire suppression system could go off, giving all the computers a nice, cool bath or sucking all the oxygen out of the room, and causing a potential personnel problem.

If your data center or other computing environment is unmanned, then it is imperative to install temperature sensors that can contact a human being who can come in and fix the problem. In the worst case, fixing the problem may mean shutting down the equipment, but since that will eliminate most of the heat generation, at least the equipment will be safe.

Systems should also have ability to shut themselves down if they begin to overheat. If a system detects internal fan failure, it should be able to spin up other fans and notify the appropriate support personnel that maintenance is required. Look for thermal protection and thermal overload notification features. Ideally, the system notices it has a problem, since it may be local to a fan or air flow difficulty and not a machine room condition. However, you can achieve some measure of thermal protection with simple environmental monitoring and an "emergency power off" switch. Crude, but effective when the alternative is data corruption.

Possibly more serious than overheating is water penetration. If water gets under your raised floor or starts accumulating on the floor, all sorts of damage can occur, including short circuits and general component damage. Electronic devices don't generally cope well with water. Water could come from cooling system failures, building leaks, water pipe leaks, or even condensation. To protect yourself from water damage, install water and humidity detectors that contact people immediately when trouble is found. Often these can be part of the same system that detects fire or cooling system problems.

The most serious environmental problem is, of course, a fire. Fires can be dangerous and possibly fatal to your personnel. Automated fire detection and suppression systems are a must, and are required by law in most areas. Support personnel need to be taught to leave the premises immediately if the fire alarm sounds; a fire suppression system that removes the oxygen from the room will surely have unfortunate effects on anyone who stays in the room. Even an accidental discharge of the fire suppression system can have negative consequences, as you have to have equipment scrubbed and prepared to come back on-line.

If the fire is serious enough, the data center will have to be closed for some period. If that eventuality is unacceptable, then you need to consider the possibility of a *Disaster Recovery* (DR) site. We discuss disaster recovery in the next chapter.

Vendor Management

Some of the most important professional relationships you are likely to have are with your vendors. In the computer industry, vendors are more than just salespeople. They can help with implementation, and they can provide knowledge and expertise that is unavailable through other channels (not to mention a nice meal or a free round of golf every now and then). As part of developing reliable and resilient systems, we strongly recommend building and maintaining relationships with your key vendor representatives. Learn what resources your vendor has to offer. Take advantage of them. But don't abuse them; believe it or not, vendors are people, too. Team with your vendors; if they like you personally, they are more likely to go the extra mile for you.

Choosing Key Vendors

When you are deciding which product to buy, a significant part the evaluation effort should go into looking at the company selling the product. With that in mind, we offer some tips that will help you succeed in product and vendor selection:

Promote vendor competition. Don't make up your mind before you can speak with them all. Each vendor can give you key questions to ask their competitors; but play it fair. Tell each vendor you are going to do this. Give each vendor a chance to guess what the competitor might say, and to shoot it down in advance. Ask each vendor who he or she considers the competition to be. Give each vendor a chance to evaluate the competition; avoid vendors who are openly hostile or angry, or just plain nasty toward their competitors. They are probably trying to hide something.

See what people are saying. Look in magazines, both trade magazines and general financial magazines; visit trade shows and conferences; poke around the web and through relevant newsgroups; ask friends and colleagues; and get out and really speak with vendor-provided references.

Find out what people are saying about the company, its people, its products, and its support. If you can't find much this way, then the company may not be a big player. Probably the most important question you can ask a reference is, "What's the worst thing about working with Company XYZ?" Sometimes, over a beer (one that the vendor buys), you can find out the real poop about working for a company from its employees; you can find out a lot this way. Are the employees happy? Why or why not? Is this relevant to your doing business with them? It may or may not be.

Test customer support. Place a test support call to see how nice support people are, and how quickly they call you back. Determine the overall quality of the response. Be fair, though—don't burden or abuse the support people. Are patches and critical problem information made available on the Internet in a timely manner? Do customers have to go look for them, or will critical problem information find the customer? Examine vendor-generated statistics on average time to close support calls. What about their customer-support web site? Can you get real questions answered there, without having to wait for callbacks from support engineers?

Look at the company's financials. While it's tempting to pick vendors on the basis of their stock performance, look at the company's operating picture. Does the company have a lot of cash, or is it heavily in debt? Are the product lines you're interested in making money, or losing market share? Is there a risk you'll be buying into a product line that isn't going to be around in a year? Are you buying into a vendor that won't make it a year given cash flow, debt, and market conditions? Look at the company's price/earnings (P/E) ratio, reported in nearly every stock quote table. A high (or not applicable) P/E ratio can indicate very low earnings, no earnings, or a money-losing company. Accounting tricks and charges for mergers can affect this number, so use it as a piece of corroborating evidence, not your primary decision factor on the financial front.

Some companies have policies that prohibit decision makers from owning stock in vendors to prevent even apparent conflict of interests. If you like the vendor enough to own the stock, make sure that your code of business conduct agrees with your investment decisions.

Look for a broad product line. Don't go with a one-trick pony (a company with only one product); it may be acquired or squashed by a richer competitor. A one-trick pony may lack the resources to keep its product competitive over the long term. If a sales rep has lots of products to sell, it is in his best interest to keep you happy over the long term. The happier you are, the more of his other products you are likely to buy. If a vendor has only one or two products to sell, once you buy them, your value to him may diminish.

Who does the vendor partner with? Just about everyone partners in the computing industry nowadays. Do you like the vendor's partners? Do you use their products? Do you like them? If a vendor you are considering does not partner with other vendors you use, how much trouble will that cause? What happens when a problem arises that looks like it's a joint problem between two vendors? Can the vendors work together to resolve it, or will they spend all their time pointing fingers at each other? A vendor who partners with lots of other vendors is more likely to be successful and to have products that are more universally interesting.

Look ahead. Get a nondisclosure presentation. See what the vendor is planning two, three, and four years down the road. Is it interesting? Is it believable? Does it fit what they are doing today? Does it play to their strengths? Have they delivered on their promises reliably in the past? What is the company vision? Is it realistic?

Cross-platform support. Can the same product be delivered on all, or most, of your critical computing platforms? How similar are the products on different platforms? Can the different platform products be administered easily and centrally?

Stick with your vendors. After you have chosen vendors you are happy with, try to stay with them. You should still evaluate products from other vendors, but once vendors are in, and you are happy with their treatment, they should be treated as incumbents; don't kick them out unless the competition is clearly superior.

Limit the number of vendors. It is much easier to work with 3 or 4 vendors than it is to work with 20. Less intervendor dissent and competition, and less of your time spent in sales presentation meetings!

Working with Your Vendors

The single most important piece of advice in working with your vendors is that you actually work *with* them, and not against them. Be a partner with your vendors. Don't always try and chisel every dime away from them; they need their profits to support you. If they represent large and successful companies it is unlikely that they are trying to rip you off; they want your goodwill, too. Vendors want to build long-term relationships with you so that you will look at their other products, and so that you can be a reference site for them in the future.

If you mistreat your vendors, who, like you, are only human, *they can take their business elsewhere*. Just as you can choose between vendors, your vendors can, if their products are any good, choose from many potential customers. If they like and respect you, you are more likely to get their time and resources. If you pay a reasonable price for their products and services, they will come back to you when they have new products they think you will like.

The same rules that apply to working with salespeople apply to working with support personnel. If you return from a meeting and find two phone messages waiting for you, who will you call back first? The person who is rude and screams and yells at you, or the one who is pleasant and only calls when he or she has a real need for your help? It's human nature; be the second kind of person.

Don't make every single support call into a crisis. If you do, your real crises won't be taken very seriously. When a support call is for a minor problem, treat it as one. You won't be sorry. When there is a genuine crisis, you will get better help, more resources, and probably a solution faster than you would if everything is a crisis.

Give your support personnel all the information they ask for. If they are asking a question, they need the information to solve your problem.

On the other hand, there are plenty of incompetent support personnel answering the phones for good vendors. If you are unsatisfied with the response you get back from support, make sure your local sales team knows all about it. (If you like the support you get, tell them that, too!) As a customer, you have the right to say, "I don't like that support person, and I refuse to work with him anymore. Get me someone else."

Similarly, if your sales rep or another member of the sales team is a jerk, then you certainly have the right to go to his or her manager and ask for a different rep for the account.

The Vendor's Role in System Recovery

Ranging from hardware service to repair damaged components to bug fixes required to prevent repeated system outages, vendor service plays a large role in system recovery and constraining the time to repair a failed system.

Hardware Service

On-site service. When on-site service is required, what kind of response can you expect? What level are you paying for? What happens if the vendor fails to meet the agreed-upon level of service?

Spare parts. How long does it take for the vendor to get spare parts to you? Are the parts stored locally, or must they come in from across the country?

Root cause analysis. The vendor can examine a recurring problem and help determine the cause of the problem, and they can do so without draining customer resources.

Software Service

Bug fixes. Once a software problem is isolated, the vendor can provide a patch (and the mechanism to apply the patch), or an upgrade to fix the problem. Patches are preferable, and should be available via ftp or a web site.

Time to resolve problems. The faster the vendor can get trouble tickets closed, the quicker your systems can be back in business.

Integration. Will the vendor take ownership of multiple-vendor problems, or point fingers? Finger-pointing slows recovery; taking ownership and being willing to work with other vendors to solve problems gets systems back on line faster.

Escalation

Know your customer service managers. They can be your best ally when things go bad. Make friends with them. Call them to praise their people when things are going well as quickly as you call to complain when things go poorly.

Know the escalation process. How do you get a support call escalated? What does that mean? Does it help? How long before a problem gets attention from engineering? Who do you call locally when things don't go right with support?

Not everything can be an escalation . . . or nothing is. Don't cry wolf!

Vendor Integration

Will your vendors support your configuration? Are "his" disks interfering with "my" operating system? What are the supported combinations of releases?

Who do you call first? Which vendor is your best route to other vendors when the vendors pass calls to each other? How do you decide where to take your first call? What if that vendor is not the right one? *Blind one-stop support calling is NOT highly available.*

Vendor Consulting Services

Who knows a product better than the company and the people who produced it? If a complex or new product is to be installed for the first time, take full advantage of the vendor's expertise. Use your vendors to implement new products, perform major upgrades of old products, and customize applications. They have most likely done this sort of work successfully before, and can do it again for you.

Yes, consulting services can be extremely expensive ($2000 to $3000 per day is not unheard of). But consultants have the ability and experience to get things done right the first time. And should the consultant run into problems, he or she has a support network to fall back on. If your local personnel do the work instead and they run into problems, who can they call? Many vendor consulting organizations offer fixed-price consulting. If the job is done easily and successfully, the hourly rate may be very high, but if things don't go as well, you are protected from hidden costs, and the vendor is has incentives to get the job done quickly and efficiently.

People and Processes

We lump a number of topics in here, including security, documentation, staff management, and escalations and coverage models. Again, you'll find many other books on these topics (particularly security), so we are trying to raise only those points that impact availability designs.

Security

System security, which by itself has been the subject of many computer books and seminars, is a critical part of system availability. The reason is simple: A breach in security can directly or indirectly cause downtime. Network breaches can keep your users out; deleted or damaged files can seriously impact your business.

Breaches can come from outside or inside. Watch out for corporate espionage. Protect your systems from disgruntled employees and ex-employees. It is very important to keep your employees as gruntled as possible! When people leave, if they were treated badly, they are much more likely to leave their ex-employer a going-away "present." When employees (and especially system administrators) depart, change any passwords they may have had. Scan all of your systems for files owned by those users, especially scheduler files that may contain time bombs. If another employee needs to take ownership of some of the files of the ex-employee, it may be best if the work of going through the files to get the required data is performed on a standalone system, especially if you are concerned about trusting the ex-employee.

Some examples of other protective measures you may choose to employ are:

Firewalls. A firewall is a system that acts as a gateway between the Internet and your internal computer systems. It monitors and restricts certain types of network traffic, and can keep hackers and other unwanted visitors from getting into your systems from the Internet. Be sure that your firewall systems are highly available; if they go down, your users may lose their ability to access the Internet at all.

Data encryption. Data on backup tapes or on your network that is left unencrypted can be read by anyone with the means and desire to do so. While it may not be easy to get to these tapes or networks, someone who truly wants to can. Data is the heart and soul of almost every organization nowadays; protect it.

Strong password selection. Make sure that all passwords into your systems are secure. Passwords should include characters from at least two or three character classes, and should be at least six characters long. Character classes are: uppercase letters, lowercase letters, numbers, and punctuation. Passwords should never be a dictionary word in English or other popular language (Spanish, Japanese, etc.). Yet they should also be easy to remember, because passwords that are written down may as well not be set at all. An example of such a password might be: "sa/ni/li." Why? The letters come from the first two letters of each word in *Saturday Night Live* (easy to remember), and are separated by a character from a different class. If your operating system permits it, spaces make excellent characters for passwords, as many automated password crackers don't try spaces.

Protect passwords. Don't give passwords to vendors or users who don't need them. If a vendor comes in and needs a privileged password to do his job, change it to something easy to remember while the vendor is around, and return it to something harder when he leaves. Run a complete security audit after the vendor is done, looking for security holes left as side effects of the work.

Limit administrative access. Restrict it very closely. Don't let more people get privileged access on your critical servers than need it. If remote administrative access is required, use secure shell (`ssh`) to build a tunnel, rather than allowing work as root to be done from a trade show or Kinko's public computing facility.

Enable auditing. While auditing certainly imposes a performance overhead (up to 15 percent on some systems), and it requires significant disk space to hold all of the logged information, auditing can also help you track down intruders and keep track of system calls made by every running application. If you're suspicious about user activities, auditing gives you some data; if your intruders are good, however, they'll clean up behind themselves and leave few clues in the audit or system logs.

Establish policies for password and key escrow. While password and encryption keys should normally be kept secret, allowing only one person to hold critical information of this nature is dangerous. If the one person who knows the encryption key to a critical corporate document gets run over by a bus, or is hit on the head and suffers total amnesia, then nobody has the key. Critical keys and passwords should be kept in escrow, such as in a sealed envelope kept in a well-known, physically secure location like an executive office or safe deposit box. If the envelope is disturbed, then the associated keys and passwords must be changed.

Data Center Security

Security has always been one of the most important features of data centers. With modern electronic-card-based access systems, access can be carefully monitored and restricted. And yet almost every data center permits outsiders (vendors, visitors, and even the occasional school field trip) to wander through, oohing and aahing over the massive and expensive equipment. Many don't just permit tours, they promote them, inviting visiting vendors, job applicants, and homicidal maniacs into the rooms containing their most important computing resources.

TOO MUCH INFORMATION

In the data center of a large and very well-known financial institution, every system has a big sign on it. The signs tell anyone who is interested what the system is, what applications are run on it, and how much it cost. Labeling systems so that administrators can find them easily is a fine idea, but this crosses the line into bragging and is a potentially huge security problem. Since access to their data centers is easily gained through a tour, a competitor could easily target a particular server for some sort of mischief or sabotage during such a tour.

—Evan

In a perfect world, data centers would be completely off limits to anyone who did not have a business-related reason to enter. Enough people have business reasons to enter, so data centers are often very crowded, even without allowing tours to wander through.

Documentation

Nobody likes writing documentation. It is slow, tedious, and takes time away from more important pursuits, like putting out fires and solving interesting problems. However, it is vital to the long-term success of any system, computer or otherwise. It is impossible to keep every tidbit of knowledge about a system in one person's head. Even if it were possible, that person might change jobs, go on vacation, or forget details. Or worse, he might think he remembers some detail, but remembers it wrong. On the other hand, visit any established mainframe shop and ask to see the "run books," and you'll find volumes of information describing how you start, stop, diagnose, and deal with every application that is in production.

Good documentation is as important to the long-term success of systems as any other component. Without it, new personnel will be hindered in their attempts to learn how existing systems are maintained. The more time it takes for them to come up to speed, the longer the systems are undersupported.

To make documentation efforts successful, documentation should be maintained online, but stored off-line. Maintain it online so that it can be easily changed; store it off-line so that it can be accessed whether systems are up or down. Store an additional copy off-site, in a reasonably secure place that can be accessed by key personnel in an emergency. Documentation should be regularly reviewed and tested. If documentation sits for months without review, testing, or updating, it will fall out of date, and become worse than not having documentation at all.

Another aspect to producing documentation is that if you are a really good SA, then you may not have a lot of ongoing problems to solve. Producing documentation may help justify your existence to upper management who doesn't understand the day-to-day work on system administration.

One reason that people are reluctant to create documentation is the fear that documenting what they do will make them less valuable to the organization, and may even make them expendable. Documentation does not make anyone less valuable to the organization; just the opposite, it frees experienced personnel from the burden of maintaining older, less interesting systems and allows them to move on to newer projects. Without good documentation, they run the risk of constantly being pulled back into old projects.

So, what do you document? To start, we recommend:

- What to do when various critical events occur

    Starting and stopping an application

    When a failover occurs

    When systems fail completely

    When a site disaster occurs

- Procedures for rolling out new systems

    Servers

    Clients

        Applications

        Monitoring tools

        Physical data center changes

- Requirements for new applications

        Log requirements

        System standards

        Interdependencies

- Network layout

- Hardware diagrams for every critical system

- Track all system and network outages

Start with that list, and see where it goes. Documentation should be written at a very low level, and on the assumption that the reader has little or no experience. It should also contain many cross-references. Don't write the same information in more than one place. If different parts of the same documents disagree, time will be wasted trying to determine which passage is correct.

Keep things as simple as possible!

System Administrators

The most important people to the long-term successful operations of your computer systems are your system administrators (SAs). System administration, especially in the Unix world, is learned almost entirely through on-the-job experience and by making mistakes (often one and the same). There is very little formal training in how to be a system administrator. There are lots of courses and books that teach the various skills required to administer systems, but there are so many varied skills involved that it is very difficult to become a totally well-rounded SA.

Some of the skills, obvious and otherwise, required by a good SA are:

Backup engineer. Must be able to take and administer backups, and locate and retrieve tapes easily and quickly. Must also arrange for off-site storage of the tapes and quick and easily retrieval in an emergency.

Evaluator of equipment and software. Must be able to examine new products, both hardware and software; cut through the marketing double-talk; and determine what products will adequately meet requirements.

Hardware engineer. The first line of defense for swapping bad disks may be your system administrator; CPU and memory module replacement may be handled by your hardware service provider, or by your own staff if you've chosen break-and-fix self-service.

Software developer. SAs are always writing bits of code to automate key tasks.

Help desk. An SA is the first line of defense when users run into any sort of problems.

Chameleon. To properly support users, an SA must understand the business, whether they're involved in equities trading, manufacturing, or data warehousing.

Fire inspector. The SA is ultimately responsible to make sure that the cables running through the floor, ceiling, and/or elevator shaft are up to local fire codes.

Security expert. The SA must maintain firewall machines at a proper level of security (strict enough to keep intruders out, but loose enough to let valid data and users pass through unimpeded), ensure that quality passwords are chosen, and ensure that departing employees' files are purged from systems promptly.

Technical writer. Documentation must be written for future SAs and for the current staff, who will be absent during vacations and training. The SA is ultimately responsible for it.

Quality assurance engineer. Before new applications can be rolled out, they must be tested. Unless dedicated QA engineers are on staff, this falls to the SA staff, too.

Technical trainer. When the user community needs to understand a new technology, it falls to the system administrators to make sure the users are adequately trained.

Town crier. Bad news (such as system outages) must be reported to his user community

Diplomat. Bad news (such as system outages) must be reported to his user community in such a way as to not make the users terribly angry.

Detective. When system problems occur, it is up to the SA to track them down and solve them.

Network technician. In general, the SA is responsible for maintaining and troubleshooting networks and associated hardware.

Salesperson. Once the SA has decided on a particular product or technology, he or she must then go and make the case to management.

New technology expert. When some new whizzy high-tech toy comes along, the SA is expected to understand it and to explain it to the more technical users, whether it be programming language, operating system, palm-top computer, or new hardware paradigm.

Relationship builder. To be successful, a good SA needs to develop relationships with the support and local sales teams from all key vendors, his users, management, customers, the local help desk, and his peers in other departments.

Night owl. A large percentage of the work an SA is responsible for must be done at night or on weekends, and usually after working a full day and week.

(Is it any wonder that most SAs have a very hard time explaining to nontechnical friends and relatives, never mind their user community and their management, exactly what it is they do for a living?)

Every site, and often every system, has different methods for maintaining their systems. Every time an SA changes jobs, he or she needs to learn the new model, and combine that with preexisting skills and experience in order to become truly useful in the new environment.

Since system administrators are the people who have to implement all of the stuff we have discussed in this book, along with countless other technologies, you don't want to be replacing your people all the time. Keep your system administrators:

Happy. Give them interesting work. Don't micromanage. Ask them what makes them happy, and try to deliver it. As long as the systems are running well, there's nothing wrong with letting them surf the web or maintain a web page during the day if they want to. (Remember all those late nights and weekends!) In Chapter 3 we talked about the six environments you might need, with the last one being the playground. Don't be afraid to let your system staff run free in the playground, because they may just come up with the next big process improvement.

Responsible. If your SA is responsible for the proper functioning of a particular system, then that person needs the authority to change things as he or she sees fit. It's not fair to assign responsibility without granting concurrent authority.

Interested. Make the work challenging and fun. Make the workplace a pleasant place to spend time. Keep things as high tech as possible.

Motivated. Reward good work. Let your SAs have cutting-edge equipment and software if they are good at what they do.

Well-compensated. If you won't, somebody else will!

Educated. Send them to training and conferences like USENIX and SANS regularly. Let them stay on the cutting edge of technology. There are entire user groups, like the 24×7 Users Group, dedicated to system and physical plant availability.

Around! If you have frequent personnel turnover, it will be very difficult to maintain your system availability.

Don't undervalue your important people. Make sure they want to keep working for you.

Internal Escalation

System administration is a 7×24 job. Unless someone is on-site 24 hours a day, as is realistic in larger sites with full-time operations staffing, the daytime staff will be responsible for off-hours crises, too. There is virtually no time that is guaranteed to be totally free of responsibility. Someone needs to be reachable at all times of the day or night in case of emergency; the best way is usually through the use of pagers. But what if the person with the pager, or coverage responsibility that night, cannot be reached in a timely manner? Pagers do not reach everywhere.

An internal escalation policy must be set into place, with a primary person, a secondary person, and an emergency backup person. If the first person does not respond to a page after a given period of time (often 30 minutes), the backup person is paged and given 30 minutes. After 60 minutes have passed, the third person, usually a manager, is paged. Since the first two people know they will be in trouble if the manager gets paged, it is in their best interests to respond quickly.

LEFT A MESSAGE WITH YOUR SPOUSE

Very early one August Sunday morning, the Stern phone rang. My wife, Toby, answered to hear a computer-generated voice, which she promptly hung up on. A few minutes later, the same call, same voice, same hang-up. "Who is it?" I asked. "Some computer telling me something about the temperature of a pie," she answered. Voice-generation software being somewhat infantile in 1988, I recognized the caller—the environmental monitoring system in my start-up company's machine room. At 5:30 A.M., the temperature wasn't "pie," it was "high"—like over 100 degrees. Our rooftop chiller had failed sometime over the weekend, and the machine room was quickly roasting the disks with the product we planned to introduce at the following week's trade show. One call to the 24-hour HVAC service, 150 feet of garden hose, and a few hundred dollars worth of fans dropped the temperature to the point at which we could safely restore power to the machine room, and by Monday things were back to normal. Moral of the story: If you're on call, your family is on call with you. Make sure that everyone knows how the escalation path reaches you.

—Hal

In addition to pagers, home phone numbers should be available, and e-mail can also be employed. E-mail is the weakest approach in an emergency, especially if the e-mail system is affected by the emergency.

Late-night phone calls and pages can be reduced through the use of automated processes that take care of the most common and invasive problems. But, if late night work is unavoidable, a tremendous amount of time can be saved by giving your administrators remote access to servers so they can log in from home and correct problems without having to get dressed and drive to the office at all hours of the night. Remote access can speed up the initiation of repairs by two hours or more.

But, plans must still be made to grant SAs access to the facilities at all hours of the day or night. In order to ensure success, SAs must have keys and access cards to the facility and to any important rooms inside; codes to deactivate burglar alarms; emergency phone numbers; appropriate security clearance and passwords; and any access codes to use phone lines at off-hours. The bottom line is that your SAs need complete 7×24 access to any and all parts of the facility that they may need to get to when a crisis is in progress. The worst thing that could happen is for your SA to get up at 3 in the morning, get dressed, drive to the office, and then be barred access to the systems he needs to get to. Never let that happen. An occasional dry run, as unpopular as that may be, is probably appropriate.

Trouble Ticketing

Ease the burden on your people through the use of automated problem detection and reporting tools. The marketplace is loaded with these sorts of tools; they come from hardware and operating system vendors with their equipment, as well as from vendors who specialize in such products, such as Computer Associates, BMC, and Tivoli. These packages allow users to submit their own problem reports, too.

Whatever product you use, make sure that trouble tickets and reports include as much detail as possible. These reports need to be reliable, detailed, accurate, verifiable, and documented. The less work an SA has to do to research the problem, the more time he can spend solving it, or moving on to the next problem.

▶Key Points

- Bad documentation, inadequate testing, and poorly educated users and administrators can be just as damaging to system availability as technical failures.

- Data centers and data center cabinets are valuable ways to maintain systems, but they are not perfect in all situations.

- Treat your vendors like people, and in turn they will take better care of you.

- Realize that your system administration staff is like engine oil. It's only a commodity when it's on the shelf; when working for you, it's your responsibility to take care of it.

- Security, a topic worthy of many books all by itself, is a critical part of system availability.

CHAPTER 14

Disaster Recovery

It's the end of the world as we know it, and I feel fine.
—Michael Stipe (R.E.M.)

And now we come to the final layer in achieving high availability. Disaster recovery is the hardest level to achieve because, almost by definition, you cannot really know what you are preparing for. Your business may be required by federal monitoring agencies to be prepared for disasters, or you may simply decide that it is within your business plan to prepare for disasters. Exactly what disasters you choose to prepare for, and equally important, what disasters you choose *not* to prepare for, are decisions that may have a significant impact upon your business's ability to continue to exist.

At the same time, most people are uncomfortable discussing true disasters because of their very nature. Disasters, whether man-made (such as acts of terrorism or war) or natural (such as earthquakes or floods), can result in changes that go far beyond the day-to-day doings at the office. They can result in loss of property and, in extreme cases, loss of life. They force you to prepare for things that you can almost never truly prepare for, and to discuss issues that few people are comfortable discussing.

This chapter focuses squarely on the physical and environmental problems that could require you to move operations from one place to another. There's another aspect to disaster recovery, namely, the point at which you throw up your hands and accept data corruption or other integrity problems that force you to reload from tape or restart from a replicated copy. We'll consider those replication problems, since you'll most commonly be handling them with replicated machines that are close to the primary machines, and the disasters are "soft" ones caused by software or systems issues, not physical catastrophes.

Many of the issues in this chapter get delicately close to legal ones. If it appears that we may be giving legal advice, we are not. We are not lawyers (regardless of what our mothers may have wanted for us). If you have legal questions regarding the issues we raise, or need to clarify what your company's or industry's regulatory requirements are, talk to your corporate counsel. It helps to start with local legal experts, who are most familiar with the particular national issues, and work your way up—with help from your management—when you run into a true disconnect between your implementations and expectations from on high.

We raise many of these issues without providing answers because many of them have no easy or generally applicable solution. Those will depend on your company, your location, your people, your DR requirements, your budgets, and many other factors. The primary goal of this chapter is to point out many of the issues that you could run into while planning for a disaster.

The single most important lesson of this chapter is that even one overlooked item could cause any and all disaster planning efforts to completely fail in the event of an actual catastrophe. Despite all of the money spent and plans made, overlooking something as simple as license keys for the applications at the disaster recovery site could cause the entire effort to fail. Every detail must be considered in advance.

The only way to be completely sure that your DR site will function if a disaster occurs is to test it ahead of time.

Disaster Recovery or High Availability?

One of our key principles says that you should not try to solve two problems with one solution. Though it does not always appear that way, high availability (or failover management) and disaster recovery are most assuredly two very different problems that need to be examined and addressed separately. Let's take a look at the two problems, and see what makes them different.

Local Failover

To achieve local failover, you need:

Servers that are colocated. For local failover, you need your servers to be located near each other. Normally they are arranged next to each other, vertically in a single rack (bad idea—remember the China Syndrome discussion), or a few meters apart in a data center. Perhaps they are a little farther apart in separate data centers, or possibly on separate floors. Farther apart than that and you may run into issues of disk cable length limitations or network latency (if it takes too long for a heartbeat to get from one server to the other, your FMS may not work properly).

Shared disks. Both servers need to see the same copy of the data, otherwise you add a great deal of complexity in keeping replicated disks in sync.

Shared subnets. The members of the failover pair (or cluster) need to be on the same subnet so that networked clients can easily and smoothly reconnect after a failure has occurred.

Clients that are not affected by the outage. The failure that local failover is designed to recover from is an isolated failure, one that is isolated to a single server, and that will not impact the clients. Generally, no provisions need to be made to keep the clients running, or to relocate client users to another location. They should continue running on their own.

Simple recovery. When the down server is repaired, it can either take over once again, or it can work as the backup server for the newly-promoted system.

Disaster Recovery

In a disaster recovery scenario, you need:

Servers far apart. In a disaster recovery scenario, the servers are located miles apart, so that the impact of a disaster will not affect both sites.

Servers with separate resources. In a disaster, you are preparing for the total loss of your main site. To achieve that, it is necessary to maintain totally separate and independent systems. No shared resources can be permitted. Not sharing resources (also called a *shared-nothing* configuration) also lifts cable length and other distance limitations. Of course, since the resources are not shared, disaster recovery also usually introduces the added complexity of WAN data replication, or some other method of transporting your critical data from the main site to the disaster recovery site.

Clients are affected, too. The nature of a disaster is such that local clients are affected too. They will probably not operate once the outage occurs; your disaster-recovery scenario may need to include plans to relocate your clients, too. Of course, remote clients who come in via the Internet or other networks may not be affected at all by the primary site disaster.

Complex return to normal. After a disaster, it may not be possible to ever return to your original site. Or, if you are able to do so, it may be in some sort of degraded mode. In order to return to the original site, it will almost certainly be necessary to reinitialize the disks with the data from the DR site. Depending on the amount of data, that is a serious undertaking that may involve massive amounts of data being replicated over the network, or shipped on backup tapes.

Do You *Need* Disaster Recovery?

The first question is the most basic one as we begin to examine this most expensive and complex aspect of maintaining system availability. Do you even need DR?

If you work in some industries, such as financial services or health care, then your industry regulators probably require you to have a DR plan. Other industries may not need them at all. And in still others, it may be a business-by-business, department-by-department, or even an application-by-application decision. How do you even decide?

Consider the implications of a total disaster. If your site fails completely, will your clients still need to be serviced? If they are in the same building as the main systems, then perhaps not. A small or medium-sized web-based business, such as a store or auction house, may be financially crippled by an outage lasting a few days, but may also be unable to fund or justify a large-scale DR effort. These companies need to weigh the costs and risks of business interruption versus business continuity. Business interruption insurance may not be the solution, because the "web waits for nobody," and an online outage means you've essentially shut the doors. A larger business with worldwide customers and worldwide recognition that cannot afford to shut down needs a DR site and a DR plan.

If your users are located in the same site as your servers, it may be necessary to include a plan to move these users to your DR site at the same time the servers move.

Of course, if you do lose your main site, and the decision is made to move operations to the DR site, will there even be people to initiate the transition and to operate the site? The DR site may be very far away from the main site. If it is unmanned, or undermanned, it will take time for your system administrative (SA) personnel to physically arrive at the DR site. Depending on the nature of the disaster, your SAs may be delayed in traffic, or totally incapacitated and unable to make it to the DR site at all.

A DR site is extraordinarily expensive. It is essentially a mirror of your main site, located somewhere relatively far away. That means data center space, work space for users, computers, furniture, security, and all the other expensive assets that are located in your main site. It may also require dedicated personnel who spend all their time at the DR site keeping things ready for a disaster.

Despite the cost, many DR sites sit idle all the time. Potentially, a tremendous amount of computing resources sits largely unused even though there are probably resource shortages at the main site. This fact can be very unnerving to the folks who approve purchasing.

Of course, setting up a DR site is a lot more than just putting a bunch of computers and networks in a big empty building, and forgetting about them until the disaster strikes. When you start to lay out the operational requirements, you'll find they cascade and create complex dependencies. The DR systems must be kept synchronized with the main site. That means hardware. It means networks. It means CPUs and memory. It means having the right quantity and power of the computing systems. It means tape drives. That also means software. It means making sure that the operating systems (and patches) and the applications are kept in sync. It means that if a disaster strikes tomorrow, your users could pick themselves up and move the DR site and get back to work. You want the disaster recovery site, and its computing environment, to look, feel, and react like your primary location. Seemingly innocuous things like the telephone handset buttons become important if users aren't immediately comfortable working in the alternative environment. The more surprises there are for the users, the longer it will take to get them back in business.

Keeping your DR site really ready requires constant diligence. Making a small change at your main site that does not make it to DR could cause things to fail when it's time to migrate. If that happens, all the expense and effort spent managing the DR site could be for naught.

Choosing Your Disaster

So, you've decided that you do in fact need to protect your business against disaster. (If not, read on anyway and see if some of these concerns are familiar; if you've heard of them, then you *do* need a DR plan, although to be politically correct you may be asked to call it something else.) The next issue to consider is exactly what disasters you'll choose to protect your business against.

We have chosen a handful of potential disasters in order to discuss some of the variations that might be required to defend against them:

Single system failure. This is a trick question! A single system failure is not a disaster at all. You may be thinking of local failover, which can be successfully defended against through the use of failover management software. Alternatively, a complete system failure that results in data corruption may be disaster-level in terms of interruptions, but again, we consider this a motivation for the data replication techniques discussed in Chapter 10.

Building-wide power failure. Unless the power will be out for an extended period, this does not qualify as a disaster either. A good uninterruptible power supply should protect you here. Since it can be almost impossible to know that the outage won't end in the next five minutes, it can be very difficult to make the decision to call a disaster. It would be very unfortunate to begin the disaster procedures, only to find the power chooses that moment to come back on. However, if you know for sure the power will be out for an extended period, then this scenario would qualify as a true disaster. You'll want to make sure that your DR site has its own independent power source; otherwise you will just be moving from one dark place to another. Space for users and clients would be required if a disaster is declared due to a power outage.

Flood. There are different causes for floods. One is a broken water main; in this case the collateral damage would most likely be limited to a few square blocks, and only to the lower floors. Many businesses might decide to simply stay home for a few days. Other businesses might try to limp along, while still others would migrate to their DR site. Another cause for a flood might be a broken water pipe on a higher floor of the building. In that case, water could easily run down through floors and ceilings, affecting operations on many floors of the building. Finally, the weather is often to blame for water penetration. During hurricane or tornado and flash-flood seasons, and at times when the ground and sewer systems cannot absorb large, sudden rainfalls, there's a risk of water ending up where you least desire it.

THE WATER DOWN BELOW

For protection from flooded basements, one site had not one, but two backup servers in two separate basements in separate buildings. The data center also had two backup generators. Unfortunately, one of the basements didn't have enough space for both the server and a generator, so they put both generators in the same basement. Of course, the two-generator basement was the one that flooded, and sure enough, power was lost.

—Evan

Fire in the data center. If a fire is serious enough, it qualifies as a local disaster, and this explains why many sites have two data centers on two different floors in the same building; they would failover systems from one data center to the other. Of course, the China Syndrome Test can be applied to data centers that are located one directly above the other in an office building. If the one upstairs has a fire, water might run down through the floor, causing problems downstairs. Smoke could just as easily get upstairs from the downstairs data center. Also realize that a serious fire may result in the closing or even partial condemnation of your building; having a redundant data center that is now off-limits doesn't help. A DR site next door would be adequate protection. If the fire was limited to the data center, then most likely no space for clients would be required at the DR site for this particular disaster.

Tornado. Tornadoes are nasty, and, of course, very hard to predict. Placing your DR site far away from the main site is good, but local geographic conditions and historical data on tornado tracks should definitely be taken into account if your main site is in an area where tornadoes are common.

TORNADO ALLEY

One customer I dealt with in the midwestern United States proudly told me how their DR is a good 10 miles away from their main site. Since the disaster they are most concerned about is tornadoes, that sounds pretty reasonable. Then they sheepishly admitted that both sites are right in the heart of the same tornado alley, and despite the distance, they felt one tornado could conceivably wipe out both sites.

—Evan

Earthquake. Hello, California. If you really want your business to survive a serious earthquake, put your DR site as far away as possible from any fault lines that the main site may be near. Otherwise even 100 miles away may be insufficient, because a serious earthquake may cause damage all along its fault line.

War or terrorist attack. Many financial institutions (who shall remain anonymous for obvious reasons) in or near major cities have their DR sites in completely unmarked and undistinguished (and in some cases outwardly squalid) buildings. Should major city landmarks become the target of terrorism or of an act of war, these buildings will be much more likely to survive than will, for example, a building in Times Square in New York with a fifty-foot-high neon sign identifying the occupants of the building.

Atomic bomb. A nuclear attack is a fine example of the sort of disaster that you may not choose to bother protecting against. As we have looked at other potential disasters, we have not really addressed potential loss of life. When an atomic bomb enters the picture, it may be time to consider other priorities. But if your business model even requires surviving this eventuality (the federal government, for example), the best defense would be multiple DR sites spread all over the world. If that turns out to be inadequate for your business, it just might not matter anymore. Remember that the original ARPAnet design was meant to survive in the event of partial failures during strategic exchanges; of course, having a highly available network doesn't help when the network clients have all been rendered useless by the ElectroMagnetic Pulse (EMP) preceding the bomb's shock wave.

The bottom line when choosing your disaster is to identify which disasters your business needs to be able to recover from, and those that your entire business will in fact survive. Don't waste your money trying to defend against disasters that your business will not survive. At the same time, don't worry about disasters that will also knock your user community out of commission. If your building floods, what are the chances that the phones will still work?

Populating the DR Site

If you are still with us, then you have decided that there are some disasters that are worth defending against. The next issue, then, is how to build your DR site, and how to get and maintain your data there.

What Actually Goes to the DR Site?

First, you need to determine what applications are important enough to protect in this manner. What applications can we simply not operate the business without? Once you have determined what applications are required, the next question is to determine what hardware and infrastructure such as server systems, desktops, disks, networks, tape drives, cooling, and power you will need to run them. We assume you have the site and the space for all this equipment. Then all that hardware must be purchased, obtained, installed, and configured. Don't forget about operating systems and patches.

Filling DR Disks

Once your systems are in place, it's time to begin filling those disks. There are several options for getting your applications and data to your DR site. Applications and data may be separate issues, depending on the method you choose for loading those disks. There are automatic and manual methods to get your data across your network.

Automatic methods include:

Hardware-based disk replication. This very reliable and popular method of wide-area data replication will get all data sent to the remote site regardless of its content or type. The downsides to hardware-based replication can include the relatively high cost and the relatively slow performance, especially over longer distances. A hardware solution may also tie you to a particular vendor for all incremental disk purchases. But for many users, these limitations may be perfectly reasonable and acceptable, which has resulted in the popularity of solutions like EMC's SRDF (Symmetrix Remote Data Facility).

Software-based data replication. Providing a newer option for replicating data, software-based solutions are generally much less expensive and can be faster than hardware-based ones. Since the replication is software-based, it does not tie the system to a particular kind of hardware. However, since the technology is relatively new, it does not have the history or the number of deployments that hardware-based replication has. One example of a software-based data replication solution is VERITAS Software's SRVM (Storage Replicator for Volume Manager).

Database or transaction-based replication. Most often provided by database vendors, database replications are designed to replicate the data from a single application. They do not always replicate the configuration files and other files that are not specifically part of the database or application that they are responsible for, and since they run at the application level, it is very likely that they will slow down the application. If performance is an issue for your database, benchmarks are an excellent idea. Both Oracle and Sybase offer replicated versions of their databases.

WAN-based tape duplication. Many backup utilities have the ability to copy a backup tape across a wide-area network to a remote data server. This work can be done during the day, when most tape drives are otherwise sitting idle. Once the data is copied across the WAN to the DR site, the tapes can be read (restored) into the disks at the DR site. The upside is that the tape drives are kept busy during the day, when they might otherwise be idle. The downside is that sending all that data across the WAN during the day is probably not what the WAN was implemented for; it will surely add a lot of traffic, slowing down the other applications that the WAN was designed for.

Extended data cables. When distances are short, and the right-of-way can be obtained, another way to achieve automatic data replication is by running extended Fibrechannel cables, possibly with repeaters, between the data center and disaster recovery site. This works well in a campus environment, or in a city where there is fiber running under the streets. It can be expensive to run those cables, especially when digging is involved. Once the cables are run, additional software needs to be in place to copy the data between sites; depending on the nature of the cabling, the software could be software based replication, or it could be plain-old disk mirroring.

As for manual methods for getting data to the DR site, there are really only two, and one of them is of extremely questionable usefulness and reliability:

Hand-carrying disks to the remote site after a disaster. This is a very risky strategy that has largely become impractical over the last few years. To hand-carry your disks, you need physical access to the disks after the disaster has struck. If the building has exploded, burned, or collapsed, that may be simply impossible. Assuming that someone can gain access to the servers long enough to rescue the disks, they need a way to carry and transport what may be several hundred disks, which may weigh several hundred pounds, depending on the size and physical makeup of the disks. (Of course, if the disks cannot be removed from their cabinets, then the cabinets must be moved too.) Assuming that you have removed all of the disks, and transported them to your remote site, there are still a couple of very important criteria that must be met: (1) there must be identical disk cabinet hardware that can receive all of the disks, and (2) the disks must all be well-labeled so that you know where to install them. In most cases, this will turn out to be a most impractical method of data replication.

Shipping (or hand-carrying) backup tapes that already contain data. There are two variations to this strategy. Tapes can be kept on-site and then hand-carried to the DR site only when a disaster actually occurs. In this case, tapes must be located, identified, handpicked, and hand-carried to the remote site. This effort can be quite time-consuming, and may turn out to be completely impossible, depending on the nature of the disaster. The other variation is that tapes are hand-carried to the DR site on a daily basis. That can be much more expensive than one-time carrying of tapes, but it will be much more reliable, since at worst the data at the remote site is always no more than one day old. There are many issues that arise when the data is hand-delivered to the DR site:

- Where do you store the off-site tapes? Is the location secure? Is it so secure that when the time comes to restore the tapes they will be hard to reach?

- How are the tapes transported to the remote site? Is the transportation mechanism secure? Are you in a business where your competitors or some other party might attempt to hijack the truck full of tapes? How can you protect yourself from that possibility?

- Who is authorized to restore the tapes? How many backup people are there should the primary people be unable to reach the backup site?

■ Should you restore the tapes every day when they arrive, or only store them every day, and restore them when the disaster occurs? Restoring them daily may cause a lot of busy work that may never be used, but daily restores also ensure that the restores work, and they mean that the data may already be on the DR systems when the disaster hits your main site. No need to wait for the tapes to be restored. Restoring the tapes regularly also ensures that the restore procedures work.

Once the Data Makes It to the Remote Site

Many other issues still must be addressed once the data makes it to the remote site, through whatever means you may have selected:

■ Can the backup tapes be read at the DR site? Is specialized software required to read them? Does the software require licensing? Do you have those licenses? How long will it take you to get the license keys?

■ Do you have to rebuild your tape indices before you can begin restoring data? How long will that take?

■ Are your application executables present at the DR site? Are they the most current versions? Will there be any incompatibilities between what you are running at the two sites? Will the associated data be accepted by the version at the DR site?

■ Assuming that your applications are present and up-to-date, do they need separate license keys to run at the DR site?

Prioritization

Once the disaster has been declared, system administrative personnel must perform whatever tasks have been identified as necessary to bring up the key applications at the DR site. It would be nice to think that this process will go smoothly and quickly, but the reality will probably not be quite that rosy. There are a limited number of qualified people who can work on starting the applications, and a limited number of workstations where they can access the systems they need, in order to begin the work. Therefore, all applications, data, and systems to be brought on line at the DR site must be prioritized.

Questions that need to be answered include:

■ What applications must be running first? What data gets restored first?

■ What applications are not needed at the DR site at all?

■ What applications are only needed at the DR site if the disaster continues past 1, 7, 14, or 30 days?

- Who gets priority for scarce resources?

- Who makes the decision that one group gets service ahead of another? A chain of command must be in place if the top decision maker is unavailable.

All of these decisions must be made BEFORE the disaster strikes, and must be signed off on by all relevant parties. Copies of the "pecking order" must be well-circulated and easily available to everyone responsible for starting applications on the remote site. (Plan ahead!)

Whatever mechanism is chosen to transport data to the DR site must take these decisions into account. The most important data should probably be on its own tapes, for instance.

Rerouting Telecommunications

All of the best disaster recovery planning in the world produces zero benefit if the remote site can't talk to your customers, suppliers, and partners, or if they can't find you. At a minimum, you'll need to be sure that you have worked out redundancy and rerouting plans for the following telecommunications equipment:

- *Telephones.* Your switches, PBXs, and voice mail systems should be available on the remote side, along with agreements from your local, long distance, and other telephone service providers for how you migrate service to the redundant site. If you rely on cellular telephones, be sure that you have clear service in the disaster recovery site. An appropriately remote location may be in a "dead zone."

- *Local Area Networking such as switches, routers, and hubs.* This sounds obvious, but if you keep the same configuration as your primary site, you'll have two (or more) independent locations with the same IP numbering and host-naming schemes. You're going to need a plan to keep them separated or to keep the redundant site isolated from public networks and your primary site network to avoid confusing intermediate pieces of network equipment. If you choose a different naming and numbering scheme, then you'll need to make sure that all of your applications, configuration files, and naming systems are configured to handle it.

- *Wide-Area Networking (WAN) lines.* Whatever connections you have to the Internet or other commercial networks must be made redundant. Typically, this involves working out an alternate provisioning agreement with your Internet service provider (ISP) and the conditions under which you move the routing from one site to another. Again, you need to worry about hostnames and IP addresses, as well as things like public domain naming service records. Your ".com name" needs to move to the alternate site, but the IP addresses used by the ISP for your edge routers may be different.

This is something to work out and test well in advance. Firewalls, packet filtering hosts, and other security measures should be configured and ready to go in the remote location.

The biggest hurdle in building a redundant communications network is ensuring that you have sufficient functionality to allow for live updates of the remote site but no conflicts in naming or addressing that could wreak havoc with your primary site. Careful planning and testing, especially of applications in the remote site, will make the transitions back and forth to the remote site much smoother.

Starting the Applications

Once your data and applications are safely at the DR site, the decision must be made to switch operations to that remote site. As with data migration, the process to move the functional control could be either automatic or manual.

In the automatic case, a software package similar to an FMS could be used to detect the total failure of the main site, and automatically migrate operations to the DR site. Unless implemented carefully, this could be a very dangerous way of doing things. The decision to go live at a DR site is a critical one, which could be extremely costly if undertaken frivolously. You don't want to have an entire bullpen full of customer service representatives on city buses and in their cars to the alternate site when you realize that the "disaster" was that someone had turned off a rack of network equipment. Refer back to our debate of manual versus automated failover in Chapter 8. Manual failover is ideal when there are multiple points of control—in the case of disaster recovery, you're controlling systems, physical locations, telecommunications and employees. This is clearly a good case for manual methods. It is the kind of decision that should be confirmed by one or more knowledgeable persons before it begins.

Automatic DR failover could be initiated inappropriately due to network faults, application faults, or due to some sort of security breach. Once the DR failover takes place, applications and data could begin to be served from a remote site on a different network in a different state. Once that occurs, either users will be unable to contact the DR servers, or the main site will fall some number of transactions behind the DR site. In the first case, the business will stop for a time, and in the second case, it will be necessary to refresh the main site with the changes that were sent to the DR site before life can return to normal. In either case, the fix becomes onerous and manually intensive.

With manual DR failover, or at least manual confirmation of the automatic DR failover decision, you can feel confident that operations will not suddenly leave the main site for no good reason. Requiring a system administrator to type "Y" or to click OK on a console someplace (possibly twice, just to be certain) is an excellent precaution. You should probably not even consider DR failover software that does not offer this feature.

At this writing, we are unaware of any generally available products that perform DR failover, although companies are working on them.

Application Licensing

An often overlooked element of maintaining disaster recovery sites is the licensing of your applications. Many vendors license their software against the host-id or other system-unique piece of data. When you migrate those applications to another system, the licenses may become invalid, causing the application to fail to start.

Know how your applications are licensed, and what the vendor sees as the implications of migrating to your DR site. Does the application vendor require a license for the DR site? What will that license cost? Some vendors charge full price for a DR license, while others charge a significantly reduced price, and still others give away DR licenses. At some vendors, the decision on what to charge for DR site software is left to the discretion of the individual account team (one more reason to be nice to them).

In some cases, it may be necessary to contact your application vendor's support center for a new DR license key. Depending on the nature of the disaster, you may be one of dozens or hundreds of affected customers, all of whom need license keys. Don't assume that you will rise to the top of the list, and get a key when you call. Plan ahead, and have your DR keys before a disaster strikes.

As you examine this issue, consider all of the applications that run on your main site, and determine whether they are needed at the DR site. All applications need to be considered—databases, disk and volume management, backup utilities, and everything else.

Accessing and Using the DR Site

Depending on how you populate your DR site, physical access to the site may become an issue before or after the population, but it will absolutely become an issue. Some of the issues to consider include:

How are the people at the DR site alerted to incoming users? If there are security personnel, or others who work there, they must be told that the people are coming. They may have some specific preparations to make before the primary staff begins to arrive.

Who has the keys to the DR site? If the DR site is unmanned, even if it is unmanned only at night or on the weekend, then someone must have the keys. That person needs to be among the very first to arrive. If he is not, then nobody else can get in. Conversely, giving out too many keys could be a security risk, especially as people leave your company.

ID cards and badges. If you issue ID cards or badges to all the key personnel, and they don't use or need them for months or years, they may have trouble locating them when the disaster occurs. If that happens, how can they gain access?

Where is the DR site again? Personnel who have never been to the DR site may not know where it is. They will need directions.

How do I get there? If your key people are city dwellers without cars (very common in New York and other large cities), they may have no way to get themselves from the main site to a DR site located in the suburbs. If the disaster is widespread, public transportation (if it even runs to the DR site at all) may not be functioning adequately.

What about new hires? Have more recent hires been given basic access information for the DR site? Do they have badges, directions, or the other information they'll need?

Can anyone gain unauthorized access when there is no disaster? At the DR site, assuming automatic data population, an unscrupulous person will find all the information he needs to really mess up your business. How hard would it be for someone to gain access when the site should be dark? In *The Velocity of Money*, a 1997 financial thriller by Stephen Rhodes, a trading floor's DR site was used to enter illegal trades.

Once everyone is inside, a slew of facilities issues arise. Mundane things like chairs, desks, computer work stations, networks (both internal and external), phones (assuming they even work), heat or air conditioning, food, and water could be the undoing of an otherwise flawlessly executed DR plan.

Personnel Issues

During a disaster, people are your most important asset. They must be informed, organized, coordinated, and coolheaded. Different people will react very differently in a disaster, and some of them will surely react in ways that would otherwise be considered uncharacteristic. Depending on the nature of the disaster, some people's priorities may shift away from their jobs to their families or their personal belongings. (Just as we are not lawyers, we are also not psychologists.)

When a disaster strikes, many important decisions will need to be made very quickly. These decisions could have significant consequences to the future operations of your business. The best way to make them is to make them in advance. Some of the questions that must be dealt with include:

Who declares that a disaster condition exists? Most likely this will be someone fairly high up the executive ladder. Everyone should know in advance who this person is, and what their first actions will be once the declaration is made.

How is the word spread? Once the disaster is declared, key personnel must drop what they are doing and begin their disaster responses. How are these key people notified that a disaster condition exists and has been declared? If each person decides on his own, then some will begin a disaster drill while others insist that things aren't so bad. If the key person declares the disaster, but doesn't tell people immediately, precious time will be lost until the message gets out.

Who are those key personnel? Who are the people who must drop what they are doing to respond? They must know this before the disaster occurs. They must also know exactly what is expected of them during the disaster.

Who is in charge? Once the decision is made, different small groups will begin their disaster routines. Each group, perhaps by floor or function within the company, will do its thing. Someone must oversee the group, and report back to an overall coordinator. Who?

What about liability issues? If one of your people is hurt or worse while getting himself to the DR site, what is your corporate liability? These issues should be worked out with lawyers well in advance.

Who reports to the DR site? Who stays home? The DR site is likely to be smaller than the main site, without adequate space for all personnel. Some people must be expected to go home during the disaster, rather than report to the DR site. These people must know their roles in advance of any disaster.

Should someone arrange to be at a well-known wired phone? Assuming the wired phone system still functions, having a single clearinghouse for decisions and for people to identify themselves and their locations might be a very wise precaution.

Who coordinates with outside parties? If the disaster is large enough, government agencies such as the local police, or FEMA (Federal Emergency Management Agency) will be involved. Someone from the organization needs to be the main contact point. The same holds for the news media. Again, depending on the nature of the emergency, television and/or newspaper reporters may be looking for information. All of that information should be coordinated through one person, particularly at companies that are concerned with their outside image.

What happens if the primary people responsible for each of these key functions is unavailable? During a disaster, some people may be incapacitated. Others may simply be out of town. If the people given some of the key tasks are unavailable, others must be designated to take their places. These people should also know their roles, and be prepared to step right into them.

Other Issues

Prepare for the original site to be totally inaccessible. It is entirely possible that you will never be allowed to return to your original site—not even to retrieve personal belongings. If law enforcement undertakes an extended investigation, they may keep everyone out of the building, or parts of it, for the duration of the investigation. The building could be damaged beyond repair or simply condemned by local authorities.

Prepare for the disaster to end at some point. Once the disaster ends (assuming it does), how will you get your data back to the original site? How will that migration take place? Will you have to schedule downtime to move back? These procedures must be documented and tested as much and as well as the original disaster procedures. The move back will probably be easier, since it can be done with a more relaxed and phased approach.

Communications. How do your key people communicate with each other? Are wireless phones good enough? In a widespread disaster, wireless sites may be affected. If they are not, it may simply be impossible to get a connection into the network, as everyone else is trying to use their wireless phones, too.

Documentation. All of these decisions should be made in advance. But if they are not adequately documented, then all the decision making work is for naught. Copies of this information should be distributed to all personnel, and kept off-site as well as on. And stored on paper.

Prioritize everything! There will never be enough hands. Document exactly what steps need to be performed and in what order. If there are extra people, steps can be performed in parallel. A good audit trail may help save jobs once the smoke has cleared.

Get sign-offs from everyone. That means management, administrators, and important and vocal users. The people who are the biggest pains in the neck, even if they have no actual authority, should be included in the sign-offs. These are the people who can cause dissension in the ranks; get these people on your side as much as possible.

Who is the final authority?   When a dispute arises that cannot be resolved easily, it may be wise to have a predesignated arbiter, who makes the final call. Remember, though, arguing and deciding take up valuable time that could be spent actually restoring systems. Sometimes it's just better to give in than to fight, especially when time is critical.

Know how long it will take to bring up your DR site.   This will surely be the longest "R" of all your MTTRs. Look into what you can do to shorten the duration. When the World Trade Center in New York was bombed in February 1993, it was a Friday. Many (though not all) of the trading floors in the building were back online at their DR sites on Monday morning. Set the expectations in your organization accordingly.

Prevent disputes.   A disaster is a very high-stress situation. Your people are likely to be extremely stressed out, and running with very short tempers. By getting buy-in and agreement on as many of these issues as possible before they actually occur, you should be able to sidestep many of the potential points of dispute.

Testing the Whole Thing

Last and most certainly not least comes the issue of testing your DR procedures. Thoroughly testing your DR procedures is the best way to have them run as smoothly as possible when the disaster occurs. Not testing them will surely compound the disaster.

Pick a weekend, and do a full dry run. Get users involved. Randomly select some key people and remove them from the test at the last minute, or even in the middle of the test, to simulate what might happen in reality. Limit advance knowledge of the details of the test disaster to as few people as possible; lots of surprises will approximate real life much better than a simple and smooth test where everyone knows what is going on. The closer your test is to reality on every level (short of actually injuring people, please), the better the test will represent a real disaster. Plan for the worst case; planning for the best case is easy.

Testing disasters can be extremely expensive work, but if the alternative is a massive expense that could completely wipe out your business, it is well worth going through the drill.

If emergency medical technicians can dry-run plane crashes, and if New York City can simulate terrorist subway gas attacks, then your business can simulate a disaster of its own.

Whoops!

There are so many issues to think about it is very difficult to address them all. Any single neglected issue can cause the whole plan to fail. Consider:

- Your key administrators, tapes in hand, arguing with the guards at the DR site, trying to get inside

- Your key people arguing with each other on cell phones, while stuck in evacuation traffic, with a trunkful of backup tapes

- Your key people being mistaken for looters as they try to rescue disks, tapes, or other key equipment

- Your key people, with no cell phone, driving around for hours searching for the DR site, which they have never been to, and which is totally unmarked

- That the disaster has also caused a total power outage at the DR site

- That the disaster occurs during a big off-site meeting

- That the disaster occurs at 11 P.M. on Christmas Eve

- Or that it occurs the Monday after most of your key people have quit to join your competitor

▶Key Points

- No aspect of increased availability is anywhere near as complex, expensive, delicate, legally challenging, or labor-intensive as disaster recovery.

- Plan, plan, plan! Nowhere in your operation is planning going to pay off better than in a disaster. If everyone knows what to do and where to go, things have a chance of actually working.

- Test, test, test! If you don't adequately test your disaster plans, you have no idea whether they will be successful. All your efforts and expense could be for nothing.

- Even one missed or untested element could cause the whole DR plan to fail.

- The value of planning and testing cannot be overstated.

CHAPTER 15

Parting Shot

Life is like a sewer. What you get out of it depends on what you put into it.
—Tom Lehrer

There is a very interesting and not unexpected side effect to spending your time designing high availability into systems. You gain a much better overall understanding of the systems that you are responsible for. Whether you are a hands-on system administrator, a manager of system administrators, or a corporate technical officer, as you move through the discipline that is high availability, you quickly learn about system capabilities, disks, networks, backups, and all of the other topics that we have covered in this book. You learn the value of spending a little more money for high quality when it is needed. This information will make you more successful at your job.

How We Got Here

In the Introduction, we discussed the concept of an availability index, which is no more than a fancy way of saying that the higher the level of availability you need, the more money it will cost you. That money is an investment in the safe and ongoing operations of your systems, and in turn your business. Failure to put the right money in the right places could, in the end, cost you and your business dearly.

The money that you spend on protecting your systems is really spent on protecting your applications. Your applications in turn run your business. Spending money (and time) to design HA into your systems is an investment in your business.

You almost certainly have a life insurance policy that will protect your family in the event that something happens to you. You have insurance on the physical plant that make up your business's facilities. But so many businesses do not carry insurance on their systems and applications, and they fail a lot more often and for a lot more reasons than buildings or people do.

HA in all of its forms is insurance. It's life insurance for your business. You wouldn't raise a family without insuring yourself, and you shouldn't run a business without insuring it and its systems. Life insurance salesman sell life insurance as an investment, not as a simple expense. HA is the same thing. If your income is $35,000 per year, would you get $1 million in personal life insurance? Probably not, although you might. If your income is $250,000 per year, would you buy $25,000 in life insurance? Again, probably not. You buy insurance according to your personal needs. As your needs change, you reevaluate your insurance needs.

If your downtime costs $100,000 per hour, is it worth an extra $25,000 to shorten every outage by 30 minutes? Of course it is. But the same $25,000 solution may be a total extravagance for a small business whose outages cost $1000 per hour. Every business is different. Every business has different requirements. The trick is to spend appropriately for your business's needs. And to reevaluate that spending as your needs change.

The trick is to figure out how much your downtime actually costs you (factoring in any government or industry requirements), and to balance the amount you spend against that. There is no single set of rules that applies to every business, just as there is no single insurance policy, or even type of insurance, that applies to everyone.

Where We're Going

We can't wrap up without at least giving a hint of where we see the state of the art in availability going over the next few years. Consider this a preview of coming attractions, or our task list for future editions:

- Standards are emerging for availability features with programming interfaces. The POSIX efforts to standardize checkpoint and resume functions, now in an early form, are a good example. Standards compliance will become another design consideration—are the standards broad enough to be useful and specific enough to eliminate a lower layer of design work?

- Networking bandwidth is increasing faster than CPU speed. Metcalfe's Law has overtaken Moore's Law as the defining force behind complex systems. Networked, highly available, and highly distributed systems will be the norm. Replication and caching will be requirements, not engineering luxuries.

- The Internet business models that "win" will focus on the entire customer experience. Internet time is real time, and customer experiences are defined by their interactions over any given time span. Fill the customer's online time with hourglass cursors and you're not a market-mover. Instead, you're moved out of the market by someone who pays more careful attention to the machine room technology supporting the online brand.

- Applications and operations teams are joined at the hip. They're joined at the hub, the router, the monitoring software, the log file, and the database as well. Those who keep their application writers and application runners synchronized and in harmony regarding constraints, costs, time, and complexity will succeed. Those who don't will be looking to take a do-over more frequently than management would like.

- While complexity increases, scale decreases. Embedded systems are the next big thing. In an appliance, you don't always get the chance to fix a bug with a patch or constrain user actions. You'll need to get things done right, with headroom, the first time, with an appreciation for every possible way in which the device can be used.

There are many sources for inspiration and skills transfer from noncomputing fields. Stewart Brand chronicles Danny Hillis' endeavor to build a clock that will last for thousands of years in *The Clock Of The Long Now;* he also writes about the design implications of physical buildings and structures that endure for decades in *How Buildings Learn.* Smart engineers have been making reliable and available products for hundreds of years, and that prior art is available for us to leverage into the world of short time scales and big web sites. Demand for availability design and verification skills will continue to grow. That's why we transcribed our knowledge in this book; it also means that the state of the art isn't standing still. We hope that with this introduction to the skill sets and design choices involved, you've become a member of this growing class of highly valued individuals.

Glossary

We use a lot of jargon and technical terminology throughout the book. It is unreasonable to expect that every reader will understand every term. To help with general understanding of technical terms, we offer the following list of brief definitions; for longer definitions, please refer to other sources more dedicated to the subject in question. Many of these definitions are also found with more detail in the text of the book. We repeat them here to help eliminate searching through the book for a particular term.

1-to-*N* failover   A failover configuration where one primary server runs several key applications; when it fails, each application fails to a different smaller server.

Administrative network   In a failover configuration, a network connection that is connected to the public network but is not highly available or publicized. It is solely for the use of the system administrators, to give them guaranteed network access into the system, regardless of the state of the application.

Advisory file locking   A mechanism to coordinate read and write access to a file from one or more processes that does not prevent an uncooperative process from doing what it wishes. Advisory file locking is the "gentleman's agreement" about sharing. See also Mandatory file locking.

AMD   A public domain alternative to the standard Solaris automounter. amd runs on a variety of Unix systems.

ARP   Address Resolution Protocol. A protocol used to map IP addresses to hardware or MAC addresses.

Asymmetric failover   The base failover configuration, consisting of one primary server that fails its services to a dedicated standby server.

Automounter   A Unix process that automatically mounts network file systems only when they are requested.

Backplane   The central communications pathway that connects all the different hardware components of a computer system.

Blocking process   A process that "gets stuck" waiting for some critical resource or system event to occur. It is stopped, or blocked from further execution, until the wait condition is resolved. Certain processes can block and cannot be interrupted until the resource they are waiting for is released.

Blue Screen of Death   In the Windows world when the operating system crashes, and the GUI goes away, the user is left with a blue screen (the color can actually be changed in the registry) that explains the nature of the crash. In the vernacular, this is called the Blue Screen of Death.

Boyle's Law   In physics, the law that says that a gas will expand to fill all available space. In computing, it says that computing needs will expand to fill all available resources.

Checkpoint   A marker (usually a file) that an application leaves behind in the event that it crashes. The checkpoint enables the application to restart at or near the point that it crashed, rather than having to restart from the beginning.

DCE/DFS   The Open Software Foundation's Distributed Computing Environment (DCE) Distributed File System (DFS). An analog to NFS, primarily available through IBM's Transarc subsidiary, that supports caching, Kerberos security including data privacy, and volume replication.

Deadman timer   A timer that is kept from expiring by a particular action. When the action stops for a predetermined period, the timer goes off. Typically used to abort a transaction after it has been in progress for a fixed period of time; the "action" of processing requests stops long enough for the application to believe a failure has occurred.

Denial of service attack   A network problem, often a directed attack, which prevents legitimate access to network resources by forcing the resources to service many small and unimportant requests.

DHCP   Dynamic Host Configuration Protocol, used to give systems IP addresses and other critical network information. Used mostly for PCs and other transient systems that need to "borrow" a network identity for short periods of time.

Directory services   Network-based lookup services that contain key-value pairs for host names, IP addresses, user information, security certificates, or just about anything else. Historically, NIS and DNS filled this role, but now LDAP is emerging as the most flexible network directory service.

DLM Distributed Lock Manager. A method that permits multiple hosts to have read/write access to the same file or files at the same time. The DLM arbitrates access between the hosts.

DNS Domain Naming Service. A network-based naming service that matches IP addresses to hostnames and allows queries to cross domain boundaries. This is the naming system for the Internet.

Dual-ported disks Disks that are physically connected to two hosts at the same time. Access to these disks may only be performed by one host or the other; simultaneous access is not permitted.

Failover The process by which the services that were running a now-failed server migrate to a functional server and resume serving their clients.

FCAL FibreChannel Arbitrated Loop. A modern high-speed disk connection medium.

FDDI Fiber Distributed Data Interface. A high-speed, token-passing based local area network medium. In the age of 10 Mbit/second Ethernet, FDDI was the rich man's 100 Mbit/second alternative. 100 Mbit and Gigabit switched Ethernet have largely replaced FDDI.

Fibrechannel A specification for the physical layer of fiber-optic cable networks.

File locking A method of controlling file access to one host or one user at a time.

Firewall A computer system used as a logical barrier between different networks in an enterprise. The most common use is as a barrier between internal networks and the Internet.

Floating point exception Performing a mathematical operation that results in a divide-by-zero, overflow, or underflow condition. Overflow and underflow are caused by dividing very large or very small numbers into each other.

FMS Failover Management Software. Software that manages failovers and service groups.

FTP File Transfer Protocol. A commonly used cross-platform file transfer utility.

Gratuitous ARP An ARP request sent by a host while configuring one of its network interfaces. The ARP request is for the host's own IP address, and is used to inform other network nodes of the net IP address to MAC address mapping created by the interface configuration.

Heartbeat network In a failover configuration, the network that is used to allow the two systems to communicate privately with each other.

Hot pluggable disks Disks that may be added and removed from a disk array while the disk array is powered up, and without having to interrupt the computer to which the disks are attached.

Hot spares   Disks that are set aside as replacements for disks that fail. When a disk fails, a hot spare can be automatically dropped into the role that the failed disk played.

Initiator   On a SCSI bus, a computer that initiates requests for data to a target.

IP   Internet Protocol. One of the most pervasive network protocols.

IP address   A number of the form A.B.C.D, where each value can range from 0 to 255, that uniquely identifies a computer on an IP network.

JBOD   Just a bunch of disks. A retronym that differentiates a set of freestanding disks from the possibly managed disks in a disk array.

Kerberos   In Greek mythology, the three-headed dog that guards the gates to Hades. Also a popular ticket-based security system.

LAN   Local Area Network. The network, usually Ethernet based, that runs in a single building.

Latency   The delay in service response. Network latency is introduced by a busy network, as well as by the delay in transmitting data across a long network cable.

LDAP   Lightweight Directory Access Protocol. "Lightweight" differentiates it from its X.500 predecessor, the "heavy" directory protocol. An up-and-coming network directory service.

LVM   Logical Volume Manager. Software that allows the attachment of logical structures to disks, to increase their availability and manageability.

MAC address   Media Access Control address, a 48-bit value that uniquely identifies a network station, or node. Note that multiple IP addresses can map to the same MAC address, if a computer has multiple network connections.

Memory Exception   When a program attempts to access a location in memory that turns out to be illegal for some reason (outside the valid range of memory, pointed to location zero, etc.), a memory exception error occurs, usually terminating the program.

Metcalfe's Law   The power of networked computer systems goes up exponentially; as you connect them together their aggregate usefulness increases as the square of the number of systems.

MTBF   Mean Time Between Failures. The average amount of time that a component will go between failures. The average is calculated from all known components of a particular type.

MTTR   Mean Time to Recover (or repair). The average amount of time it takes to get a system back on line after some sort of component failure has occurred.

Multicast   A network protocol that allows a single message to be sent to more than one host on the network, but not necessarily all hosts.

Multihosting Connecting a disk or other peripheral resource to more than one computer at the same time.

Multiinitiator A SCSI bus that has more than one initiator device on it.

Multipathing A connection from a computer to a disk drive that runs over more than one cable.

NFS Network File System. A protocol allowing network-based access to a filesystem.

NIC Network Interface Card. An I/O card that connects a system to a network.

NIS Network Information System. A Unix-based service that allows administrative information to be shared among many hosts in a LAN.

NLM Network Lock Manager. The adjunct protocol for NFS that handles file locking requests over the network.

N-to-1 failover A failover configuration where one system acts as the standby for several active hosts at the same time.

N-to-M failover A failover configuration where many systems in the same cluster back each other up, usually with a set of complex rules to decide where particular services will fail in a given situation.

Parallel application An application that can run on more than one processor at a time, accessing the same file or database. Parallel databases may run on more than one system at a time, possibly sharing the same data sets.

Ping A network utility that sends a "hello, you there?" message to another host. The message is more properly referred to as an ICMP echo request.

Port Number A particular socket number on a system at which an application is listening. Ports can be well-known, for services like mail or telnet, or automatically assigned when the client-side application doesn't care what value it uses. The four values of source IP address, source port, destination IP address, and destination port uniquely identify every TCP/IP socket connection.

Private disks In a failover configuration, the disks that contain a system's OS and other unshared files.

Private network See heartbeat network.

Process table A list of active processes running on a system at a particular time.

Public disks In a failover configuration, the disks that are switched from one server to the other. They contain the data that are required to deliver critical services.

Public network The network over which a server contacts its clients.

RAID Redundant Array of Independent (or Inexpensive) Disks. A set of standards for arranging disks in various ways to make them more resilient to failure and/or to make them perform faster.

RAID-0 Striped disks. A RAID level that adds performance but decreases availability by sharing the I/O load over several disks.

RAID-0+1 Mirrored stripes. A combination of mirroring and striping that increases both performance and availability.

RAID-1 Mirrored disks. A RAID level that increases availability by copying the contents of one set of disks to a second, allowing the two to work as peers.

RAID-1+0 Striped mirrors. A combination of mirroring and striping that results in the highest possible availability, without hurting performance.

RAID-5 A RAID level that achieves availability, at the cost of performance, by calculating the parity of all the disks in a striped set.

Rdist A utility for distributing application software between systems, across a network.

Retronym A word that describes something that only needs a name to differentiate it from something newer. Examples: analog watch (as opposed to a digital watch), JBOD (as opposed to a disk array).

RIP Routing Information Protocol. A public domain protocol for working out efficient network routes.

Rolled forward Database transactions that are completed from their log entries after a crash.

Rolled back Transactions that were in progress and that are aborted after a database failure, putting the system in the pretransaction state.

Round-robin failover A failover configuration where system A fails to B, B fails to C, C fails to D, etc., until Z fails back to A.

Route A network path between two systems.

Routing cost metrics A value assigned to a route to help routing processes find the most efficient path from one system to another.

RPC Remote Procedure Call. Protocol for allowing one system to send requests to another.

SAN Storage Area Network. A modern high-speed model for connecting storage devices (disks and tape drives) to the systems that need their resources.

SCSI Small Computer Systems Interface. A common medium for connecting disks and systems.

Service group In a failover configuration, the combination of disk resources, applications, and network identities that can be cleanly failed over between systems. (Also called a package in some operating systems.)

Shared disks See public disks.

Shared nothing An alternate way for two systems in a failover configuration to share their data. It requires replication to get the data from one system to the other.

SLA Service Level Agreement. A written document that sets forth commitments between users and administrators for system recovery after a failure occurs

Split-brain Syndrome The bane of failover configurations, a very rare condition where more than one server attempts to take control of a set of shared disks, resulting in data corruption.

SSH Secure Shell. A tunneling mechanism that creates an encrypted remote shell from one system to another.

SSL Secure Socket Layer. A security handshaking system that creates an encrypted socket, typically between an Internet browser and a web server.

Stateful A system that requires some knowledge of the clients and servers, and their current points of execution. This state needs to be preserved or recovered in the event of a failure.

Stateless A system in which every request contains enough information for it to be processed independently of all others. Ideal in theory, but very hard to implement because some operations like file locking simply require state.

Striped disks See RAID-0.

Subnet Part of a TCP/IP network. Subnets are used to fragment a larger TCP/IP network into smaller physical segments, each with a part of the logical IP address space.

Symmetric failover The most common failover configuration, where two systems each run critical services, and in the event that either one fails, the survivor takes over for it, and runs both sets of services at the same time.

Target On a SCSI bus, a disk or tape drive that responds to requests for data placed by an initiator.

TCP Transmission Control Protocol, the "other half" of IP, that provides reliable data delivery over a socket connection.

Thread An execution path through an application. Simple applications may only have one thread, but more complex applications may have multiple threads that are executed in parallel for speed and efficiency.

Trunking   Putting together more than one network connection, so that they act as one for data transmissions. Striping for networks.

UDP   User Datagram Protocol, an unreliable transport on top of IP used most commonly for broadcasts and other traffic in which the sending application takes care of recovery.

Unicast   A retronym that refers point-to-point network transmission, from one sender to one recipient. The opposite of broadcast.

Windows SMB   Server Message Block, a file-sharing protocol for Windows machines.

Write cache   A dedicated block of memory in a disk array, used to speed I/O operations to the array.

XOR   Exclusive or. A bitwise mathematical operation used to calculate parity in some levels of RAID (4 and 5). The result of an XOR of 0 and 0 is 0; of 0 and 1 is 1; of 1 and 0 is 1; and of 1 and 1 is 0.

A List of URLs

Throughout the book, we make references to vendors, products, organizations, and public-domain software who have a presence of the World Wide Web. As a courtesy, we offer a list of their URLs:

Baydel: www.baydel.com

BMC: www.bmc.com

CERT: www.cert.org

Cisco: www.cisco.com

Columbia Data Products: www.cdp.com

Computer Associates: www.cai.com

EMC/Data General: www.emc.com

Hewlett-Packard: www.hp.com

IBM: www.ibm.com

Informix: www.informix.com

Intel: www.intel.com

Legato/Qualix/Full Time Software/Vinca/Octopus: www.legato.com

Linux: www.redhat.com, www.linux.com

Microsoft: www.microsoft.com

Network Appliance: www.netapp.com

Nortel: www.nortelnetworks.com/index.html

Novell: www.novell.com

Oracle: www.oracle.com

Perl: www.perl.com

Rational/Pure/Atria Clearcase: www.rational.com

SCO: www.sco.com

St. Bernard: www.stbernard.com

Storage Technologies (Storage Tek): www.storagetek.com

Sun Microsystems: www.sun.com

Sybase: www.sybase.com

Syncsort: www.syncsort.com

Tivoli: www.tivoli.com

Tripwire: www.visualcomputing.com

VERITAS/Open Vision/Seagate Software NSMG: www.veritas.com

Index

Page references followed by an italic *t* indicate material in tables. Commercial hardware and software products are indexed without the manufacturer's name as an adjective. All terms containing numbers are indexed as if the number was spelled out. Thus, "1-to-1 failover configuration" would be located as if spelled "one-to-one failover configuration."